D1315376

WITHDRAWN
FROM THE RODMAN PUBLIC LIBRARY

WILLOUGHBY

Welcome to the Suck

Narrating the American Soldier's Experience in Iraq

Stacey Peebles, *1976*

Cornell University Press
Ithaca and London

RODMAN PUBLIC LIBRARY.

38212005620791
Main Adult
956.704 P373
Peebles, Stacey L. (Stacey
Lyn), 1976-
Welcome to the suck :
narrating the American
soldier's experience in

JAN -- 2012

Copyright © 2011 by Cornell University

All rights reserved. Except for brief quotations in a review, this book, or
parts thereof, must not be reproduced in any form without permission in
writing from the publisher. For information, address Cornell University
Press, Sage House, 512 East State Street, Ithaca, New York 14850.

First published 2011 by Cornell University Press
Printed in the United States of America

Library of Congress Cataloging-in-Publication Data

Peebles, Stacey L. (Stacey Lyn), 1976–
    Welcome to the suck : narrating the American soldier's experience in
Iraq / Stacey Peebles.
        p. cm.
    Includes bibliographical references and index.
    ISBN 978-0-8014-4946-8 (cloth : alk. paper)
    1. Persian Gulf War, 1991—Personal narratives, American.   2. Iraq
War, 2003——Personal narratives, American.   3. Persian Gulf War,
1991—Literature and the war.   4. Iraq War, 2003——Literature and the
war.   5. Iraq War, 2003——Motion pictures and the war.   I. Title.
    DS79.74.P44   2011
    956.7044'24092273—dc22   2010044422

Cornell University Press strives to use environmentally responsible
suppliers and materials to the fullest extent possible in the publishing of
its books. Such materials include vegetable-based, low-VOC inks and
acid-free papers that are recycled, totally chlorine-free, or partly composed
of nonwood fibers. For further information, visit our website at www.
cornellpress.cornell.edu.

Cloth printing   10 9 8 7 6 5 4 3 2 1

RODMAN PUBLIC LIBRARY

CONTENTS

Acknowledgments

I owe a special thanks to David Mikics, who encouraged this project from its inception, read every chapter multiple times, and offered invaluable feedback. I am also grateful to Peter Potter for championing the idea for this book and providing kind and detailed guidance every step of the way.

I would like to thank Wayne Lesser and Tom Palaima for all these years of friendship, ideas, collaboration, and support. My thanks to Sue Collins for her perpetual encouragement, and to Karen Fang, Elizabeth Klett, and Kat McClellan for sharing coffee, research goals, frustrations, and successes. Iain Morrisson's, Dan Price's, and Ralph Rodriguez's comments on chapter 1 in its earlier incarnation as an article were very helpful.

Thanks to Tony Hilfer, who would have loved this adventure. And especially thanks to Barbara and Gene Peebles for all their love, and to Richard Power, my reader first and last.

An earlier version of Chapter 1 was published as an article in a special issue of *PMLA* on "War" in October 2009. I am grateful to the Modern

Language Association of America for permission to reprint overlapping material. I also thank Alice James Books (www.alicejamesbooks.org) for permission to reprint excerpts from Brian Turner's book, *Here, Bullet* (Copyright © 2005 by Brian Turner).

Introduction

Being a Soldier makes me proud, it's the in between part that can be tough.

—from the military blog "American Soldier," posted 29 January 2006

Near the end of *Jarhead,* his 2003 memoir of the Persian Gulf War, Marine infantryman Anthony Swofford writes about celebrating with his company when they learn that the war is suddenly over. "The music plays throughout the day, Hendrix, the Stones, the Who, music from a different war," he complains. "Ours is barely over but we begin to tell stories already" (335). Like many other soldiers from the Gulf War and the Iraq War, Swofford finds himself drawn to 1960s rock and roll and other touchstones of the Vietnam era, yet he is eager to show how this war, *his* war, is unique. He is effectively "in between" the old war stories and the new one that he and his fellow soldiers will help to tell. The only thing to do, as he and his comrades demonstrate, is to start talking.

Most people have become familiar with what life was like for a soldier in Vietnam through the popular representations of that war. Films like *Platoon* and *Full Metal Jacket* as well as books by Philip Caputo, Michael Herr, and Tim O'Brien follow the experiences of young men, usually drafted into service, encountering thick jungle, guerrilla warfare, and rock and roll, while gradually descending into disillusionment and political cynicism. It is an engaging narrative, and a pervasive one. But as Swofford notes, the soldier's experience in Iraq is a different story.

This book explores this new war story in prose, poetry, and films about the American soldier's experience in the Persian Gulf War and the Iraq War—or, in soldier's lingo, in "the Suck." Among the many changes in the soldier's experience, such as the effects of large-scale advances in medical and communications technology and the greatly increased presence of women in the military, what is most evident in these narratives is the soldier's desire to be truly "in between," to break down and transcend the cultural and social categories that have traditionally defined identity. Ultimately, however, that desire is thwarted. War, and contemporary American war in particular, enforces categorization even as it forces encounters across the boundaries of media, gender, nation, and the body.

Different wars make for different stories, although some elements of the war experience are constants. Accounts from Homer to O'Brien describe the soldier's initiation into battle and how he begins to identify himself as a fighter. They reveal how life as a soldier affects his conception of manhood or masculinity. War can make (or unmake) the man—and today it is a proving ground for women as well. Stories of war depict the soldier's encounters with the enemy and with the civilians of another culture, groups that are not always easily distinguished from one another. And they portray the aftermath of war, a homecoming that in many cases is shaped by physical or mental trauma. But these features of life as a soldier are experienced and expressed differently in different wars. Think how the shock of the trenches for new soldiers reared on Kipling has come to define World War I, or how the Vietnam War affected our national perception of disability. Stories from contemporary American wars—the Persian Gulf War and the much lengthier Iraq War—are only now beginning to be told. This new narrative, as stories about war always do, reveals what it means to fight in a particular war as well as how that fighting reflects the politics and culture of the nation. (The war in Afghanistan predates the Iraq War and will likely outlast it, as political and military attention shifts to that conflict during the Obama presidency. But to date, that war has inspired fewer and less prominent works of literature and film than the wars in Iraq.)

This book explores the different aspects of the contemporary American soldier's experience while paying particular attention to a paradox of these late twentieth- and early twenty-first-century wars. The soldiers fighting in the Persian Gulf and Iraq wars and represented in these narratives have grown up in a culture of mediation, where it has been more acceptable than ever before to subvert or transcend traditional categories and norms of behavior, gender, and ethnicity. Similarly, developments in the accessibility of multiple media enable experiments with virtual or alternate identities, while advances in military and medical technologies offer the promise of a fighting self supplemented by such things as GPS-guided Humvees, night-vision goggles, online communications, and even robotic appendages. As young people, these soldiers have been encouraged to revel in their individuality, challenge restrictive categories, and make ample use of technology to do so. Contemporary American culture traffics in identities that are cyborg, hybrid, avatar.

But war thwarts these impulses to challenge binary modes of thinking and move beyond the need for categorization. The literature and film of these contemporary conflicts reveal soldiers who revel in the availability of communications and media technology, ready to live virtually as the star of the ultimate war movie. That media savvy and extensive knowledge of pop culture, however, is anything but a balm for the realities of war, and only exacerbates their sense of isolation and impotence. Other soldiers express dissatisfaction with traditional gender roles, most notably the dictates of masculinity, but their attempts to construct a viable alternative fail. Some arrive in Iraq ready to reach across national and ethnic divides and make a difference, but the invasion's execution prohibits them from doing so, reinforcing their sense of being strangers in a strange land. Finally, traumatized and injured veterans find that after such radical changes to the mind and body, the most sophisticated treatment and technology in the world can't always make them whole again. In these stories, many veterans return to the United States to discover the unexpected pain of being "in between" war and home, not able to fully exist in either state. This "blended" identity is not what they bargained for—but it is a common phenomenon nonetheless, and one that demands our attention.

Political commentators on the Iraq War have often referred to the conflict as "another Vietnam." Although there are certainly similarities in the length of the engagement and the public's growing disapproval of America's continued involvement, it would be wrong to assume that the soldier's experience is the same, or that it is represented in the same way. In Vietnam, most soldiers were drafted, yet their expectations of war were often romantic, shaped by the novels and films of World War II. Their ensuing disillusion was political—America wasn't quite what they thought it was. Ironically, the all-volunteer military in Iraq often seems *already* cynical, hardened against idealistic patriotism by their knowledge of things like the Watergate and Iran-Contra affairs. The first political memory for many soldiers today is an image of Monica Lewinsky, a stained dress, a president's indignant denial. And of course, their knowledge of what war is like is shaped by the Vietnam movies so many of them have watched over and over. Yet soldiers in these new war stories also feel betrayed—not necessarily by their nation, which many already believe is on a fool's errand in Iraq, but by the personal resources they expect to carry them through. They are politically cynical, but personally idealistic, believing themselves to be beyond the strict categories of race and gender, to be technologically and culturally savvy. But these resources fail them as well.

The stories of soldiers—who are also citizens, spouses, students, and employees—give us the grunt's-eye view of the events and consequences of the conflict at hand, often in opposition to reports from military leaders, politicians, and the media. Their stories have the power to change our national narrative. Right now, that national narrative *is* changing, and the soldiers, writers, and filmmakers addressing these contemporary wars are literally and figuratively on the front lines of those changes. They are innovators, as the stories they choose to tell as "first responders" will set the terms for other representations to follow. They may also set the terms for us. On 31 August 2010, President Obama announced the end of the combat mission in Iraq, saying that "it's time to turn the page" while also noting America's long-term partnership with Iraq and the reality that violence will not end with the end of the combat mission ("Remarks"). Operation Iraqi Freedom may be over, but the United States is still very much "in between" possible conclusions to—and about—the Iraq War.

Keep on Telling It

Though digital technology has dramatically changed the way soldiers' stories about contemporary war are told, war stories themselves are nothing new. Interested audiences have immersed themselves in the travails of battle as described in epic verse, displayed in museum exhibitions, lamented in song lyrics, and illustrated in great works of art and photography. Readers might page through the works of Homer, Thucydides, Polybius, and Virgil, marveling that ancient and modern combat are so different in some ways and so similar in others.[1] The great war stories of antiquity are many and various, though the last century saw its share of memorable and instructive representations of war. These stories are often categorized as either celebrations or critiques of battle—or, to use Sarah Cole's terms, "enchanting" or "disenchanting." "*Enchantment* refers to the tendency to see in violence some kind of transformative power," she writes, while disenchantment "is not a passive recognition of spiritual flatness but the active stripping away of idealized principles, an insistence that the violated body is not a magic site for the production of culture" (1631). In this sense, a work like Stephen Crane's *The Red Badge of Courage* (1895) is a double-edged sword. Written at the end of the nineteenth century about the Civil War, the book takes pains to emphasize realistic depictions of the physical conditions of battle and the psychological consequences of fighting while also highlighting the transformative power of the war experience. At the end of the book, soldier Henry Fleming has overcome his crippling fear and shame. The trials of battle have forged his identity, and he swells with pride at his newfound maturity and masculinity. "Scars faded as flowers," Crane writes in the book's final scene. "He was a man" (211).

In the twentieth century, many of America's most celebrated war writers wouldn't gloss over the pain and suffering of battle quite so easily as Crane, choosing instead to accentuate the disenchantment of war. Any "greatest hits" list of modern war literature is of course both subjective and incomplete, but many agree that Dalton Trumbo provides one of the starkest views of the horrors and consequences of war in his novel *Johnny Got His Gun* (1939). The stream-of-consciousness narration tracks the thoughts of a young World War I veteran, Joe Bonham, who slowly realizes that he has lost his arms, legs, sight, smell, and hearing. He has been reduced to almost nothing, but his mind continues to fight for control and for some way to communicate. "It was like a full grown man suddenly being stuffed back into his mother's body," he reflects about his traumatized state. "He was lying in stillness. He was completely helpless. Somewhere sticking in his stomach was a tube they fed him through. That was exactly like the womb except a baby in its mother's body could look forward to the time when it would live" (80–81). War makes Henry Fleming a man, but it takes away Bonham's masculinity along with everything else. When he finally discovers that he can communicate with the doctors and nurses by tapping with his head in Morse Code, they discourage his "speech" by drugging him. He wants to tell the world about the effects of war, but the world, it seems, is not ready to listen.

In stark contrast with World War I, World War II was a terrifically popular setting for inspiring stories of bravery and courage, young men fighting for "something greater" that justifies even the most extreme sacrifice. Yet some novelists upended the conventions of stories about the "Good War" in order to portray experiences that are surprisingly harsh, absurd, or otherwise disenchanting. Norman Mailer's first novel, *The Naked and the Dead* (1948), went against the grain by depicting a group of World War II soldiers engaged in an existentialist struggle with their commanders, each other, the conditions of war, and the natural world around them on the fictional Japanese island Anapopei. James Jones similarly dared to show World War II as something other than a righteous and courageous success in *The Thin Red Line* (1962), also set in the Pacific. In that story, instead of fighting for the cause, or their country, or even each other, the soldiers fight to achieve what Jones calls "combat numbness," a desirably blank emotional state that enables them to temporarily forget their fear and anxiety. Combat numbness is somewhat paradoxical, at least in Jones's description—soldiers "turn on" to the visceral excitement of combat in order to "turn off" their troubling emotions.[2] Paradox and absurdity, however, reach new heights in Joseph Heller's *Catch-22* (1961) and Thomas Pynchon's *Gravity's Rainbow* (1973). Pynchon interweaves descriptions of apocalyptic, technological, and sexual paranoia, and Heller articulates the paradox of war generally. "There was only one catch," he writes, "and that was Catch-22," the epitome and embodiment of war's absurdity. Catch-22 "specified that a concern for one's own safety in the face of dangers that were real and immediate was the process of a rational mind." To be afraid in life-threatening situations is perfectly reasonable—but not acceptable:

> Orr [one of the pilots] was crazy and could be grounded. All he had to do was ask; and as soon as he did, he would no longer be crazy and would have to fly more missions. Orr would be crazy to fly more missions and sane if he

didn't, but if he was sane he had to fly them. If he flew them he was crazy and didn't have to; but if he didn't want to he was sane and had to. (55)

The logic is as deadly as the bullets. And all the logic in the world, absurd or sound, can't save the protagonist Yossarian from the ultimate recognition of human mortality. After treating a wound on his comrade Snowden's thigh, reassuring him all the while that it isn't lethal, that he will be fine, Yossarian opens Snowden's flak jacket and the man comes apart in his hands. He "heard himself scream wildly as Snowden's insides slithered down to the floor in a soggy pile and just kept dripping out" (449). This is Snowden's secret, the real truth of war and life: "It was easy to read the message in his entrails. Man was matter, that was Snowden's secret...Ripeness was all" (450).

That secret—the trauma of war that can come spilling out, unbidden and unsuspected—became the center of many Vietnam War stories as well. That war was experienced as disenchanting not just by individual soldiers, but culturally, politically, and historically. Vietnam is a specter that has not yet been exorcised, an understanding that Larry Heinemann exploits to powerful effect in his novel *Paco's Story* (1986). There, the enigmatically named Paco Sullivan washes dishes with his scarred hands and never speaks about what happened to him in the war. That story is told by the novel's narrators, the ghosts of Paco's former comrades-in-arms. They literally haunt him, showing up most often at night, while Paco seeks the release of sleep: "It is at that moment we would slither and sneak, shouldering our way up behind the headboard, emerging like a newborn—head turned and chin tucked, covered head to toe with a slick gray ointment, powdery and moist, like the yolk of a hard-boiled egg, and smelling of petroleum" (137–38). The images are vivid and startling, appropriately nightmarish. But the acknowledged master of Vietnam's lingering ghosts is Tim O'Brien, whose works like *Going after Cacciato* (1978), *The Things They Carried* (1990), and *In the Lake of the Woods* (1994) portray the Vietnam War and its aftermath as inextricably bound up in the language and psychology of trauma. He writes about war's "surreal seemingness," how the extreme nature of the experience challenges familiar notions of truth and fiction and the very action of storytelling itself. That challenge gives O'Brien's work its narrative energy.[3] In some cases, he writes in *The Things They Carried,* "you can't even tell a true war story. Sometimes it's just beyond telling." But a few pages later, he adds, "You can tell a true war story if you just keep on telling it" (71, 85).

Writers like these have kept on telling war stories for centuries, and the most contemporary are discussed in the chapters that follow. Filmmakers, of course, have taken on the task with a younger medium. The first war film, *Tearing Down the Spanish Flag,* appeared in 1898 as the Spanish-American War began and showed hands (intended to be those of American soldiers) ripping away the Spanish flag in Havana and replacing it with the Stars and Stripes. Though quite short at ninety seconds, the film was a big hit, drawing crowds to nickelodeon theaters. The filmmakers J. Stuart Blackton and Albert Smith went on to make more films for the Vitagraph studio, including another 1898 release, *The Battle of Manila Bay.* For this film, they "recreated Admiral George Dewey's famous victory in the Blackton family bathtub; Smith took close-ups of cutouts of battleships that Blackton moved around in the water, while Mrs. Blackton puffed cigarette smoke at the lens to give the effect of gunfire from the ship's cannons" (Holsinger 190).

War films—and their special effects—have come a long way, and as cameras grew lighter and more portable fictional films achieved greater degrees of verisimilitude and documentaries could take audiences right into the middle of the action. In 1918, D. W. Griffith's *Hearts of the World* used footage of World War I shot the previous year near the British front lines. Lewis Milestone's 1930 adaptation of Erich Maria Remarque's *All Quiet on the Western Front* was shot on a California ranch rather than on the battlefield, but with over 2,000 veterans serving as extras its depiction of the devastated, almost lunar landscape of the front and the horrific consequences of mechanized warfare set a new standard for stark realism (Feaster). World War II was occasion for more collaboration than ever before between Hollywood and the military, with directors like Frank Capra explaining *Why We Fight* (1943–1945), and films like *Wake Island* (1942) and *Guadalcanal Diary* (1943) echoing the morale-boosting, patriotic messages of the military to the public.[4] The World War II story remained popular for decades with releases like *Stalag 17* (1953), *The Longest Day* (1962), and *Patton* (1970). Two big-budget World War II dramas were released in 1998—Steven Spielberg's *Saving Private Ryan* and Terrence Malick's adaptation of *The Thin Red Line.*

The Vietnam War worked somewhat differently on film. Initially, Hollywood was loath to tell stories about a war that was unpopular and seemingly unwinnable. John Wayne's *The Green Berets* (1968), which was a Vietnam War movie that relied on the conventions of the World War II film, was largely deemed a failure. *M*A*S*H* (1970) took the opposite tack, and its story about a group of medical personnel in the Korean War was understood to be implicitly about Vietnam. It wasn't until years after the war ended that Hollywood began to address the Vietnam experience in earnest in films like *The Deer Hunter* (1978), *Coming Home* (1978), and *Apocalypse Now* (1979), an interest that continued into the 1980s with *Platoon* (1986) and *Full Metal Jacket* (1987). The Persian Gulf War, as brief as it was, hasn't often served as subject matter for films, though *Three Kings* (1999) and *Jarhead* (2005) were well received. The Iraq War has inspired both documentaries and, especially since 2007, an increasing number of fictional films. (These will be discussed in detail in chapter 4.)

The Digital Battlefield

Though fictional films and documentaries continue to tell the stories of contemporary war, the public no longer relies on the direction and funding of a film studio or a major media organization to communicate the sights, sounds, and stories of battle. Anyone with access to reasonably up-to-date communications technologies can offer a portrait of or opinion about the contemporary war experience. The distance between the front lines and the home front can be virtually (if not actually) negated—and this is, as many have noted, undoubtedly one of the most significant changes to affect this new war experience and, in turn, these new war stories.

These communications technologies—often referred to as new media— rose to prominence in the years following the Persian Gulf War and have multiplied rapidly since America's invasion of Iraq in 2003. E-mail is ubiquitous, blogs have become as influential as mainstream news sources, and social networking sites like MySpace and Facebook have millions of users. Given even basic Internet access, soldiers can easily communicate with friends and family back home using e-mail, or make their stories and comments public by blogging. Blogs by soldiers and veterans who write from within the war zone or after their return home are referred to as milblogs, or military blogs, though this category can also include blogs written by military spouses, parents, and embedded reporters. The website milblogging.com (owned by military.com) claims to track 2,810 milblogs in forty-five countries as of September 2010. Thomas Conroy and Jarice Hanson have noted that all milblogs can be traced to a single blogger who wrote to counter the media's coverage of 9/11 (25). "Sgt. Stryker's Daily Briefing," begun in November 2001, was written by a blogger with the pseudonym John Stryker, borrowed from the Marine Sergeant played by John Wayne in *The Sands of Iwo Jima* (1949). In the "About Me" section of the blog, Stryker writes that he is an aircraft mechanic in the Air Force, and that he uses a pseudonym to "prevent his jealous and wrathful employer from smiting him from on high for voicing contrary opinions." His entries cease in January of 2002.[5]

Whether milbloggers are writing from a pro- or anti-war stance, they often set their task as providing a counterpoint to what the mainstream media or the military has to say about the war. Like bloggers generally, milbloggers seek to communicate against the stream of large-scale media institutions, which they believe aren't telling the whole story. And so they write their own story, making it digitally available for anyone who wants it. Some of the most popular milblogs have been published as books, including Colby Buzzell's "My War," Jason Christopher Hartley's "Just Another Soldier," and others like "Blackfive" and "Boots in Baghdad" that have been collected in the anthology *The Blog of War,* edited by Matthew Burden.

Blogs can include images, though they are primarily venues for text—for the written stories and opinions about the experience of war. Sites like YouTube, Google Video, and LiveLeak, however, allow soldiers to upload short videos taken with cell phones or small digital cameras that are easy to carry and use. Thus soldiers can tell their war stories through moving images, which are often supplemented by commentary or a soundtrack. Kari Andén-Papadopoulos has noted that like many milblogs, soldiers' videos "have introduced new and sometimes highly controversial perspectives into the documentation of warfare that military and media elites are struggling to contain" (17). Many videos celebrate soldiers working for the good in Iraq and emphasize humanitarian efforts that the media highlights less often, though even those that do can reveal sights and sounds of war that are institutionally verboten. Andén-Papadopoulos writes about how new media have changed the terms of the debate about images of war:

> Since the Vietnam War, news organizations and media scholars have debated the question of whether, and how, explicit images of the violence and carnage of war should be broadcast. For soldiers serving in Iraq, however, this is not an issue. They are clearly not impartial or external observers of the war, who abide by the dictate to serve the so-called "public interest." They are combatants documenting the war as they wage and experience it. (21)

Although the government would prefer to portray war as "clinical and even compassionate," online videos can reveal U.S. soldiers participating in seemingly indiscriminate violence against Iraqis, verbally abusing Iraqi children, or physically abusing animals, all of which have caused public outrage (18). Andén-Papadopoulos lists five categories of YouTube videos made and uploaded by soldiers during wartime: videos that show "combat action, routine patrolling, colloquial interaction with Iraqi civilians, recreation in the barracks, and tributes to fallen comrades" (20).[6] He goes on to consider several videos that have been widely circulated, such as "Lazy Ramadi," a parody of *Saturday Night Live*'s "Lazy Sunday" skit. In it, two National Guard staff sergeants make light of their dangerous posting, and the video—itself a parody of a parody—has spawned many imitators that also make fun of the war's grim outlook. Other videos aren't so lighthearted. In March 2008, a clip was posted (that has since been removed) showing a Marine, David Motari, throwing a puppy off a cliff. "The 17-second clip generated international attention and sparked outrage from animal rights groups around the world when it came to light," and Andén-Papadopoulos adds that it also resulted in Motari's expulsion from the Marine Corps.

The military, as one might imagine, has something to say not only about the actions these blogs and videos describe, but about soldiers' access to and use of new media in the first place. The military—the institution that commands and manages troops and the waging of war, as distinguished from the individual soldiers who fight it—acknowledges both the advantages and disadvantages of that access. On the one hand, the morale boost available to soldiers by fast, cheap, and frequent communication with loved ones back home is invaluable, as is the cathartic effect of sharing one's story in a creative way. On the other is the threat some communications pose to the military's message and even its operations. Writing in the *Military Review* in late 2007, Army Major Elizabeth Robbins weighs these issues, ultimately concluding that the risk of soldiers revealing too much information or negative opinions is outweighed by the ability of new media—and particularly milblogs—to "reveal the Army's human face" and educate the public in the "values, beliefs, and humanities of those in uniform" (111, 112). In order to manage that risk, Robbins calls for more and better training in information security and electronic communications, and a document that clearly outlines the acceptable and unacceptable uses of new media (116–17).

In fact, such regulations were released by the Pentagon in April 2007, stating that military personnel must consult with their supervisor and their operations security officer before posting to blogs or forums, restrictions that led some to bemoan the impending death of high-quality milblogging. Colby Buzzell is one milblogger whose posts may have contributed to the military's decision to pursue regulation, and who felt the effects of those policies. As he discovers, digital texts would be subject to review and what some called censorship. Images, however, fared worse. In March 2007—around the same time that the Pentagon published its regulations—the Department of Defense created its own channel on YouTube, called Multi-National Force—Iraq. This channel features videos that, according to Andén-Papadopoulos, adhere to "traditional norms of propaganda" and are designed to "counteract the prolific posting of damaging video clips by its own troops" (19). This effort was accompanied by an announcement in May that the military was blocking soldiers' access to YouTube, MySpace, and eleven other websites (Sipress and Diaz).

Of course, Americans aren't the only ones with access to new media, and Iraqis run the risk of harsher penalties than U.S. soldiers if they are caught voicing critical or unsanctioned opinions. When the new Iraqi Constitution was ratified in 2005, it included a basic guarantee of free speech, but that freedom has been poorly defined and defended. As Sophie Redmond reported in 2007, Article 38 of the constitution "renders respect for the right of freedom of expression conditional upon respect for public order and morality. This significantly limits the operative scope of the right and introduces the possibility for Iraqi authorities to restrict certain types of expression on the simple basis that these would not accord with notions of public order and morality" (4). In addition, journalists and media workers of all types are extremely vulnerable to threats, harassment, kidnapping, and attacks by insurgents. Redmond calls their working conditions "the worst and deadliest in the world for their profession," and notes that murder, not crossfire, is their leading cause of death (8).

Nonetheless, many Iraqis keep telling their stories in both traditional and new media, and their voices are also heard around the world, providing a portrait of the experience of war quite different from that offered by U.S. soldiers, regardless of their political views. Two of the best-known Iraqi blogs are Salam Pax's "Where Is Raed?" and Riverbend's "Baghdad Burning," both of which are written in English and have been published as books in the United States.[7] Salam (the blogger's real first name, though "Pax" is a pseudonym) began his blog as a way to keep in touch with his friend Raed, who moved to Jordan for his studies. The blog begins as an irreverent, cynical take on life in Iraq and the approaching war, and Salam shows off his detailed knowledge of politics as well as pop culture. One entry from September 2002 lists the music he likes to listen to while pulling a double shift at his job as an architect:

Toufic Farroukh: *Drab:zeen* (really good arabic / jazz / dance fusion)

Röyksopp: *Melody A. M.*

Timo Maas: *Loud* (and take a break when 'that's how I've been dancing' comes up to jump around)

David Bowie: *Heathen*

Lamb: *What Sound*

"And remember," he adds, "never ever try to do work or drive while listening to Björk or Aphex Twins—they do strange things to brain cells" (5). Before the war begins in earnest, even his bad days are described with a light touch: "Real-Life™ by GOD Inc. is not the greatest software available," he observes. "The system crashes whenever I run the damn program…The SIMS are much more fun. Just felt like sharing that" (11). Salam mocks other Iraqis who seek to communicate in English less fluently than he does: "I am compiling a Top Five list of my favourite Iraqi anti-Bush slogans in English. At the moment I have two competing for the top spot: 'Bush Go Hell!' and 'Down Down Bush and his Tail Blair!'" (21).

After the invasion, however, Salam's posts become less frequent and less buoyant. "American civil administration is having a shortage of Bright Ideas," he writes on 9 May 2003. "Why does it feel like they are using the let's-try-this, let's-try-that strategy? Trial and error on a whole country?" (167). After the British newspaper the *Guardian* sought him out in Baghdad in 2003, Salam began writing a series of columns for that publication, one of many bloggers whose online popularity led to opportunities to write in more traditional—and, notably, Western—venues. Today he continues to blog on a different site, salampax.wordpress.com.

Riverbend (also a pseudonym) was inspired to blog in part by reading Salam's posts, and writes her first entry on 17 August 2003. In that initial post, she gives her vital stats: "I'm female, Iraqi, and 24. I survived the war. That's all you need to know. It's all that matters these days anyway" (5). The next day, she vents her frustration about stereotypes of Iraqis and the accusations (leveled at Salam and eventually at her as well) that they are not "really" Iraqi. "You know what really bugs me about posting on the internet, chat rooms or message boards?" she asks. "The first reaction (usually from Americans) is 'You're lying, you're not Iraqi.' Why am I not Iraqi, well because, a. I have internet access (Iraqis have no internet), b. I know how to use the internet (Iraqis don't know what computers are), and c. Iraqis don't know how to speak English (I must be a Liberal). All that shouldn't bother me, but it does" (6). New media isn't only for Westerners, after all, nor is cultural sophistication. Riverbend explains that she was born in Iraq to Iraqi parents, that she lived abroad for several years when she was younger, and that after returning to Baghdad she studied English in school. "There are thousands in Iraq like me—kids of diplomats, students, expatriates, etc.... you wouldn't believe how many young Iraqi people know so much about American / British / French pop culture.... Iraqi TV stations were constantly showing bad copies of the latest Hollywood movies" (20).

Before the war, Riverbend worked at an Iraqi database/software company, and she grieves the loss of that "geeky" freedom and responsibility. Like "Where Is Raed?", Riverbend's blog reveals a detailed knowledge of politics, often explaining the goings-on for the benefit of non-Iraqi readers. She also describes the rituals associated with different holidays and festivities, and takes special care to note how the lifestyles and liberties women enjoyed before the war have been drastically curtailed. Like her, they have had to give up jobs and the freedom to walk unescorted by a man, and must now dress much more conservatively for fear of attack. Riverbend is media-savvy, and as Salam does, she often provides links to other blogs and articles and then posts her own responses. In April 2004, she wonders about why the world isn't allowed to see the war the way she does:

> I think Western news networks are far too tame. They show the Hollywood version of war—strong troops in uniform, hostile Iraqis being captured and made to face "justice" and the White House turkey posing with the Thanksgiving turkey...which is just fine. But what about the destruction that comes with war and occupation? What about the death? I don't mean just the images of dead Iraqis scattered all over, but dead Americans too. People should *have* to see those images. Why is it not ok to show dead Iraqis and American troops in Iraq, but it's fine to show the catastrophe of September 11 over and over again? I wish every person who emails me supporting the war, safe behind their computer, secure in their narrow mind and fixed views, could actually come and experience the war live. I wish they could spend just 24 hours in Baghdad today and hear Mark Kimmett talk about the death of 700 "insurgents" like it was a proud day for Americans everywhere. (254)

Just days later, Americans would be privy in a new way to images revealing the consequences of war and occupation—though these images showed the suffering of Iraqis contrasted with the seeming enjoyment of Americans. When the Abu Ghraib scandal broke in late April on *Sixty Minutes II* and in the *New Yorker,* the digital pictures of Iraqi prisoners bound, humiliated, and tortured quickly made their way around the world both in traditional news sources and on the Internet. Writing in early May, Riverbend describes her own and her community's incredible anger over what the pictures revealed. Everyone, she says, is livid. "There was a time here when the people felt sorry for the troops," she writes. Locals would watch the young Americans sweating in the heat in ill-fitting uniforms and pity their sense of displacement and discomfort. "That time has passed," she continues. "People look at the troops now and see the pictures of Abu Ghraib" (261).

But Iraqis aren't just looking at the Americans and the images they create. Many insurgent groups have been historically media-savvy, using the Internet for communications, recruiting, and the distribution of propaganda, some of which has been aired on stations like al-Jazeera or the BBC. The 2006 trial and sentencing of Saddam Hussein was seen all over the world, and videos of his hanging appeared as products of both tradi-tional and new media. The execution was filmed by an official government videographer, and the somber, discreet result was aired on Iraqi and Brit-ish television in an attempt to legitimize the decision to pursue a punish-ment that was both swift and severe. But, as Vian Bakir writes, unofficial footage of the event was covertly captured by a security guard using a cell phone camera. The guard uploaded his footage to the Internet, which was promptly and widely distributed. In the official version, Saddam stands silently as the charges are read, and the hanging is not shown. The un-official footage, however, shows Saddam denouncing America and being taunted by witnesses. He begins to recite the Shahada, the Muslim decla-ration of faith, but is prevented from completing it when the door opens underneath him. Saddam falls and dies, and the camera lingers on his face (Bakir 12). The execution became controversial, Bakir notes, "because the rapid and widespread dissemination of unofficial footage captured by mo-bile phone directly contradicted the official sanitized version" (8). War has always been an ugly and messy business, but new media have created new windows into that mess, windows that are accessible to anyone with an Internet connection in any part of the world.

Soldiers and citizens living and working in Iraq have provided some of the most prominent and well known of those windows, and their blogs, pictures, and videos do often serve to contradict or counter the messages of larger and more powerful institutions. Those institutions also have an interest in the use of new media, and the military establishment has a lon-ger history than most realize in communications and simulation technolo-gies. Battlefield communications are instrumental in the implementation of successful strategy, and simulation—the virtual modeling of scenarios for both training and strategic purposes—is a pursuit that dates back to the development of chess or the Asian game Go. Ed Halter, in his history of war and gaming, writes about the ancient Greek game *petteia,* the Vi-kings' *hnefatafl,* and the Welsh *gwyddbwyll,* all evidence of how "[c]ultures around the world have shaped games to represent war, and in turn have used this theme of war to enhance the experience of playing games" (6). Games like Grosses Koenigsspiel, or "King's Game," developed by Christo-pher Weikhmann of Ulm in the mid-1600s, were specifically designed to teach nobles how to serve as military officers, and do so in a way that pro-vided entertainment as well. The game included pieces to represent a king, a marshal, chancellors, heralds, lieutenants, bodyguards, and others, and could accommodate eight players on a board of almost 700 squares (36).

Three hundred years later, armies were still seeking the most effective ways to simulate battlefield action. In 1976, the military asked the Defense Advanced Research Projects Agency (DARPA) to build scale models that they could use for training. DARPA then worked with Nicholas Negroponte of MIT's Media Laboratory to simulate battlefield situations more effectively by using video editing. That program would eventually become the Department of Defense's Modeling and Simulation Coordination Office (Guest 151). When in 1980 Atari released *Battlezone,* a futuristic tank battle game, the Army modified it so that it would have controls similar to those in a Bradley Infantry Fighting Vehicle (Herz and Macedonia 7). *Doom* was released in 1993, and introduced gamers to the first-person shooter perspective and 3-D graphics; the game allowed players to assume the role of a renegade Marine fighting demons on Mars. In 1996, the Marine Corps Modeling and Simulation Management Office adapted *Doom II* into *Marine Doom* by editing the commercial version to simulate the conditions of urban combat. This version, which was used to train four-person fire teams, "ostensibly taught concepts such as mutual fire team support, protection of the automatic rifleman, proper sequencing of an attack, ammunition discipline, and succession of command" (7). Other commercial games that have been adapted for use by the military are *Tom Clancy's Rainbow Six: Rogue Spear, Delta Force 2,* and *Microsoft Flight Simulator.*[8]

The online war game *America's Army* was launched on 4 July 2002 by the Army's Modeling, Virtual Environment, and Simulation Institute at the Naval Postgraduate School, and went further than all previous efforts in combining the goals of the military and the entertainment industry. As Ed Halter reports, in May 2003 Black Hawk helicopters appeared in the skies above Los Angeles and disgorged a group of U.S. Special Forces who rappelled to the ground and charged into the L.A. Convention Center, where the Electronic Entertainment Expo was in full swing (vii–viii). They were there to promote *America's Army;* Halter notes that the game had more than five million registered users in 2005 (ix). Quite a few of those players were actual Army soldiers. Players with a valid military e-mail address could request that their avatars wear an Army logo, something that more than 6,000 players were doing in early 2005 (xiv).

Games like *America's Army* and *World of Warcraft* are considered by many to be harbingers of the next stage of new media—immersive, multiuser virtual worlds that go far beyond the one- or two-way communication of blogs and video-sharing sites. Combat is, as ever, a primary interest of gamers, whether it happens in the urban, vaguely Middle Eastern environment of *America's Army,* or the fantasy role-playing world of *Warcraft.* The virtual world called Second Life is also immersive and multiuser, though it differs from the others because it has no particular narrative or purpose for the players to pursue. A player's representative, or avatar, can engage in combat if the player wishes, but can just as easily construct virtual buildings, purchase virtual clothing or other goods, dance, chat with other avatars, or even meditate. The choices are not quite infinite, but they are extensive enough to generate excitement. In writing about Second Life, Tom Boellstorff notes that the appeal of virtual worlds can be understood in terms of potentiality—they "approach the actual *without arriving there*" (19). Indeed, much has been made of players' ability to embody an avatar of differing race, gender, physical properties, or even species. A Second Life character named Wilde Cunningham has achieved some renown, as he is an avatar played by a group of nine men and women with cerebral palsy. "Many residents with actual-world disabilities found that Second Life broadened their social networks," writes Boellstorff. "Residents often noted with astonishment that they would interact with someone for weeks or months before learning that they had an actual-world disability like hearing impairment or stroke-related paralysis" (137). In a similar vein, James Cameron's 2009 mega-budget film *Avatar* tells the story of a disabled veteran who, by virtually inhabiting the body of an alien being that is ten feet tall and a vivid blue, can engage in all the activities expected of a sci-fi action hero.

What better way to transcend boundaries and escape the forces that have traditionally circumscribed identity? Online worlds like Second Life would seem to provide just that—a chance to live virtually and revel in potentiality. In many ways the virtuality is freeing. Avatars in Second Life can fly, teleport instantly anywhere in the world, have blue skin—or no skin at all. But for all the advantages, this world—like the real world—isn't perfect. Non-white avatars have been known to encounter discrimination, and W. James Au tells the story of a woman who changes her avatar's appearance from blond and tan to African American and encounters a number of negative reactions from both friends and strangers in the virtual world (73). And conflict is inevitable. As Au puts it, "For the first decade of its popular use, the Internet has been a marvelous way of bringing people from around the world together online—mostly so they can learn just how much they can't stand each other. For every instance of individuals and communities coming together online in a positive way, there are surely thousands more where the interaction is fraught and divisive" (103). Hate speech and harassment are just as easy—if not easier—to engage in virtually as they are in person.

The Second Life idyll, then, begins to look more and more like the real world. And just like life in the real world, war can be hard to escape. In April 2003, as U.S. troops were entering Iraq, players from a different online game entered Second Life. The other game, which allows players to fight in scenarios based on World War II, is a "complex, massively multiplayer simulation," reports Au, "and so the people who play it tend to be older history buffs and experts on weapons and tactics of the era; many are veterans, active-duty military, or Army brats" (106). They were drawn to the Outlands area of Second Life, a kind of free-fire zone where combat was acceptable. Many Second Life players initially welcomed the World War II gamers. Eventually, however, conflict began between the gamers and the Residents (as Second Life players are called) that soon erupted into full-scale battle. One particular area of the Outlands became a surreal territory that saw all manner of weapons and combat engagement. "Someone imported audio clips from *Full Metal Jacket*," notes Au, "so R. Lee Ermey's deranged, hyper-obscene drill sergeant rants echoed through the place, giving it that extra tinge of madness" (111).

But it wasn't just combat that invaded the virtual world—the politics of combat did as well. On one of the walls marking the territory's boundary, players began to post signs of support or protest of the war in Iraq, and those political associations informed the virtual combat. Ironically, Au writes, according to one of his sources, some of the World War II gamers "originally hoped Second Life would offer a respite from the politically heated Iraq-related talk that had scorched up their game's off-topic discussion boards, in the run-up to the invasion" (107). In the original Residents' virtual idyll, virtual combat appeared and spoiled their dreams of peace and quiet. But for those who would fight for fun as an escape from real-world politics and divisiveness, the idyll shatters just as easily. War, whether virtual or actual, always shows up. There are at least two Iraq War memorials in Second Life honoring the fallen soldiers, and one player, Derek LeTellier, recreated the destruction of the World Trade Center. As Tim Guest reports, LeTellier built two tall virtual buildings, and then knocked them down. When the towers fell, they caused virtual havoc—the "world" crashed, and all players were ejected (4). When the servers were restarted, LeTellier built a virtual screen, on which he showed images of the virtual 9/11. Other players gathered to discuss whether the display was appropriate or not (13). "I have a question," one player wrote, commenting on Second Life's coverage of the event. "When does Third Life come out so we can escape our second one?" (qtd. in Guest 16).

The Second Life of War

As it turns out, even avatars can't escape the problems of politics, discrimination, and conflict. We shouldn't discount the personal innovation and experimentation that technologies like Second Life allow and encourage. But the desire and potential for transcendence, for a different way of being, that is so evident in many of these virtual worlds is often at least partially thwarted by the inevitable intrusion of what might be called "real life"—the discomfort, disgruntlement, and disagreement that is so much a part of human interaction. The disappointment that results from the realization that living virtually doesn't mean living idyllically or even that much differently echoes the disappointment seen in stories of contemporary war. This makes sense—if the everyday conflicts of real life are disrupting and disenchanting, then the lethal conflict of war would be much more so.

It's true that some aspects of the war experience may initially seem freeing. New recruits shuck their old selves like husks, emerging from boot camp with less hair, different clothes, strong bodies, and new skills. And in some ways war *is* a kind of second life, where many of the rules of civilian life don't apply. In the virtual world, avatars can elude the laws of biology and physics, and can even kill other avatars without serious consequences—death, in Second Life, is overcome with the click of a mouse. Soldiers have similar freedoms—they are given access to complex and lethal technologies that enable them to see in the dark, to move over otherwise impassable terrain, and, of course, to kill. For soldiers, killing in the context of war is presented as a pragmatic, political, and even moral necessity, a complete inversion of the legal and moral tenets of civilian life. Soldiers can kill, do kill, must kill, and the possession of that lethal power can at times be intoxicating. Initially, it can seem like one is the star of one's own movie or living in a very realistic game. But in this life—the second life of the soldier at war—the sense of freedom one might experience when old restrictions are lifted and old ways of living are so dramatically changed is counterbalanced, and for many, outweighed by other limitations. And the limitations of a soldier's life can be devastating. They must dress alike, walk alike, talk alike, and identify themselves within a strict hierarchy and against a specific enemy, but the most extreme limitation is that of life itself. Injury, pain, and death are real and immediate, and the shattering experience of both attacking and being attacked can result in lasting physical and mental trauma. In war, the realities of biology, physics, and psychology can hit home with a vengeance—and there's no way to log off.

Trying to exist "in between," in a space of potential and possibility, isn't so easy, especially on the battlefield. In this book, I examine a selection of contemporary war stories from the Persian Gulf War and the Iraq War. How do soldiers fighting these wars experience them? I show how these newest war stories have a new twist, even as they address familiar, even ancient subjects: the initiation into battle and the ways that older war stories influence that initiation; the effects of war on ideas about manhood and masculinity; encounters with the enemy and, more broadly, with another culture; and the aftermath of war, especially as shaped by injury and trauma. These are common aspects of the war story that other artists like Homer, Crane, and O'Brien have kept on telling. The new twist in the new stories, however, is the palpable desire to transcend categorization, to live in between what traditional boundaries, norms, and standards would dictate. That transcendence—weighty currency in a contemporary American society enmeshed in notions of multiculturalism, mediation, and new media—proves to be an elusive ideal for soldiers fighting these most recent American wars.

In this book I discuss two Gulf War memoirs by Anthony Swofford and Joel Turnipseed that provide a portrait of soldiers living and fighting on the cusp of the major political and technological changes that would begin in earnest just a few years later. The Iraq War, a much longer conflict, has given rise to more and various representations; I cover a blog by Colby Buzzell, memoirs by Nathaniel Fick and Kayla Williams, a collection of stories by

John Crawford, poetry by Brian Turner, and the documentary and fictional films *Alive Day Memories* and *In the Valley of Elah*. The chapters that follow discuss Swofford's and Buzzell's initation into war; Turnipseed's, Fick's, and Williams's struggles with notions of masculinity and identity; Crawford's and Turner's encounters with Iraqi soldiers and civilians; and *Alive Day*'s and *Elah*'s depictions of postwar trauma. There are other works, of course— many others, and more coming out every day. I chose these because they are each prominent and much-discussed examples of this first wave of new war narratives and because the thwarted desire for transcendence that they represent is such a powerful and poignant part of the stories they tell.

These stories are about and, in most cases, written by American soldiers. Some soldier-authors begin to write during the war, as Crawford and Turner do, continuing and pursuing publication after they are back home. For Iraqis writing about war, there may be no separation between the home front and the front lines, giving the war experience an immediacy that's apparent in Salam Pax's and Riverbend's blogs. Translated works of Iraqi fiction and nonfiction have been less available for American audiences, though some by authors like Dunya Mikhail and Betool Khedairi have gained distinction. Although the focus of this book is the war stories of American soldiers, I have also included brief considerations of these Iraqi works—where the pain of thwarted desire is that much sharper and more grievous.

The 2009 film *The Hurt Locker* begins with a quotation from Chris Hedges. "War is a drug," he writes, "a potent and often lethal addiction" (2–3). Yes—it was true for Achilles, and it is true for Sergeant First Class William James, the protagonist of that film and a character I discuss in some detail in the conclusion. Yet the film's title refers to a place of pain, the internal or external experience of suffering that can't be negated by the adrenaline rush of combat. Soldiers often use the phrase to refer to a way of coping with the chaos and confusion of war. After a scalding experience, what can you do that will enable you to get up, go outside the wire, and continue to do your job? Put that experience in the hurt locker, and deal with it later. Luckily, many soldiers haven't kept that hurt locker closed indefinitely, and open it to write or otherwise tell their stories—as Brian Turner does in his poem also titled "The Hurt Locker." These stories are thrilling, painful, lovely, horrific, and intimate. It benefits all of us if, when the locker opens and the voices begin, we listen.

1

Lines of Sight

Watching War in Jarhead *and* My War: Killing Time in Iraq

War is the world's second-oldest form of entertainment. From Achilles and Cúchulainn to Krishna and the Volsungs of Icelandic saga, our most enduring stories are about war and war heroes, and the post-Neolithic art found on every continent except Antarctica suggests our fascination with the images of battle as well. Getting caught up in the representation of war allows for the vicarious (and safe) enjoyment of its thrilling and troubling spectacle and the chance to take a peek at life and death in extremis. That spectacle can be captivating even for those in the midst of war, where the investment in the deadly goings-on is much more dire. The desire simply to see, politics and morality aside, can be overwhelming. "Part of the love of war stems from its being an experience of great intensity," notes Bill Broyles, in his famous essay "Why Men Love War." "[I]ts lure is the fundamental human passion to witness, to see things, what the Bible calls lust of the eye and the Marines in Vietnam called eye fucking" (56). War, after all, can be the show to end all shows. "For all its horror, you can't help but gape at the awful majesty of combat," Tim O'Brien writes in "How to Tell a True War Story." "You admire the fluid symmetries of troops on the move, the harmonies of sound and shape and proportion, the great sheets of metal-fire streaming down from a gunship, the illumination rounds, the white phosphorous, the purply orange glow of napalm, the rocket's red glare.... It's astonishing. It fills the eye. It commands you. You hate it, yes, but your eyes do not" (80–81).

Broyles and O'Brien frame this passion to witness actual war as an illicit pleasure, unlike, one assumes, reading the *Iliad* for a college class. As battle rages and real people die, morality would perhaps dictate that you should look away and not desire to see such horrible things. Of course you hate it, says O'Brien—any "normal" person could not possibly approve of such pain, suffering, and destruction—but you love watching, too. And so you indulge in visual lust. New soldiers often anticipate this very pleasure, the chance to see things that people aren't supposed to see. In decades and centuries past they might have fed their anticipation by listening to the stories of their elders or reading war histories, but since the advent of films—and more particularly, videos—they have the opportunity to view and re-view representations of what those sights might be like. In two recent memoirs, the former infantrymen Anthony Swofford and Colby Buzzell have portrayed the experience of preparing to fight the Gulf War and the Iraq War while watching films about the Vietnam War with something like the illicit pleasure that Broyles and O'Brien describe. Those films are most often thought to be antiwar, and yet instead of reflecting somberly on the carnage at hand, Swofford and Buzzell thrill to the violent and sexy spectacle of fighters like them violating social and moral taboos.[1] They watch raucously, confident in their own agency as military men who will soon wield power and violence the same way they wield the gaze.[2]

Swofford and Buzzell are indeed enchanted by these films, and ready to be initiated into the theater of war. That initiation, however, occurs differently than they expect. In this chapter, I explore what happens when these watchers go to war, as described by Swofford in *Jarhead,* his 2003 memoir of the Gulf War, and by Buzzell in *My War: Killing Time in Iraq,* his 2005 memoir of the Iraq War. These two men have since emerged as first-person spokesmen for the soldier's experience in late twentieth- and early twenty-first-century war. Swofford has since written pieces for *Harper's Magazine* and the *New York Times,* and published a novel *Exit A; Jarhead* was adapted for the screen in 2005. Buzzell's *My War* received the 2007

Lulu Blooker Prize, for books based on blogs, or "blooks," besting 110 entries from fifteen countries (Pilkington). Buzzell now writes regularly for *Esquire* and has been featured on National Public Radio's "This American Life." Both appeared in the Public Broadcasting Service documentary *Operation Homecoming: Writing the Wartime Experience* alongside such venerated war writers as O'Brien and Paul Fussell, anointed by the media as the latest members of a literary cadre of veterans turned authors.

Swofford and Buzzell notably emphasize the voyeuristic delight they take in watching war onscreen before and during their military service. But after they enthusiastically consume the illicit pleasure of these war films—this "military pornography"—they experience a kind of identity crisis, in which they recognize the vulnerability of their own position as representations themselves. These soldiers fight as representatives of the nation, and watchers are certainly not immune to being watched as well. What results is a lingering uncertainty about what war means for them, as significant points of reference like the movies and the military itself are emptied, at least in part, of their seductive power. Technology enables them to sit in the dark and live in the cinematic, virtual world of the Vietnam War; unfortunately, however, real war admits no avatars. Swofford and Buzzell find that the gaze that seemed to give them such power has been turned on them. They feel objectified, and in response, Swofford roils with sexually coded anger and frustration, while Buzzell chooses to amplify his own display by starting a blog. They are both exposed—as spectacle and as targets—and their discussion of that exposure reflects the pleasures and concerns of new media technologies as well as the complex networks of information and force mapping out America's ongoing presence in Iraq.

Jarhead and *My War* are compelling texts in part because they show the relationship between the contemporary experience of war and the changing technologies of representation. War stories, after all, are being told in new ways. As late as the Vietnam War, soldiers were limited to writing letters that the military could censor and to watching movies communally, if they were given access to a projector and film reels. Since the 1990s the increasing accessibility of media like video and digital texts has greatly affected these soldiers' expectations of and reactions to combat and, in turn, the way in which a noncombatant readership encounters Swofford's and Buzzell's representations of that experience. These lines of sight, all targeting the spectacle of war, reveal the contemporary intersections among war, media, and agency.

Iraq, 1991

Jarhead was published to much acclaim in March 2003, just sixteen days before the Iraq War began; positive reviews appeared in the *New York Times, Newsweek,* and the *Boston Globe.*[3] In the book, Anthony Swofford chronicles the making of his military self. A crucial step in this process occurs early in the story, when a group of young Marine Corps recruits gathers to watch Vietnam War movies like *Apocalypse Now, Full Metal Jacket,* and *Platoon.* It's 1990—Iraq has just invaded Kuwait, and they are on eager standby to join Operation Desert Shield. Swofford describes them all reveling in the representation of the jaded warriors they want to become.

> For three days we sit in our rec room and drink all of the beer and watch all of those damn movies, and we yell *Semper fi* and we head-butt and beat the crap out of each other and we get off on the various visions of carnage and violence and deceit, the raping and killing and pillaging. We concentrate on the Vietnam films because it's the most recent war, and the successes and failures of that war helped write our training manuals. (5–6)

And indeed the films provide a different kind of training. Swofford acknowledges that directors like Francis Ford Coppola, Stanley Kubrick, and Oliver Stone may have intended their films to be antiwar but that he and his fellow soldiers (or soldiers-to-be) "watch the same films and are excited by them, because the magic brutality of the films celebrates the terrible and despicable beauty of their fighting skills" (6–7).

The director Sam Mendes, in his 2005 film adaptation of Swofford's book, dramatizes this sequence by showing the recruits ecstatically singing and shouting along as they watch the "Ride of the Valkyries" helicopter attack in *Apocalypse Now.* That scene, in Coppola's 1979 film, was intended to be by turns thrilling, memorable, and deeply disturbing. Lawrence Weschler reports that Coppola was initially reluctant to allow the footage to be used in *Jarhead,* because, as the film editor Walter Murch says, "he apparently wasn't pleased at the prospect of his complex film being reduced

Figure 1. In the film adaptation of *Jarhead* (Universal Studios, 2005), a group of Marines about to leave for Iraq cheer the "Ride of the Valkyries" sequence in *Apocalypse Now.*

so narrowly to the aspect of its use as military pornography—and in the end, Sam [Mendes] had to plead with him personally to secure his tentative approval for use of the Valkyrie sequence" (qtd. in Weschler 68).

Vietnam War films can be fun to watch in part because they make ample use of 1960s rock and roll, music that has been so identified with that conflict that Swofford resents his comrades for playing it during "his" war. David James has argued that representations of the Vietnam War use rock and roll to invoke that war's unique "mix of terror and ecstasy" and "allow it a place in the interlocking myths and apparatuses of the mass media" (85, 80). Works like Michael Herr's *Dispatches* (1977), a personal and often surreal history of the conflict, and Hal Ashby's *Coming Home* "rewrote genocide as rock and roll" by displacing the devastating and confusing aspects of the Vietnam War onto the aural and commodified pleasures of popular music (80). For Swofford those aspects of war *are* the source of his communally experienced visual and illicit pleasure—no displacement necessary. According to him, the violence of the movies may be "terrible and despicable," but it is also "magic." Compare the experience Swofford describes with watching a typical World War II film like *Thirty Seconds Over Tokyo* (1944) or *The Longest Day* (1962), where viewers are encouraged to take righteous pleasure in identifying with the heroes onscreen. Instead, Swofford locates himself and the others "in the wrong," on the other side of what traditional morality would dictate, and they love it. Or, perhaps more accurately, they lust after it: "Fight, rape, war, pillage, burn. Filmic images of death and carnage are pornography for the military man; with film you are stroking his cock, tickling his balls with the pink feather of history, getting him ready for his real First Fuck" (7). The visual and illicit pleasure of these movies is acknowledged here as distinctly sexual, though it is still distinguished from the "*real* First Fuck," the ultimate initiation into the authentic experience of combat.

Watching these movies gives Swofford a powerful sense of agency on several levels. He identifies completely with the onscreen soldiers while the enemies become, quite literally, objects, their wounding and death the source of great viewing pleasure.[4] Swofford gets to be a voyeur—that is, he can visually penetrate the spectacle onscreen and take pleasure (and specifically sexual pleasure) in its offerings without being vulnerable himself.[5] He also has the promise of both lethal and, as he notes, sexual penetration—again, without any kind of reciprocal openness. Swofford sees watching, fighting, and fucking as roughly equivalent, and at this point in his military experience he is firmly established in the position of power: he watches, he will fight, he will fuck. He has been primed for this potent blend of intoxicated and intoxicating sexuality and violence. He is ready for war as he has seen it: "Now is my time to step into the newest combat zone. And as a young man raised on the films of the Vietnam War, I want ammunition and alcohol and dope, I want to screw some whores and kill some Iraqi motherfuckers" (7).

In the 1990s movies were a readily available resource for fostering that agency—and, with the advent of videotape, a resource more easily copied and transported. However, the voyeuristic consumption of military pornography that Swofford describes is hardly a new development. In 1985 Richard Holmes published *Acts of War: The Behavior of Men in Battle,* one of the first psychological and sociological studies of the experience of the common soldier. Holmes notes that "[t]he soldier's preconception of battle is shaped, not only by his upbringing, education, and training, but also by the influence of the art, literature and film to which he has been exposed. The arts, in their broadest sense, play a more important role in creating images of war than is generally recognized" (59). And this is true for wars and soldiers throughout history and across cultures. John Milius, who wrote *Apocalypse Now* with Coppola, says that unlike his co-author he is "proud to join the long line of military pornographers, right up there with Homer and Shakespeare and Tolstoy and Hemingway" (qtd. in Weschler 73). Often, however, soldiers go to war and find that their own experiences are quite different, sometimes maddeningly so, from representations of previous wars that have informed their conception of and conscription into military service. Holmes also points out that "[t]he risks of such gulfs between preconception and reality are colossal. Battle is a traumatic experience at the best of times. But if it produces not only all the stresses of noise and danger but also the dislocation of expectation, then the risks of failure and breakdown loom large" (73). For a soldier directly encountering the violence of war, that violence is suddenly and often traumatically made real by the perception of pain or the presence of the dead and wounded—what Elaine Scarry calls the incontestable reality of the body (56).

World War I poets railed against the aristocratic and chivalric fancies that pressed them into service, into trenches and inhumanly mechanized warfare. Wilfred Owen bitterly accuses those who

> tell with such high zest
> To children ardent for some desperate glory,
> The old Lie: Dulce et Decorum est
> Pro patria mori.

Later, many Vietnam veterans-turned-authors would hold a special place of enmity in their hearts for the scores of patriotic World War II movies they saw as kids. In his novel *The Short-Timers* (1979), from which Kubrick's *Full Metal Jacket* was adapted, Gustav Hasford describes a group of American soldiers in Vietnam watching *The Green Berets*. As I mentioned in the introduction, this 1968 film was the first to address the war in Vietnam, though it starred and was co-directed by John Wayne, an icon of World War II movies. In Hasford's book, the soldiers delight in the screening, but not because they find the film realistic, or even plausible:

> I prop my boots on the seats and we watch John Wayne leading the Green Beanies. John Wayne is a beautiful soldier, clean-shaven, sharply attired in tailored tiger-stripe jungle utilities, wearing boots that shine like black glass.

Inspired by John Wayne, the fighting soldiers from the sky go hand-to-hand
with all of the Victor Charlies in Southeast Asia. He snaps out an order to an
Oriental actor who played Mr. Sulu on "Star Trek." Mr. Sulu, now playing
an Arvin officer, delivers a line with great conviction: "First kill…all stinking Cong…then go home." The audience of Marines roars with laughter.
This is the funniest movie we have seen in a long time.

Later, at the end of the movie, John Wayne walks off into the sunset with
a spunky little orphan. The grunts laugh and whistle and threaten to pee all
over themselves. The sun is setting in the South China Sea—in the East—
which makes the end of the movie as accurate as the rest of it. (38)

These soldiers maintain a cynical distance from the representation of
the same war they are ostensibly fighting. Unlike Swofford, who watches
Vietnam War movies and finds them titillating, or pornographic, Hasford's soldiers see *The Green Berets* as merely obscene, a gross misrepre-
sentation that provokes only hilarity. Grizzled and experienced, they
understand the difference between their war and the movie's version of
it, which not everyone has the chance to figure out, according to Michael
Herr. In *Dispatches,* he writes, "I keep thinking about all the kids who got
wiped out by seventeen years of war movies before coming to Vietnam to
get wiped out for good…We'd all seen too many movies, stayed too long
in Television City, years of media glut had made certain connections difficult" (209). What kind of connections does Herr mean? Maybe the connection between the idea of death and its material fact, its incontrovertible
evidence. Maybe the reminder that it is not always sweet and right to die
for one's country, as Horace (quoted by Owen) and John Wayne would
have it. And maybe the realization that the power of a penetrating gaze
or weapon is short-lived, that one can just as easily be found in someone
else's lines of sight.

In Swofford's account, that sense of power begins to unravel when the
men travel overseas and their war experience begins in earnest. They are
consumed with thoughts about wives and girlfriends whose fidelity is always suspect; at the same time, they begin to realize that they can be taken
as objects as well. Swofford obsesses about his sometime girlfriend Katrina, who, he imagines, sleeps with other men but always comes back to
him because combat "seems sexy" to her, because she has a "military fetish"
(69). He can also be watched, fetishized, made into a symbol for someone
else's gaze. As a jarhead, Swofford realizes, "[t]hough you might be an

individual, first you are a symbol, or part of a larger symbol that some people believe stands for liberty and honor and valor, God and country and Corps. Sometimes this is correct, sometimes this is foolish. But either way, you are part of the goddamn thing." You are also all the other jarheads in the world, the ones with poor grammar, with the "silly regulation mustachio," the ones drunk at high noon, the ones "fighting and warring and cussing and killing in every filthy corner of the godforsaken globe, from 1775 until now, they are you. This is troubling and difficult to admit, and it causes you unending anguish, and you attempt to deny it, but it's true. Even now" (119–20).

Swofford reacts to Katrina's apparent betrayal by adding her picture to the Wall of Shame, a post covered in pictures of and comments on women who are cheating or are assumed to be cheating. "It is not necessarily a bad thing," he muses, "to be able to tell the story of your woman's betrayal" (92). He attempts to deny his status as betrayed, as object or symbol, by reclaiming the privileged status of the viewer, though that status has been compromised. To that same end, he joins another movie-screening session, ready to sit back and be pleasured by the entertaining display. "And the pleasure of the violent films," Swofford tells us, "is like the pleasure of cocaine or a good rough fuck" (64). This time, however, the soldiers are delighted to find that military pornography and actual pornography have become interchangeable, because someone has spliced scenes from a homemade sex tape into a Vietnam War flick. "The barracks full of unsuspecting marines cheered a screen full of jungle carnage as the on-screen marines charged a VC bunker, then in midcinematic combat frenzy the barracks went silent when the screen turned from overwhelming firepower to the sleek power of sex. After a few seconds, the room erupted" (65).

As becomes clear, one grunt's wife made the video of herself having sex with a neighbor as an act of cinematic revenge. The Marine in question screams in recognition, and they turn off the video—at least until the next night, because, as Swofford puts it, "[W]hy not, the damage is done and when is the next time you'll be able to witness infidelity? And fuck that poor jarhead anyway. He's down at sick call on suicide watch, and as soon as the docs okay him, he'll be on an emergency-leave flight to the States, he'll be the fuck out of the desert" (65). Even though the cuckolded jarhead has been humiliated by his wife's flamboyant betrayal, Swofford refuses to deny himself the chance to watch—and watch again.

Despite his posturing, Swofford has begun to realize that he, too, may have gotten screwed, and not just by his girlfriend. The anger he and the other soldiers feel at the unexpected reversal of their agency boils over when they are forced to demonstrate their protective gear for visiting reporters. That gaze rankles. They are ordered to play touch football in their cumbersome protective suits and gas masks, which they do until a grunt named Kuehn takes another down in a tackle. The game "degenerates," and the soldiers decide to demonstrate a "field-fuck," much to the displeasure of their staff sergeant. A field-fuck, Swofford explains, is "an act wherein marines violate one member of the unit, typically someone who has recently been a jerk or abused rank or acted antisocial, ignoring the unspoken contracts of brotherhood and camaraderie and esprit de corps and the combat family. The victim is held in the doggie position and his fellow marines take turns from behind" (20–21). Swofford is a bit coy here, but sexual penetration is clearly imitated rather than actual. The "violation" of the "victim," however, makes the rules clear—break with us and suffer the consequences. Yet what happens this time is less a punishment of Kuehn than an expression of the frustration and rage the soldiers feel at having their agency eroded. In sexual pantomime, Swofford and the others take turns being violently sexual agents, but it is painfully clear to the men that the powerful act of penetration here is only an act, and their phallic mastery just a phantom:

> I stand back from a turn with Kuehn. I feel frightened and exhilarated by the scene...a pure surge of passion and violence and shared anger, a pure distillation of our confusion and hope and shared fear. We aren't field-fucking Kuehn: we're fucking the press-pool colonel, and the sorry, worthless MOPP suits, and the goddamn gas masks and canteens with defective parts, and President Bush and Dick Cheney and the generals, and Saddam Hussein, and the PRC-77 radio and the goddamn heavy E-tools that can't help us dig deep enough holes; we're fucking the world's televisions, and CNN; we're fucking the sand and the loneliness and the boredom and the potentially unfaithful wives and the bad food and the fuckhead peaceniks back home.... [W]e're fucking our confusion and fear and boredom; we're fucking ourselves for signing the contract, for listening to the soothing lies of the recruiters, for letting them call us buddy and pal and dude, luring us into this life of loneliness and boredom and fear; we're fucking all of the hometown girls we've wanted and never had; we're angry and afraid and acting the way we've been trained to kill, violently and with no

remorse. We take turns, and we go through the line a few times and Kuehn takes it all, like the thick, rough Texan he is, our emissary to the gallows, to the chambers, to death do us part. (21–22)

Swofford is exhilarated, but his exhilaration differs from the thrill of watching war movies. The field-fuck allows the soldiers to finally express their anger, fear, boredom, and loneliness and—paradoxically—represents every way they have been objectified as soldiers and as men. The seemingly rough and aggressive act is actually neither; Kuehn eagerly plays along with the playacting. The display is fundamentally an expression of impotence.

Somewhat ironically, Swofford claims his right to speak near the end of the book based on this erosion of agency rather than its development. He is no longer the subject but the object of the gaze, the fighting, the war: "because I signed the contract and fulfilled my obligation to fight one of America's wars, I am entitled to speak, to say, *I belonged to a fucked situation*" (254). As Swofford discovers, being the object can have its advantages as well, though they are less obvious. The field-fuck, after all, transforms the rather tame and humiliating performance of a sweltering football game into a rebellious act of defiance against the observing officer and reporters. They are telling the story not just of their women's betrayal, as they do on the Wall of Shame, but of their betrayal by the president, the nation, the world. (Colby Buzzell also discovers the power to be gained by making a display of himself, though technology allows him to take that display much further than Swofford does.)

Swofford's move from wielding the voyeuristic, objectifying gaze to feeling objectified himself reflects the failure of his identification with the soldiers he watches onscreen. Before, he fully desired and expected to do everything that he watched the movie characters do; he was ready for his own "real First Fuck." Many of the famous Vietnam War movies he and the other soldiers watch so ardently end with a sensual and intimately represented kill. In *Platoon,* Chris kills Sergeant Barnes, who urges him to "do it." In *The Deer Hunter,* Mike watches Nick shoot himself in the head during a game of Russian roulette. In *Full Metal Jacket,* Private Joker kills a wounded female sniper, who urges him to "shoot me"; after he does shoot her, another member of his squad calls him "hard core." Finally, in *Apocalypse Now,* Willard ritualistically kills Kurtz, who, one can argue, has encouraged Willard to do exactly that. These killings are all done at what Dave Grossman has called "sexual range," the closest possible killing range. In his popular and influential study *On Killing,* Grossman explores the experience of killing at six different distance ranges, including maximum or long-range killing, hand-grenade range, edged-weapon range, and finally sexual range. In this last, closest range, killing is characterized by an intimate physical proximity, a sense of primal aggression, and the orgasmic discharge of a weapon (134–37). The sexual-range killings depicted in these four Vietnam War films are morally problematic to say the least, but they do present moments where the ambiguities surrounding the experience of the Vietnam War are there to be pondered and considered, if not resolved. They are all climaxes.

Swofford never reaches this climax—he never kills. Late in the book, he and his sniping partner prepare to take long-distance shots at Iraqi soldiers in an airfield, but their commanding officer denies them permission to shoot. Instead they wait, angry and frustrated, until they rejoin their company, which is wildly celebrating the sudden end of "our little war" (235). Swofford rather tellingly calls his feelings about this a "lack of satisfaction" (239). Swofford's disappointment and failure to identify with what he sees as this most essential part of the war experience lead him to doubt its very existence. "Did we fight?" he asks. "Was that combat?" The soldiers are later allowed to fire their cache of captured Iraqi weapons, and they do so, exploding massive amounts of ammo in the desert:

> We fire and fire the AKs, a factory of firepower, the fierce scream of metal downrange and discharged cartridges and sand flying everywhere, now all of us shooting in the air, shooting straight up and dancing in circles, dancing on one foot, with the mad, desperate hope that the rounds will never descend, screaming, screaming at ourselves and each other and the dead Iraqis surrounding us, screaming at ourselves and the dead world surrounding us, screaming at ourselves, at the corpses surrounding us and the dead world. (244–45)

As in the field-fuck, the soldiers here express their aggression, fear, desire, and in this case the lust for identification with their beloved movie heroes, but shooting at the sky is an equally impotent gesture. It stands in for the killing that, at least in Swofford's case, wasn't done—the lethal penetration of another person. About that lack, that combat virginity, he is deeply ambivalent, and he considers himself to be "less of a marine and even less of a man," then "no better or worse a man," and finally as someone who has perhaps earned "some extra moments of living for myself or that I can offer others, though I have no idea how to use or disburse these extra moments, or if I've wasted them already" (247, 248, 257).

In the end, Swofford's attempted identification with the violent, seductive images that enraptured him fails, reflecting broader concerns about the role of media in shaping the public's view of the conflict. The Gulf War was, officially, a brief affair. On 17 January 1991, coalition forces launched the air campaign of Operation Desert Storm, which featured, to some acclaim, the F-117 Nighthawk Stealth Fighter, one of the first aircraft to bomb Baghdad in the early morning hours. The war ended on 27 February 1991, a mere one hundred hours after the ground campaign began. As a whole, the Gulf War was a show of overwhelming American force and technology; civilians at home watched round-the-clock, real-time coverage of smart bombs gliding soundlessly into their appointed targets. The United States could do anything, it seemed, even conduct a painless war with surgical precision. Media coverage assured the public that the war was just, efficient, and, after late February, over and done with. Subsequently, however, reports and images would leak out that indicated otherwise: the carnage on the Highway of Death, the collateral damage of misdirected attacks, the illness that would come to be called Gulf War syndrome. Questions lingered, just as they did for Swofford. What happened when those "smart" bombs missed their intended targets, as happened, it turns out, the majority of the time? (Gellman). Why was Saddam Hussein still in power, if victory had been as total as it seemed? What exactly had been the role of the media in packaging that victory for an enthralled public?[6] How many Iraqis had been killed, and what were the survivors' lives like after the war?

Iraqis themselves describe the war quite differently. Written in Baghdad in 1991, Sinan Antoon's poem "A Prism; Wet with Wars" begins

> this is the chapter of
> devastation
> this is our oasis
> an angle where wars intersect (3)

Antoon comments on the fatigue felt by Iraqis at the onset of yet another war, so soon after the end of the Iran-Iraq War, which lasted from 1980 to 1988. The poem ends with "HAPPY NEW WAR!" (4). Dunya Mikhail makes a similar point in her poem "Between Two Wars":

> eventually we forget
> how, in the short lull
> between two wars,
> we become so old. (18)

Disillusion and fatigue is not preceded by the exhilaration of new war, as it is in so many American war stories. Instead, for those living in Iraq, war is devastatingly familiar.

In 2003 war in Iraq returns for both the Americans and the Iraqis. Swofford's memoir appears that year, and thus the narrative of his deep ambivalence found a particularly receptive audience. In *Jarhead,* Swofford assumes that he can fly under the radar, that the power of his position makes him impenetrable. He is backed, after all, by the force of a great nation, represented by comrades-in-arms who, in his telling, are used to consuming the spectacle of bloodshed for their entertainment. Yet, as Swofford discovers, the lines of sight run both ways. Just because you watch others in a theater or through the scope of your rifle doesn't mean that others aren't watching you. In the end, you are equally vulnerable to consumption. In 1990–91, the national entertainment of sorts that the media's war coverage provided for Americans was useful to others too. CNN was widely pirated in Iraq, disseminating information about troop numbers and bombing attacks, as well as showcasing clips of Saddam Hussein. That dedication of airtime "raised questions about who was using whom," notes Holly Cowan Shulman. "Was CNN using Saddam as a news maker—or was Saddam using CNN to get himself broadcast around the world, knowing that, unlike CBS, ABC, or NBC, CNN coverage would be run straight on television newscasts around the world?" (116) These questions anticipated those that would arise about Osama bin Laden's use of videotaped messages after the attacks of 11 September 2001, and during the Iraq War, in his attempts to use the media grid to his own advantage.

Who *is* using whom? Swofford and his nation may have won the war, but the social and political sense of victory that followed would provide no lasting satisfaction. "I am still in the desert," Swofford notes early in his book, as indeed we are (15). As he learns, you can't fly stealth forever.

Iraq, 2003

Questions about who is watching whom have become more complex during the Iraq War. From 1991 to 2003, networks of communication and information grew considerably in scale and accessibility, and the public became savvier about the technologies of display. Flying stealth is no longer an option or even a goal, and this new war comes home not just on CNN but via e-mail, blogs, and YouTube. Colby Buzzell became a soldier some twelve years after Swofford and quickly staked his claim in both the real and virtual fields of fire.

Like his literary and military predecessor, Buzzell describes watching war movies en masse with fellow soldiers before flying to Iraq. In *My War: Killing Time in Iraq,* the published version of his blog, Buzzell says that they fill their idle time with "all the classic war flicks"—*Apocalypse Now, Full Metal Jacket, Platoon, Hamburger Hill, Patton, The Dirty Dozen,* and others—which they watch in groups and individually, on portable DVD players that are readily available. "Most of us grew up watching these movies over and over again and can recite word for word countless lines from each," he notes, adding that "most of us were probably here in the Army because we watched these movies one too many times" (73). Buzzell frequently uses movies, and war movies in particular, as points of reference for his own experience; as he notes, his wartime identity is fashioned by what he watches. He writes a creed for his M240 Bravo machine gun inspired by *Full Metal Jacket* and says that a battalion commander's speech reminds him of *Patton* (49, 57). A briefing on improvised explosive devices (IEDs) evokes the *Red Asphalt* videos from driver-education class, and completing his deployment paperwork "was kinda like the part in the movie *Pearl Harbor* where Ben Affleck and Josh Hartnett go from station to station getting checked out" (65, 66).

Later, on the ground in Iraq, when his unit returns fire on a mosque in Mosul, Buzzell remembers that he "went up and down that tower three or four times, yelling, '*Get some!*' every time I fired a burst (like they do in the movies)" (135). Buzzell also notes that the Stryker armored vehicles could be improved with the addition of external loudspeakers. "Remember in the movie *Apocalypse Now,* when they had the speakers hooked up to the Air Cav helicopters?" he asks, revealing the same enthusiasm Swofford does for this clip. "Well, we need to do the same goddamn thing with the Strykers" (208). He adds that on a joint raid with the Iraqi Civil Police, Counter Intelligence brings along speakers to play a recording in Arabic. Before the mission actually begins, however, they use the speakers to play music:

> I'm not sure exactly what [the recording in Arabic] says, but I think it says something like: Do not be scared, we are Coalition Forces, we come in peace and to help. Do not shoot us, or we will shoot and kill you. That kind of crap. Anyways, when we were driving out the main gate to the FOB [Forward Operating Base] to do this joint mission we had the loudspeakers blasting "Ride of the Valkyries," theme song from *The Good, The Bad, and the Ugly,* "The Star-Spangled Banner," and the *Rocky* theme song. It motivated the hell out of us all. In fact, it even motivated the Iraqi Police, I remember looking over at them and they were all getting into it big time. (208)

Buzzell creates a "Stryker Soundtrack" playlist on the thirty-gigabyte iPod that he brought to Iraq, which he keeps in an empty ammo pouch in his flak vest and carries on missions (146). He listens to music while on patrol and in guard towers, effectively providing, to quote the title of this section of the book, "my war soundtrack." His choices are most influenced by punk, heavy metal, and movies. He includes some of the music he mentions playing on the speakers as well as the "Imperial March" from *Star Wars,* "Paint It Black" by the Rolling Stones (featured at the end of *Full Metal Jacket*), and Kenny Loggins's "Danger Zone," which he notes is the "*Top Gun* song" (147). Even the titles and subtitles of his entries often reference well-known movies: "Dumb and Dumber," "Sleepless in Mosul," "Men in Black," and "Dude, Where's My Weapon?"

His many film references make Buzzell seem even more enraptured by these popular images of war—and popular images generally—than Swofford. Yet near the end of the book, Buzzell flatly denies that his own experience bears any resemblance to what he's watched. He frames this

Figure 2. A scene from Colby Buzzell's story "Men in Black," featured in *Operation Homecoming: Writing the Wartime Experience* (PBS, 2007). The story is based on Buzzell's blog entry of the same title. Illustration by Christopher Koelle. Used by permission of The Documentary Group.

revelation not as a disappointment but merely as a fact, mentioned as he recounts flying home after his service has been completed:

> Now if this was the movies, they'd have the guy sitting in the plane on his way back to the world, looking out the window, with maybe the Green Day song "Time of Your Life" playing in the background, and he's reflecting on the war, about all his buddies that he's lost, all the dead bodies he's seen, and all the life-changing experiences and epiphanies that he went through and whatnot, but for me it seemed to be the opposite. I was not really thinking about Iraq at all, in fact it actually felt like I was never there. (352)

Buzzell alludes to film and pop culture as shorthand, to convey an impression or mood, but he rejects the notion that his experience as a whole resembles a movie in any way. Like Swofford, he fails to fully identify with the cinematic representations of soldiers, and he claims his own war story as something quite different. But unlike Swofford's, his realization doesn't trigger the explosive anger and fear for which Swofford finds partial relief in a field-fuck. Buzzell describes his time in Iraq as a blank—an empty space, flat, lacking any emotional content whatsoever. His hardened

cynicism distinguishes him from Swofford both in the way that he reacts
to the experience of war (which is, as always, very different from the war
stories he watched so keenly) and in the language he uses to describe that
experience.

Buzzell may dismiss his service in Iraq as something to be survived and
then forgotten, but the story of that service becomes a space of rich and
emotional content for many others when he begins recording it in a blog.
If television provided a new way to "see" the Vietnam War on the nightly
news, and if the Gulf War "made" CNN, then digital technology and
the Internet have changed the way the United States both conducts and
watches war in Iraq. Tactically speaking, the Gulf War and the current
wars in Iraq and Afghanistan have showcased a revolution in information
technology that has affected everything from surveillance to targeting and
ordnance. Available technology has also transformed soldiers' ability to
communicate, whether within the military or with friends and family back
home, and in this regard the experience of the soldier in the Iraq War is
unique. Swofford could write letters, phone home occasionally, and watch
videos with his buddies for entertainment, but Buzzell and his fellow soldiers have access to portable DVD players, MP3 players, digital cameras,
and, of course, the Internet. If, as Donna Haraway noted, "modern war is a
cyborg orgy," a large-scale staging field for hybrids of machines and organ-
isms, Buzzell the soldier fits right in with the new digital infrastructure of
military intelligence, communications, and weaponry (150).

Buzzell repeatedly notes how soldiers take digital pictures at every opportunity, including during battles; Buzzell himself snaps a few during the
onset of the firefight at the Mosul mosque (133). Others strap tiny digital
camcorders on their helmets and use them to film raids and missions (349).
He adds that everyone who has a digital camera also has a laptop and that
everyone who has a laptop has a program on it to edit movies. Many soldiers gather footage from each other, edit it together, add a sound track,
and make their own war movies. "Some of the videos that I saw produced
by soldiers are about as good as anything I've seen Spike Jonze do. Almost
every single soldier in my platoon was going home with a video that stars
them" (350).

Everyone wants to be a star, at least for family and friends back home,
but Buzzell's milblog distinguishes him even among all the other soldiers
recording the war in various ways.[7] The work of recording one's thoughts

wasn't new to Buzzell. Before joining the army, Buzzell kept a journal as a way to pass the time, and as a record and evaluation of his life it eventually led him to the military. "One of the turning points that finally made me want to join the military was the day I came home from work, exhausted, and I picked up my journal and started reading it from beginning to end. It was the most depressing piece of literature I'd ever read" (52). Faced with the monotony and lack of promise in his life, "I said fuck it, and got my ass down to that recruiting station" (53). He bought more journals when he got his orders to ship out for Iraq, so he would have "something to do when I got there" (53).

After a couple of months in Iraq, a similar thing happens. He reads his war journal from beginning to end and doesn't like any of it. "What bothered me was that the experience of 'combat' so far was nothing like I had expected it to be. War, thus far for me, was quite possibly the dullest, most anti-climactic experience I'd ever been through in my entire life, and the only thing I was really combating in Iraq was boredom.... What kind of war journal is that?" (104). For Buzzell, war—like life—is boring and literally without climax, lacking sexualized thrills and any kind of familiar story line. Swofford reacts to this lack by engaging in field-fucking and firing weapons uselessly into the air. These acts express his frustration and powerlessness, but they also hint at the potential power of performance or display upon which Buzzell seizes more fully. Instead of taking delight in the objectification of others or seeking the sexual pleasures of watching and fighting, Buzzell decides to create a show of his own, one that will showcase his cynical voice.

In June 2004 he reads an article by Lev Grossman in *Time* called "Meet Joe Blog" and finds out more about blogging. He fails to find a milblog written by anyone but REMFs (rear-echelon motherfuckers) or the voice of anyone "who saw for themselves up close and personal what it was really like out here" (114). He posts his first entry on 22 June 2004, under the name CBFTW—CB for his initials and FTW for the tattoo on his arm ("Fuck the world"). He doesn't tell anyone about it, including family back home, saying that he would "feel weird if people I knew read my personal writing." He equates writing to exhibitionism: "To me, showing somebody else your writing is kinda like showing somebody a naked photo of yourself, and quite honestly, I didn't want anybody to laugh at me." With the blog and his status as an anonymous writer, he can remain "totally invisible and nameless" (110). Here Buzzell somewhat apprehensively invites the public's gaze, and we see how the workings of watching have changed from Swofford's (and, to a lesser extent, Buzzell's) ecstatic and sexually charged viewings of war movies. Swofford watches others who are metaphorically naked to his gaze, all from the anonymity of a screening-room chair, while Buzzell presents his "naked" self for anonymous others to observe and consume. The lines of sight have been reversed—yet Buzzell maintains, or attempts to maintain, a kind of revelatory power. Swofford wants to see things he shouldn't, and Buzzell wants to show those things to others, though Buzzell's desire is fueled less by a heady mix of sex and power than by a cynical impulse to reveal the truths of war. This difference is notable in their language as well. Neither writer is at all shy about cursing, but while Swofford's "First Fuck" is a raw and passionate equation of combat and intercourse, Buzzell's imperative to "[f]uck the world" is a jaded rejection of everything outside himself.

Buzzell calls his blog "My War: Fear and Loathing in Iraq," taking the title from a Black Flag song, the lyrics to which he includes, and the subtitle from Hunter S. Thompson, one of his favorite writers. He also adds a picture of Picasso's *Guernica,* which "kinda reminded me of Iraq," and the text of "the Infantryman's Creed," a song he memorized in basic training (116). Finally, he adds a Smiths album cover with a picture of a soldier whose helmet reads "Meat is Murder"—in yet another reference to *Full Metal Jacket,* he calls that "the whole duality-of-man thing"—and a disclaimer that he steals from a female officer's blog, indicating that his views are not necessarily those of the government (116). He literally constructs his presence online with a mixture of various media that reference the military, punk, gonzo journalism, and representations of war. All this media, however, serves to introduce and foreground the main attraction: Buzzell as the textual voice of the soldiers' war in Iraq.

The site quickly becomes popular, and Buzzell begins receiving dozens of e-mail messages a day, all praising his efforts. Articles about the blog appear in the *News Tribune* of Tacoma and later in the *Wall Street Journal* (Cooper; Gilbert), and NPR features it in a report, "Soldiers' Iraq Blogs." The Army takes note. Buzzell is part of a movement, and the movement begins to draw attention; eventually, Buzzell comes to be known as the "Blogfather," because so many other milbloggers are influenced by his work (Spector). This is, after all, a sea change in the way soldiers' voices are heard by the rest of the nation and the world. "Since World War I," notes John Hockenberry in *Wired,* "the military has opened the letters soldiers sent back home from the battlefield and sometimes censored the dispatches of war correspondents. Now mail leaves the battlefield already open to the world. Anyone can publicly post a dispatch, and if the Pentagon reads these accounts at all, it's at the same time as the rest of us." Since Hockenberry made that observation in 2005, however, the rules have changed, partly in response to the ad hoc nature of the disciplinary actions taken against Buzzell. After Buzzell writes about a "mad mortarmen goose chase," he is confined to his forward operating base (FOB) and prohibited from participating in missions with his platoon, a form of de facto censorship. His confinement is later repealed, and he responds by immediately posting the First Amendment:

> I'm not stupid. I know soldiers don't have freedom of speech. But I posted the First Amendment because I wanted it to be my middle-finger salute to whoever was confining me to the FOB. I also dropped the Fear and Loathing subtitle to create speculation that the Army was telling me what I could and could not write, which kinda worked because it created a buzz on the "blogosphere," as they call it. If the Army wanted to play fuck-fuck Army games with me, fine. Game on. (290)

Buzzell initially invites the head games of the military brass, but in time those games wear him down. His blog becomes "more of a headache," and he decides to give it up (319). But he refuses to go quietly. He determines to "go out with a bang" and do something to "stick it to the man":

> Like, I thought that maybe I should finish my set with a little bit more attitude instead of just walking off the stage, maybe I should end my set the same way a punk band might end their set to the very last show, which would be to just slam the guitars up to the amps, create as much static and feedback as possible to the point that the audience's ears just exploded, and then to smash my guitar and equipment on stage into a million fucking pieces. (319)

Buzzell wants a punk climax, an act that is characterized by both display *and* aggressive penetration. He wants a show that is amplified, that will blow everyone away. To achieve this, he asks Jello Biafra, the lead singer for the Dead Kennedys and a proponent of "becoming the media," to write a final statement on the blog. Biafra does, stating that "we are the real patriots here, not the unelected gangsters and scam artists who started this war" and that "[a]s long as people in the field speak up we have a chance of preserving the truth" (320). The army reacts by telling Buzzell in no uncertain terms to cease posting. But Buzzell is satisfied. He has managed to turn his objectified status into a display that is also a weapon.

The Internet is a weapon the military would prefer soldiers didn't have. About the same time Buzzell's book won the Blooker Prize, the Pentagon released official regulations governing blogs and other online material. An April 2007 operations security document states that personnel are required to consult with both their immediate supervisor and their operations security officer before sending letters or e-mailing messages or posting to blogs or other Internet forums (sec. 2–1). Already, some note that blogging like Buzzell's may be a thing of the past (Pilkington). But many soldiers have defied the threat of punishment and kept posting, betting on the military's inability to monitor all of cyberspace. When Haraway says that the preeminent technology of cyborgs is, in the end, writing, she could be talking about Buzzell, whose physical self is technologically enhanced and who exists in the blogosphere as a virtual soldier. Cyborg politics, she notes, is "the struggle for language and the struggle against perfect communication, against the one code that translates all meaning perfectly" (176). Buzzell's struggle to counter—or at least complicate—the military's and the mainstream media's message about Iraq reflects the recent proliferation of political engagement online, from the popularity of blogs like "Daily Kos" to viral videos of political candidates' gaffes and bon mots. If the 1990s were marked by the rise of the Internet and a concomitant concern and excitement about the sexual content available there—content that Swofford probably would have loved, had he had access to it during his own service—the years since have seen a comparable debate about the websites, blogs, and online videos that have become remarkable influences on political discourse.[8]

Buzzell as blogger is a groundbreaking figure in the cyberscape of contemporary media, but what it all finally means for Buzzell himself is less clear. He notes that after his service the military will have him on inactive reserve status for six additional years, "so there's that very slight possibility that I just might be called back up to fight in some other terrorist-infested cesspool someday. Especially if the North Koreans ever get crazy on the soju and start tossing nukes at us, then I'm really fucked" (353). His postwar employment options, he says, are few: data entry, valet parking, FedEx delivery. "And if that doesn't work out, I guess I can now write the word 'Veteran' after the word 'Homeless' on my cardboard sign" (353–54). He ends the book with a tongue-in-cheek acknowledgement: "Thanks to everyone who helped make this book possible, especially my recruiter. Without your help none of this would have happened" (355).

Given the developments in communications technology and the proliferation of media coverage, Buzzell operates in a more complex and layered representational network than does Swofford, and he is both more aware of that network and savvier about its manipulation. Likewise, this second war in Iraq was undertaken with a heightened awareness of the labyrinthine interconnections of contemporary communications and the many vectors of modern American display. Information about war, as the military and the soldiers realize, can be fragmented, can come through a multitude of channels, can be spun one way and then the other. Unfortunately, as this conflict has excruciatingly demonstrated, the same is true for force. President Bush's claim in May 2003 that the mission in Iraq was accomplished because the United States military had overthrown Saddam Hussein proved patently false, and growing numbers of Americans have come to doubt the purpose and justification of that mission. Lessons on the mutability of force—old ones, though perhaps first learned in earnest during the Vietnam War years—continued in the ruined urban streets of Iraq, where force rarely presents itself clearly as something to be assessed and reckoned with. Instead, it filters through a network of alleyways and communities, revealing itself suddenly in a car speeding toward a checkpoint or in a hidden IED. All the savvy in the world about these kinds of networks can't always prevent you from being "really fucked," as Buzzell puts it. Despite skillfully reclaiming an agency based on the combined power of display and aggressive penetration, in 2008 Buzzell was called back to active duty in Iraq. He writes about his callback in an *Esquire* article titled "Welcome Back"; after reporting, he was released as nondeployable because of severe post-traumatic stress disorder. "I can't do it again," he tells the examining physician. "I think I'll lose my mind" (212).

Iraqis feel similarly, as war returns yet again, but for them, release or reprieve is impossible. In "To an Iraqi infant," Sinan Antoon asks:

> do you know
> that your tomorrow
> has no tomorrow?
> that your blood
> is the ink
> of new maps? (10)

For Antoon, the networks of force are traced in the blood of innocent Iraqis who suffer the ultimate—and final—loss of agency. On the eve of America's "shock and awe" campaign, Abdul Razaq Al-Rubaiee writes that

> Tomorrow the war will have a picnic:
> Turn off the moon hanging over the roof
> So it won't dim the tracers and flares
> That light up war's path. ("Tomorrow the War Will Have a Picnic")

War is indeed a spectacle. Once that spectacle has reached out and touched you personally, however, the celebration—the "picnic"—becomes simple irony.

"We are still in the desert"

Swofford and Buzzell both describe new ways of watching war as afforded by the accessibility of media, though neither gets to possess what he sees onscreen—the seductive and illicit combination of sex, violence, and power, all wielded from a position of impenetrable agency. Each reacts to his inability to attain that degree of agency with an anti-authoritarian display that provides an outlet for his frustration and, in Buzzell's case, a different kind of power, one based on the construction of self as text rather than as imitation of an image. Swofford and Buzzell have continued to live their lives as a textual display, finding new identities as authors. In that sense, Buzzell really does owe something to his recruiter.

As Elisabeth Piedmont-Marton has argued, Swofford's literary ambitions are clear within the story of *Jarhead,* and his reading habits speak to that, though they are perhaps less noticeable than some of his other activities. He writes about reading the *Iliad,* Xenophon's *Anabasis,* and Camus's *The Stranger* while overseas, though he comments much less on these texts than he does on the films viewed communally. One assumes, however, than in his private encounters with reading materials like *Hamlet,* Nietzsche, and Camus's *The Myth of Sisyphus,* which contemplates the absurdity of being human in a meaningless world and the rationale behind suicide, he seeks more than an adrenaline rush. Buzzell's text, by its very nature, is much more raw and immediate. His writing ambitions are less polished by intervening years of reflection and introspection, but he too emphasizes that he reads voraciously. In one entry, he provides a long list of what he emphasizes is *"some* of" his reading material, including various histories of Iraq, classic war studies by Sun Tzu and von Clausewitz, Vonnegut's *Slaughterhouse-Five,* Michael Herr's *Dispatches,* and Heller's *Catch-22* (176).

Samuel Hynes notes in *The Soldiers' Tale,* which covers memoirs of the two World Wars and the Vietnam War as well as testimonies of war atrocities, that "[i]n most war narratives there is nothing to suggest that the author is aware of any previous example: no quotations or allusions or imitations of earlier models, and no evident knowledge of previous wars." Hynes calls war writing "a genre without a tradition to the men who write it" (4). This is clearly not the case for Swofford, Buzzell, or any of their comrades. These soldiers are deeply engaged with the images and texts of soldiers who preceded them, though the agency that their engagement provides varies throughout their stories. And these stories of agency desired, lost, and reappropriated show both the personal and political effects of the changing technologies of representation, as books share shelf space with DVDs, digital cameras, and laptops.

The Vietnam War films *Apocalypse Now* and *Full Metal Jacket* both briefly feature film crews who are "shooting the war." In the former, Coppola famously cast himself in the cameo role of a director, shouting at soldiers in the middle of a war zone, "Don't look at the camera! Just go by like you're fighting!" The soldiers, uncomprehending, stare in amazement. The camera apparatus itself also inspires amazement. Though certainly more mobile than in the past, it is still large, cumbersome, and not easily operated. The very size and weight of the camera restricts the kinds of stories it can tell and the documentation it can provide. The recent developments in digital technology create, among other things, cameras and other recording devices that are small, light, and as mobile as the soldiers themselves. The war story, as many writers, filmmakers, and journalists have realized, can now be told through a kaleidoscope of lenses.

Buzzell's blog in particular is an early and significant example of the influence of digital texts on the public conception of war and on the military's attempts to control that conception. Although Buzzell's use of images is minimal (and none appear in his published book), he notes that other soldiers quickly adapt to the use of developing digital-imaging technologies. Now pictures can be taken and sent via e-mail, "home movies" can be shot and edited, and the images of life at war can be recorded and shared in a number of ways. In fact, the extension of digital culture as suggested by Swofford and Buzzell has been featured in a number of films about the Iraq War. (For more detail see chapter 4.) The fictional films *Redacted* and *In the Valley of Elah,* both released in 2007, use the conceit of soldiers' digital photos and video to reveal the "dark secret" of the horrific effects of war, and Errol Morris's documentary *Standard Operating Procedure* (2008) examines the circumstances surrounding the infamous Abu Ghraib photographs.

Swofford and Buzzell, soldiers initially intoxicated by watching war, find an ameliorative outlet for combat's inevitable trauma by creating their own narratives and sharing them through means that are variously traditional and digital. As Buzzell notes, others do the same, using text as well as still images and films. But Swofford and Buzzell don't seem to want their readers to hoot and holler the way they did at those Vietnam War films. War should not look good, they suggest, for the noncombatant audience or for the soldiers themselves. And in the end, however war does "look" in its ongoing representations, the experience of real war always exists outside of the frame. This is true even for Swofford and Buzzell, who write in the face of that realization. The final scene of the HBO miniseries *Generation Kill* (2008) emphasizes this point as well, as a group of soldiers gathers to see the movie that one of them has created to commemorate their invasion of Iraq. They watch on a laptop as shots of smiling soldiers posing and clowning around are intercut with images of explosions and Iraqi corpses, both military and civilian. The initially delighted expressions on the faces of this small audience gradually give way to somber resignation. One by one, they walk away from the show.

2

MAKING A MILITARY MAN

Iraq, Gender, and the Failure of the Masculine Collective

What makes a man? It's an old question, but the critic Susan Jeffords frames it in a new way. What, she asks, does a man make? Jeffords has argued that during and after the Vietnam War, the power of the masculine collective, a community forged in war and represented extensively back home in the United States, effectively remade or "remasculinized" the American cultural landscape. Jeffords's argument leads us to a consideration of our contemporary moment, and the stories some soldiers have told about their service in the wars in Iraq. How do they represent themselves and, more particularly, their gender, after their experience of violence and war? Does her argument still apply to these new American wars and their effect on American culture?

In fact, things have changed. Several of the memoirists writing about Iraq emphasize the ruptures in their own sense of masculine identity and the corollary failure of the masculine collective, indicating a different experience of gender and culture than Jeffords identifies in and after Vietnam. In this chapter, I consider memoirs by three veterans. Joel Turnipseed was a Marine reservist during the Persian Gulf War who worked in the Sixth Motor Transport Battalion, or "Baghdad Express," and later published a memoir by that name in 2003. Nathaniel Fick was a Marine Corps officer who served in Afghanistan and the Iraq War, and published *One Bullet Away* in 2005. Kayla Williams, one of the growing number of female soldiers serving in the military, worked as an Arabic translator for Army military intelligence in Iraq, and her memoir *Love My Rifle More Than You* appeared in 2005.

Turnipseed, Fick, and Williams all struggle with their conceptions of masculinity, and military masculinity in particular. Notably, each describes gender and masculinity as a kind of performance rather than an essential quality, which would perhaps indicate a greater freedom or at least flexibility with regard to gender norms. Turnipseed explicitly discusses his desire to use dress, speech, and text to "act the part" that he wants to play, while Fick identifies his competence and worth as a soldier in his ability to perform the role of the hard military man. Williams's narrative in particular demonstrates her desire to reach across gender boundaries and be considered a true brother in arms. But in each case, the writer's performance of masculinity fails to be sustainable or sustaining in the context of war. Turnipseed, Fick, and Williams all describe that failure as well as the sense of isolation from their fellow soldiers that occurs as either cause or effect. Theorists of cultural performance like Judith Butler, Marjorie Garber, and Judith Halberstam celebrate the freedom that comes, they argue, when we decide to play a role, and particularly when we manipulate and vary the role that we play.[1] Obviously, however, some venues are more amenable than others to this kind of experimentation. Creating order out of the chaos of war often necessitates many forms of binary thinking. If one does not define oneself against the enemy, for instance, one will not be an effective soldier—that is, one will not be able to kill. And that need for binaries creeps into other aspects of the soldier's experience and identity.

So what does make a man? Mark Twain famously asserted that what makes a man is his wardrobe, because "naked people have little or no influence on society" (6). Though in these paparazzi-saturated days the latter part of his statement may no longer hold true, certainly the construction of appearance and the cultural assumptions associated with fashion, grooming, bearing, and accessories are significant elements in a critical discussion of masculinity. In war, however, it is commonly understood that what makes a military man is a little more than just his uniform. The initiation into the military includes the requisite haircut, assignment of a service number, and issuing of equipment and, of course, standard clothing. All this begins the process of "soldierization," or the identification of the self as soldier—but the completion of that process is understood in more abstract terms.

In notable cases, becoming a complete military man means achieving the status of a hero, standing out as exceptional within the larger machine of war. The hero is typically one who fights with great skill, usually at close range, and for the right reasons. In many real and fictional war stories, heroic action is less dependent on following the rules or dictates of leadership than on the character of the hero himself—he simply *knows* what is right, and his actions will eventually bear this out. In that sense, the meaning-making structure of heroism sometimes proves thinly constructed. In war, after all, those who are lauded as heroes are typically those who kill the most enemy soldiers. They may also be soldiers who risk their own lives or the lives of their comrades in order to demonstrate their worthiness, their warrior mettle. If I am a hero, the thinking goes, then in the end I will be justified and redeemed, just like Achilles or Sergeant York. Some soldiers will take enormous or ultimately fatal risks for that justification, so strong is their desire for the coherence of action, character, and experience that heroism would seem to bring.

More often, and perhaps more appropriately, the true soldier or military man is defined by a sense of honor, which can be thought of as an adherence to the set of rules that establish what is right on the battlefield, and what actions are acceptable and unacceptable. These rules are at least in part determined by those in the position of leadership, on the field and off. Simply put, honor means doing one's duty, whatever that is and however difficult it may be. Richard Holmes has noted that more often than not, honor in war may simply dictate not running away when the chips are down:

> But, in a more specific sense, it is individual soldierly honour that impels a man to rejoin his unit when he has every reason not to, and prevails upon him to remain at his post even though flight would save him ... [These codes of honour] are designed to make the social consequences of flight more unpleasant than the physical consequences of battle. The one ... might lead to

pain, mutilation and death, but the other produces, with much greater certainty, personal guilt and public shame. (301)

Honor, then, compels a man to act like a man. But underlying honor is another, deeper motivation. According to Holmes, the consequences of behaving dishonorably are both personal and public—public in the sense that honor is a quality defined and experienced among other soldiers. (The people back home may certainly praise a returning soldier, but he is praised for deeds done in war, not on the homefront.) And so it becomes clear that in the military, the man is most often truly made by the presence and acceptance of other military men. Comradeship, the bond of trust forged between men fighting together, would seem to be as old as fighting itself. That bond provides the impetus to fight as well as a sense of identity, and can be even more powerful than patriotism or a sense of righteous cause. If a love for "king and country" can seem a bit abstract under fire, then a love for the soldier next to you, with whom you have shared hardships and searing experiences, can be a much more tangible reason to keep going.

"The white heat of ideology or the burning zeal of religion may sustain the few, or even, at particular moments in the world's history, inspire the many," Holmes notes. But in battle, when soldiers have to keep trying to kill those who are trying to kill them, "neither ideology nor religion give much incentive for the one to get up and sprint to the next cover, or for the other to drive steadily across a field already scorched by his comrades' oily cremations. For the key to what makes men fight—not enlist, not cope, but fight—we must look hard at military groups and the bonds that link the men within them" (291). That comradeship can take the form of simple friendship as well as the "desire to display bravery in the company of brave men" (305).

In *On Killing,* Dave Grossman elaborates on this point, and emphasizes the potential for ideology to fail under fire:

> Numerous studies have concluded that men in combat are usually motivated to fight *not* by ideology or hate or fear, but by group pressures and processes involving (1) regard for their comrades, (2) respect for their leaders, (3) concern for their own reputation with both, and (4) an urge to contribute to the success of the group. Repeatedly we see combat veterans describe the powerful bonds that men forge in combat as stronger than those of husband and wife. (89–90)

And Joanna Bourke notes that comradeship has become a ubiquitous element of memoirs and conceptions of battle. "Whether called 'mateship,' 'the buddy system,' or 'homo-erotic relationships,' the power of love and friendship in enticing men to kill has been widely commented upon... The importance of comradeship in enabling men to 'carry on' is at the heart of most histories of 'life at the front': so much so that it has become a cliché of military, cultural history" (129–30).

Acceptance by one's fellow soldiers and the proper "display of bravery" under duress and in their company constitutes the full achievement of military masculinity, and provides a frame for a master narrative about war and the self. True to the conception of gender and identity as performance, a single display may not always be enough. For the real man to remain real, multiple demonstrations may be necessary as the circumstances dictate. This is a modern way of talking about something very old, something the ancient Greeks would have understood instinctively. What good is a great kill if there's no one there to see it? *Kleos,* or glory, needs an audience, after all. In Book VI of the *Iliad,* when Hector's wife Andromache begs him to stay with her inside the walls of Troy, he refuses, although he knows that Troy is destined to fall. When that happens, his wife will be dragged into slavery, his son and parents killed. "Yes, Andromache, I worry about all this myself," he tells her,

> But my shame before the Trojans and their wives,
> With their long robes trailing, would be too terrible
> If I hung back from battle like a coward. (Homer 6.463–66)

For Hector, the horror of shame, of failing to properly perform, is greater even than the horror of losing his family to atrocity. Display and acceptance, then, make the man, and comradeship provides the required venue.

Jeffords focuses her attention on that comradeship with regard to Vietnam. She notes that the primary trope in representations of Vietnam is the blurring of categories, and the confusion that arises when opposing categories can no longer be distinguished: America versus Vietnam, participants versus observers, us versus the enemy, soldiers versus civilians. Writers like Norman Mailer and Michael Herr "translate these oppositions into aesthetic terms by overtly discussing the status of fact and fiction, history and myth, truth and falsehood" (48–49). Jeffords is prescient. A year after her study appeared in 1989, Tim O'Brien published his collection *The Things They Carried,* which makes ample and brilliant use of exactly this quality.

But, as Jeffords argues, one category is always exempt from this blurring, and that is gender. It is true, she notes, that the "defining feature of American war narratives is that they are a 'man's story' from which women are generally excluded," but the use of gender in representations of Vietnam goes further (49). Gender is "not simply another of the many oppositions that mark Vietnam representation," she argues. Instead, gender is the difference that does not participate in the confusion that characterizes the other oppositions (53). Sustaining that difference allows the patriarchy to reassert itself, even under the pressures of feminism and the anti-war movement. Comradeship in war, generalized as what Jeffords calls the masculine collective, is thus "projected as a basis for the regeneration of society as a whole" (74). Hence, the post-Vietnam era features such films as *First Blood* (parts I and II), *Missing in Action,* and even, in Jeffords's reading, *The Deer Hunter.*[2]

And what of the present moment? Twenty-first century America may certainly be in need of regeneration, but the expression of military might—both individual and national, masculine and cultural—has folded in on itself. The confidence once seen in expressions of strength and essentialist masculinity is no longer the norm. But Turnipseed's, Fick's and Williams's descriptions of their experiences of masculinity and community reveal both the potential for a more flexible conception of gender and military identity as well as the considerable obstacles to achieving that potential in the context of war.

The Philosopher in the Theater of War

> The man, most man,
> Works best for men: and, if most man indeed,
> He gets his manhood plainest from his soul.
>
> —ELIZABETH BARRETT BROWNING, "Aurora Leigh"

> A hairy body, and arms stiff with bristles,
> give promise of a manly soul.
>
> —JUVENAL, *Satires*

Joel Turnipseed begins his 2003 memoir of the Persian Gulf War, *Baghdad Express,* with an epigraph from Paul Valéry: "Une philosophie doit être portative. / A philosophy should be portable." As he explains in the book's

opening, Turnipseed joins the Marines after high school, and as a reservist
spends four months AWOL, what he calls "a period of separation" when
he didn't go to reserve drills (22). In 1990, he is called up for active duty in
Iraq, and works in the Sixth Motor Transport Battalion hauling ammunition and explosives across the desert. This becomes the greatest logisti-
cal effort in Marine Corps history, and is dubbed the "Baghdad Express."
Turnipseed, a self-styled philosopher, goes to war as a test of himself, but
also as a test of his *idea* of himself, as he indicates with his choice of epigraph. Early in his memoir, the notion of self that Turnipseed describes
could hardly seem more different than the typical "hard men" of the Corps
(the ones that Nathaniel Fick describes extensively). The day Turnipseed
is activated as a truck driver, a colonel tells the group of reservists exactly
what kind of men they are, with no room for doubt: "You are motivated,
dedicated, die-hard, ass-kicking, sand-busting, Saddam-hating, fearless,
brass-balled, spit-polished, de-luxe, hi-tech, combat warriors" (7). Turnipseed, however, cuts something of a different figure:

> I sat beneath a tree, decked out in khakis, white oxford and dark-green car-
> digan, wearing gold and tortoise-shell glasses. I smoked my pipe and tried
> to look philosophical, holding a fountain pen over a blank page of my jour-
> nal. The other Marines threw rocks and footballs at each other, smoking
> and joking. (9)

Turnipseed's memoir as a whole is an attempt to negotiate or reconcile
these two identities: that of intellectual, aloof philosopher and hard, smart-
ass Marine. He is, in many ways, a consummate performer, and tries on
these and other personalities during his time at war. In this scene, Turnipseed is ostentatious about the difference between his appearance and behavior and that of the other soldiers, and about the fact that his wardrobe
and accessories would be more appropriate for a college professor than
for a Marine about to fly to Saudi Arabia. His description of this moment,
however, emphasizes that he is *performing*—he is "decked out," or fully
costumed, and he does not philosophize (as the journal pages are empty),
but merely attempts to "look philosophical." Turnipseed is only too happy
to try on different ways of being, and specifically, different ways of being
masculine. For him, the self is a show. But which show is the right one?
Turnipseed's heightened awareness of the slipperiness and malleability of

identity may allow him greater freedom of expression, but it also leads to a lingering uncertainty about what he's really "made of" as well as a sense of isolation from his fellow soldiers. In war, one may have to pick a side—and a self—after all.

Shortly after the colonel's rousing speech, the men gather to watch CNN reporting on the war's beginning. As many did, Turnipseed finds the coverage of this performance remarkable and deeply engrossing:

> CNN exploded on the screen, sending a riot alert through our nervous systems. Anti-aircraft fire and flares lit up the Baghdad skies, and sirens screamed beneath the rumble of bombs. The men who had been sleeping on the floor began queuing up at the two pay telephones, and the first few rows of seats filled with men craning their necks backward, eyes glued to the spectacle. (11)

A spectacle it is indeed, and the men watch with personal interest as tracers flash in Baghdad and Lou Dobbs, Wolf Blitzer, Richard Roth, and Charles Jaco report on SCUDS fired into Israel from Iraq. "CNN—we were so tuned in they had a direct coax link to our cerebral cortex," Turnipseed remembers. "SCUDS in Tel Aviv. CNN. Electric night in Baghdad. CNN. Sirens in Dahran. CNN. Generals with wicked in-flight video in Riyadh. CNN, giving new meaning to 'theater of war'" (13). But the theater becomes Turnipseed's too, a test to see how well his own performances will hold up.

Turnipseed's choice of this particular theater would seem to be at odds with his philosophical ambitions, and for a time he goes AWOL. But when he is given a chance to be discharged following that "period of separation," he relents and instead makes up his missed drills in order to stay a Marine, a decision that means being sent to Iraq after Saddam Hussein's invasion of Kuwait (23). He stays, and calls himself "a dream recruit: messed up enough that I had nowhere else to go; smart and aggressive enough to want to prove something" (23). If not for the activation, he claims he would have been effectively homeless (21). To be a Marine, at least in his understanding, is his only option: "In the end, as it was in the beginning, the Corps was all I had" (23). And so his motivation is based both on economic necessity and on the desire to test himself, to try on a tough, manly identity. This conception of war and the military as the ultimate exam to be passed, the proof of a successful and truly "hard" performance, is one that Fick and Williams emphasize as well, to differing degrees. Notably, none characterize their service as just that—the opportunity to serve, to sacrifice for one's country or the good of other peoples. This may be an acknowledged side effect of their military careers, but it is not the primary motivating factor. What matters here is what makes the man; what a man makes is of secondary importance.

Turnipseed's first act after learning he will go to war is to buy a pack of Camels and smoke his first cigarette. This moment of self-conscious change precedes a longer discussion of his notion of identity. "This awkwardness, this abruptness, was not new to me," he notes (25). As a child, he moves constantly, "a different school in a different city every year from kindergarten to tenth grade. It made me a connoisseur of loneliness" (25). Because, as he says, he has no one to show him "who or how to be," he samples all kinds of identities, drawn from *Saturday Night Live* skits, Elvis Costello, *Mad* magazine, and zines from hippie communes. "I was a total freak," he asserts (25–26). None of the experiments are consistently satisfying, however. He wants something solid, something that will finally prove both "what is" and what *he* is. And so the turn to philosophy:

> I took to philosophy to build, brick by unassailable brick, a bunker of truth, inside of which I could work on the greater labor of building an unassailable happiness. This was the only thing that mattered—and I had a sense, heading to war, that I would somehow complete this task in the desert, where wisdom had always been achieved. (26)

For Turnipseed, identity may be malleable, but the truth he speaks about is sturdy, real, and unchanging. His bunker will be hard and impermeable, and the happiness he constructs in that place of invulnerability will provide the center for a new and more stable or "authentic" identity. Turnipseed is not so different from Fick, a self-described "hard Marine" who enlists because he wants to do something "so hard no one could talk shit to me" (4).

Truth-seeking aside, war will certainly be a different stage for Turnipseed, and he prepares by trying on his new camouflage costume in the library of his family's home, "wishing to surprise everyone with the suddenness of the transformation" (27). "A *Metamorphosis*!" he announces, stepping into the living room, clearly aware of the irony in his reference to

Kafka and perhaps wondering about this most recent self-invention (29). But he can't remember a time, he muses, "during which I didn't want to erase and reinvent myself" (30). And so he ships off into the strange world of war, the perfect venue for dramatic metamorphosis.

He struggles, however, with the union of philosophy and war, the two seemingly disparate parts of himself. "I had tried, on the drive up, to wrap my philosophy around this unsettling fact: even though I felt deep within me that this was a stupid war, an avoidable war, I wanted very badly to see the worst of war" (62). Turnipseed writes "KNOW THYSELF" on his combat helmet, but it seems less like an instruction for others than a plea for his own well-being. Eager to play his role well, Turnipseed embraces activities like smoking and physical labor, but his relationships with others continue to be as strained as those he had in his previous incarnations. He may be a "connoisseur of loneliness," but he also tends to consider himself superior to those around him; despite his honesty, the overall effect is not a positive one. He grows frustrated with a bald, splotchy-faced military chaplain who spends "a good fifteen minutes doing the tiresome 'love' thing with me, *agape, philia,* and *eros*" (82). Tiresome as Turnipseed may find him, the chaplain later talks to him about Aristotle, Aquinas, Dante, and Boethius, for which Turnipseed grants him some grudging respect. He refers to the chaplain's religion as "shams and hypocrisy," but also indicates that he thinks Marines engage in something like the same thing. "Aren't you a Marine, Turnipseed?" the chaplain asks, and the would-be provocateur is disarmed: "I stood naked in my disgust, and tried quickly to cover myself with a fig leaf of dissimulation. 'It's a sort of philosophical obliquity thing'" (82).

His philosophy has indeed grown more oblique, and at times he attempts to claim he's abandoned it altogether, as when he receives a letter from his old friend Mark. The letter quotes Kierkegaard, Nietzsche, and Emerson, but Turnipseed feels like it's been sent to someone who is no longer around:

> Mark is still talking to me like I'm a transcendentalist. What the fuck? If I was going to be a hero of anything, it was going to be as camp smart-ass and champion smoker of two eighty-five cent packs of Camels a day. I had lost myself and didn't know what to make for a metaphor: like a book mis-shelved on the stacks; like a grain of sand in the desert; like what? Like

nothing but what I was—another Marine in camouflage carrying a rifle and a pack with a radio. (97)

Like Anthony Swofford in *Jarhead,* Turnipseed feels both the comfort and the despair in being "just another Marine," like so many others. But for him, becoming indistinguishable from his comrades denotes a successful performance, a previous self successfully rather than tragically lost. Yet he's not quite ready to give up on philosophy—after all, he does claim that it should be portable, adaptable to changes in setting and even identity.

Nowhere is Turnipseed's strange and shifting negotiation between his philosophical self and his desired identity as a smart-ass Marine more striking than in the descriptions of his relationship with a group of men referred to as the Dog Pound. After his fellow reservists from Minneapolis are ordered to relocate north without him, Turnipseed moves his gear into a tent with a group of African-American men from Philadelphia who also work the Baghdad Express. "You just been moved into the Dog Pound," a fellow soldier tells him (113). When the Dog Pound asks him "how the fuck you live up there" in Minnesota, the tone of his response contrasts jarringly with the other soldiers' mode of speech and bears the heightened markers of intellectual identity: "Well, you know, I sleep, eat food. Perambulate now and again. Read, chat on the phone once in a while. I mostly enjoy the time I spend relaxing and reading in the coffee shops" (121). When he arranges his belongings, his journals and books, he notes that all he lacks is "a tawny port and a good smoke" (122).

Turnipseed claims to want to be a smart-ass hero rather than philosopher, but when he meets this group of men who so clearly embody the former, his reaction is to intensify his performance as "professor," as the men sometimes call him. He finds the Pound appalling and seductive, and describes his philosophical "bunker of truth" as overrun by popular culture, presumably wielded at least in part by the Pound:

> I unpacked my journals and books, but I couldn't read. I just sat and stared. I was exhausted, but awake. And my exhaustion was more than physical. I had long been trying to set myself up in conscious opposition to society, always comparing surface to some hidden reality—which I would discover in books and philosophy. I no longer had the energy to process every perception as part of a syllogism. As for standing in opposition—my frontal assault

on society wasn't going too well: the barrels of my guns were smoking and I was out of ammo. I was down to throwing paperback editions of Wittgenstein from my foxhole, wielding an empty fountain pen. But the enemy kept sending their hordes, sounding their trumpets as they stormed the dead white barricades: whole divisions of Warner Brothers and Disney, Def Jam and Columbia, Wal-Mart and K-Mart and 7-11, Ray-Ban and Kodak, Nike and Gatorade, of Hatches and Farmers and Ebberses from privates to corporals to the Colonel's, chains of command and fast-food chains—it was just too much to overcome. (122)

Turnipseed's desire to always stand in opposition—to be a smart-ass for the philosophers and a philosopher for the smart-asses—is clearly articulated here, yet the nature of this "defeat" is a bit ambiguous. If he means to ironize his own stance, to subtly mock it with the use of metaphors of war and assault, then the fall of the dead white males has a sharp comic edge, and nicely illustrates this turning point in Turnipseed's self-perception. If, however, he's serious about mourning the influx of pop culture on the "dead white barricades," then he's just described himself as a bigot, and a failed bigot at that.

Regardless of the motivations behind this change of heart, he doesn't stick with it. One of the next acts he describes is explaining Plato's *Republic* to the other men. He insists that his relationship with the Pound, despite his misgivings, is somehow close and comfortable: "It's hard for me, now, to capture the tone of my rapport with the Dog Pound," he admits. "[I]t was natural, arch, warm, and funny. There was an immediate ease to our back-and-forth play" (123). Later, Turnipseed takes the "play" further and adopts their speech patterns, a wild deviation from his previous mode of conversation. When two of the men joke around, each claiming to have seen the other's mother selling cheap blow jobs outside a truck stop, Turnipseed joins in. "[A]in't neither one of 'em makin' a livin' wage," he says of the women, "'cause the two of you takin' all the business with that booty you been givin' away for free just outside the gate" (129).

"We had a great thing going, the Pound and me," he says, and in a kind of culminating assertion of blended identity, he attempts to rap the ideas of Henry Thoreau (134, 140). Turnipseed would appear to have found a masculine community that accepts him, or at least seems to, and provides for a happy balance between his philosophical and smart-ass selves. His rap for them is a performance of both. He is pleased that this community takes him in despite their differences. Their expressions of masculinity may be various, but each of them is, after all, male: "the boys in the Pound cared for me just because—I was a Marine, they were Marines; I was a man, they were men" (151). Military *maleness* is the real glue here, and for a while at least, he can stop worrying about how to behave. That acceptance into the utopic community of the Pound is abruptly terminated, however, when his original tentmates return to the area. Unceremoniously Turnipseed drops his newly acquired speech patterns and rapping attempts, and leaves the Dog Pound behind. His friendship with them proves to be as ephemeral as his various performances.

The ground war in Iraq is over in approximately one hundred hours. In the immediate aftermath, Turnipseed is sent to a POW camp, where he observes the beleaguered figures of "hundreds, perhaps thousands" of Iraqis, and the experience of seeing the horror of such suffering becomes his personal war story, the one he says he will be able to tell again and again (160, 156). Some of the other men take pictures, posing in front of the prisoners, and Turnipseed simultaneously condemns and sympathizes with the impulse: "so that I could understand at one remove, or not at all, to look at myself standing before a forty-foot tractor-trailer bed filled with hollow men. Maybe I could inscribe lines from Eliot's 'Hollow Men,' read so well by Brando in *Apocalypse Now,* on the back of the photo? It would be so intense, so *cool* to have later" (162). Like his comment about the "dead white barricades," Turnipseed may well be mocking his own desire for that intense coolness, but the desire exists nonetheless. The POWs aren't people, but just extras in Turnipseed's ongoing show—he wants to be able to look at *himself* in front of them. He even associates the moment with another show, Brando's performance of Kurtz performing Eliot. He can't seem to understand the moment without reference to other spectacles, and in the end, he is disgusted at what he calls his "inability to put a word or thought to my experience" (165). If there is a right word or perfect gesture, he realizes, perhaps it is just that: "Nothing." As Colby Buzzell writes in *My War,* Turnipseed finds that the experience of "real Iraq" is a blank.

The war ends, and Turnipseed is unharmed. Like Swofford, he has not killed anyone. He witnesses no atrocities or deaths, and thus feels somehow cheated (183). Back home, he visits the Post Exchange at Camp Pendleton and finds a biography of Wittgenstein and a García Márquez book about Simón Bolívar: "It was like a new world had come into being, where I could simultaneously be a nasty drunk Marine and a philosopher man-qué" (198). But this resolution entails a change of categories. Previously, he wanted to be a smart-ass and a philosopher. Desiring instead to be a "nasty drunk" and a failed philosopher is a capitulation, and he frames it as such; he says that in the end, he "gave up the desire for otherworldly perfection philosophy demanded of me and embraced the shadows" (200). This "new world" is not one where he can perform however he wants to and embrace differing modes of masculinity. The only way to do so, as he says here, is to fail at both, to be "nasty" and "manqué." And he does so alone, without any close comrades.

Turnipseed's war story is a kind of kaleidoscope, a self-portrait from a man whose idea of identity was either fractured or self-consciously playful long before he was faced with the gauntlet of war. *Baghdad Express* is like a one-man play. Turnipseed is alternately a coffee-shop philosopher, a new Marine, a smart-ass, an honorary African American, simply "a man," and even a cartoon. Throughout the book, episodes in Turnipseed's story are glossed with black and white narrative cartoons drawn by Brian Kelly, with Turnipseed appearing as a cryptically simple figure in glasses and his signature Delphic helmet. Around the time of the publication of *Baghdad Express,* Turnipseed adds another identity to his bag of tricks, and changes his last name to Hernandez when he marries a woman of that surname ("About Joel Turnipseed"). He also starts a blog called "Hotel Zero," making full use of the technological developments since his war experience to continue his writing and his reflections on identity.[3]

Baghdad Express is a trickier book than *Jarhead,* the other well-received memoir of the Gulf War to which it is often compared. Elisabeth Pied-mont-Marton has argued that Turnipseed's is the better book, because it functions as a "sharp critique of exactly the kind of self-involved recovery narrative that Swofford engages" (270). Piedmont-Marton notes Turnip-seed's unapologetically fierce addiction to cigarettes (as chain smoke swirls though most of the scenes set in Iraq), and draws the reader's attention to one of the cartoons. That cartoon first shows a chart indicating how many inches of materials such as concrete, sandbags, clay, or snow are required to adequately protect against attacks with different kinds of mortars, shells, and bombs. The following page shows a similar chart. It lists the amount of time spent alone with works by Plato, St. Augustine, Kierkegaard,

Figure 3. In one of Brian Kelly's illustrations for the book, *Baghdad Express: A Gulf War Memoir* (Borealis Books, 2003), Turnipseed contemplates his many selves reflected in a mirror. "I wanted to live the examined life," reads the caption, "but which life?" Used by permission of Minnesota Historical Society Press.

Nietzsche—or, alternatively, bourbon—required to recover from child abuse, a drunk father, a shitty life, or Ayn Rand (51–52).

Turnipseed may indeed be critiquing the idea of recovery, and Piedmont-Marton is correct to note that the narrative of healing is a common one used in novels and memoirs of war. One wonders, however, if a more primary target of his critique is the idea of an authentic identity itself, rather than the recovery of one. "Know thyself," his helmet says, but what does Turnipseed, or anyone, really know? His shape-shifting is self-conscious and usually fun to observe—the reader waits for his next costume change or accessory appropriation, and applauds what is often a performance of masculinity somewhat incongruous in the military world. Yet if his affiliations to personal modes of being are fleeting, his attachment to other soldiers is even more so. He and the Pound are fast friends, but he ditches them just as fast, and more often describes himself as isolated, even alienated from the war and the world around him. Trying to play different roles has consequences, and he doesn't seem to be able to successfully perform as both a philosopher and a smart-ass.

The Iraqi poet Dunya Mikhail fled her country in 1996 for Jordan and then the United States; she writes about the experiences of war and exile, of being *forced* to assume new and different identities. "I don't know a thing / about my role in this new play / and all my lines / will mean nothing to the audience" ("The Foreigner" 44). She contrasts herself with Americans, her new neighbors, who travel for distraction and pleasure—they are tourists rather than immigrants or refugees. Like Turnipseed's, Mikhail's is a failed performance undertaken as a response to war, and one that also results in isolation. The motivations for that performance, however, are quite different. "And I will spend a lifetime," Turnipseed writes in the final line of the book, "trying to explain the complex of emotions—anger, pride, love, honor, ambiguity, betrayal, and hope—that inhere in the motto *Semper Fidelis:* Always Faithful." His statement raises the question, at least with respect to Turnipseed himself: faithful to what? Or (more to the point) to whom?

The Hard Man Beyond the Pale

> The tragedy of machismo is that a man is never quite man enough.
>
> —GERMAINE GREER, "My Mailer Problem"

Turnipseed's *Baghdad Express* appeared in 2003, twelve years after his military service in the Gulf War. Nathaniel Fick's 2005 memoir *One Bullet Away: The Making of a Marine Officer* appeared only two years after the conclusion of his service in Afghanistan and the Iraq War. Though Turnipseed (as a reservist) and Fick (as an officer) fight in different ways in different wars, they are similarly well educated in philosophy and the classics, and each sees combat as a way to test himself, to forge his identity into greater clarity—as a way to make the man. Like Turnipseed, Fick begins the first section of his memoir with a classical epigraph about that very topic, this one from Thucydides: "We should remember that one man is much the same as another, and that he is best who is trained in the severest school." As a former classics major at Dartmouth, Fick has an affinity for time-tested meditations on war, justice, good, and evil, and has clearly taken Thucydides' advice to heart. He describes his experiences in the Marine Corps Officer Training School, the Basic Course, the Infantry Officer Course, the Recon Indoctrination Program and Basic Reconnaissance

Course, and SERE (Survival, Evasion, Resistance, and Escape) training, as well as commanding a weapons platoon on the ground in Afghanistan and Iraq. That "severest school" makes the man—the truly masculine as opposed to the undifferentiated male. When everyone is the same, performance is what counts. And to perform well is to be "hard," a term that Fick uses repeatedly. For Fick, however, being a hard man ultimately requires a willingness to protect his soldiers and also to sacrifice them if the situation calls for it. The hardness that brings the soldiers together can also tear them apart. That, Fick realizes, might be too hard, and by the end of the book he describes his own "unmaking" as well.

In fact, the complications inherent in Fick's quest for a kind of time-less masculinity are indicated right from the beginning. Someone with Fick's education would surely be aware of the context of the Thucydides quotation he chooses to introduce his narrative. The line is taken from Archidamus's speech during the debate at Sparta, as the Lacedaemonians discuss how to properly respond to the growth of the Athenian empire. Archidamus, the Lacedaemonian king and a "good and prudent man," urges caution (I.79). "At my age, Lacedaemonians, I have had experience of many wars," he begins, "and I see several of you who are as old as I am, and who will not, as men too often do, desire war because they have never known it, or in the belief that it is either a good or a safe thing" (I.80). He urges a careful consideration of forces, resources, and strategy, and above all, more time to think about the consequences of declaring war. "Our hopes ought not to rest on the probability of their making mistakes, but on our own caution and foresight," he notes immediately before making the statement that Fick uses (I.84). In Archidamus's understanding, that severest school is less an incubator for aggression or a hunger for glory than it is for prudence and thoughtfulness. The natural end of training is not always battle.

Archidamus, however, loses the debate. Another speaker urges Sparta to defend its honor and "attack the evil-doer" with "the Gods on our side," and Sparta votes for war (I.86). It's a war that Sparta ultimately wins, but only after many years of lives and resources lost. On the surface, Fick's choice of epigraph simply denotes his desire to excel, to prove himself through severe training that will be hard and make him hard as well. But taken in its context, the quotation perhaps reveals Fick's belief that good men and soldiers, well trained in that severest school, can still be betrayed by less thoughtful leaders using powerful rhetoric. To fight well is a laudable goal, but Iraq in 2003 makes Fick wonder for what—and for whom—he is fighting.

Fick begins his story, as so many war memoirists do, by explaining his decision to join the military. He is excited about cultivating his competence, endurance, intelligence, and most of all, manhood. After his years at Dartmouth, he balks at the choices of law and medical school that entice so many of his classmates. "I wanted to go off on a great adventure," he says, "to prove myself, to serve my country." Service is important, but proof is tantalizing: "I wanted to do something so hard that no one could ever talk shit to me. In Athens or Sparta, my decision would have been easy. I felt as if I had been born too late. There was no longer a place in the world for a young man who wanted to wear armor and slay dragons" (4).

Doing something "so hard" will in turn make Fick hard, and therefore protect him from shit, from contamination. He will be impenetrable. Hardness, for Fick, will preserve the boundaries of his masculine identity, which, he seems to feel, are somewhat set upon in contemporary America. Personal skill and strength no longer count for much, or so he thinks, in an era circumscribed by the long arm of technology and luxury. He pines for a "simpler" time, like those he has studied, although he is perhaps aware of the irony that there was *never* a place for a young man who wanted to slay dragons, armor notwithstanding.

Fick doesn't specifically say so, but he may be referring not just to chivalric stories but to a specific recruiting commercial aired by the Marine Corps. Reporter Evan Wright was embedded with Fick's platoon in Iraq, and wrote about his experiences in a series of articles for *Rolling Stone* and later in a book *Generation Kill,* which is the basis for HBO's 2008 miniseries of the same title. Wright spoke with the other members of the platoon, who frame their desire to join the military in similar terms. "Most Marines can remember the exact moment they decided to enlist," Wright reports. "A lot of them were sparked by a specific TV commercial. In it, a cartoon Arthurian hero slays a fire-breathing dragon, then promptly morphs into a Marine in dress blues standing at attention with a silver sword at his side" (26). The masculine icon of yesteryear still has a great deal of persuasive power and cultural currency. Perhaps, it suggests, there are dragons to be slain after all.

Like Turnipseed, Fick wants to be someone else, though Fick frames this desire in more extreme terms than Turnipseed. Teach for America or the Peace Corps, he decides, wouldn't be enough. "I wanted something more transformative. Something that might kill me—or leave me better, stronger, more capable. I wanted to be a warrior" (4). With the latter in mind, he applies for the Marine Corps Officer Candidate School (OCS), which will be the first of many "rites of passage" he describes in precisely those terms. In OCS, Fick is immediately struck by the differences between his time at Dartmouth and the classroom instruction in the Corps:

> The curriculum seemed ridiculous at first. My liberal arts education had valued discussion, debate, and nuanced interpretations of complex ideas. But in combat, we were told, there's rarely time for discussion and debate. Complex ideas must be made simple, or they'll remain ideas and never be put into action. The leadership traits were bearing, courage, decisiveness, dependability, endurance, enthusiasm, initiative, integrity, judgment, justice, knowledge, loyalty, tact, and unselfishness. We drilled them, and every other list, over and over again. (18)

In June 1999, he takes the oath of office as a Marine Corps second lieutenant. Even though he acknowledges in retrospect that he "had no idea what it meant to be a Marine," he does notice a difference in himself, "a subtle change in my worldview. My tolerance for abstract theories and academic posturing had evaporated. Instead of classes in philosophy and classical languages, I gravitated toward national security and current events" (30). He begins to repudiate the academic study of the ancient texts he loves so much in favor of more modern concerns. He prefers deeds over speech—and maybe Archidamus did talk too much, after all—but his conception of the ideal self is still firmly rooted in a sense of tradition and literally old-school masculinity. Listen as he describes his decision to train as an infantry officer:

> I wanted the purity of a man with a weapon traveling great distances on foot, navigating, stalking, calculating, using personal skill. I couldn't let a jet or a tank get in the way, and I certainly wasn't going to sit behind a desk. I wanted to be tested, to see if I had what it takes... The grunt life was untainted. I sensed a continuity with other infantrymen stretching back to Thermopylae. Weapons and tactics may have changed, but they were only accouterments. The men stayed the same. In a time of satellites and missile strikes, the part of me that felt I'd been born too late was drawn to the infantry,

where courage still counts. Being a Marine was not about money for graduate school or learning a skill; it was a rite of passage in a society becoming so soft and homogenized that the very concept was often sneered at. (33)

This passage provides an excellent snapshot of the way Fick sees himself, his goals, and the place of a masculine identity in contemporary society. Masculinity is a pure state, certainly not achievable by wardrobe or accoutrements. In fact, those things are impediments. True masculinity is to be distinguished from "society," which is characterized by softness and sameness and, one assumes, feminization. Fick also sees and desires sameness in masculinity, but here the quality is a positive one—it is the deep vein of authentic identity.

Interestingly, however, Fick characterizes this distinguished masculinity as less of an essence than a performance. The proof is in your actions, in the tests you pass. You don't pass the tests because you are already excellent— you are excellent only if and when you pass the tests. Given everyone's basic similarity, you must perform in order to make yourself different, although that difference is in turn an identification and similarity with other outstanding men. This masculinity resists commodified society; it is pure and aesthetic. It is the phallic life and identity of the hard man. He recognizes these qualities most readily in the Spartans, whom he mentions repeatedly.[4] Fick's language intensifies even further after he completes the Basic School and moves on to the Infantry Officer Course. "None of us called it IOC," however. "It was 'the Brick House' or 'the Men's Club.' IOC was, in our terms, all balls, men only. If the Marine Corps was a last bastion of manhood in American society, IOC was its inner sanctum" (45). Fick wants to go all the way, to penetrate into the deepest, most untainted center of masculine identity, where maleness has not been softened or compromised.

Fick graduates from IOC in September 2000, and as each of the twenty-eight men receives his diploma, he recites a martial quotation to the room. Once again, Fick pays homage to the Spartans with their infantry creed: "When you return from battle, you will either bear your shield or be borne upon it" (54). The military as a whole is preparing for the next fight, and wondering what it will be like. The Marines in particular have begun training their officers in things like "low-intensity conflicts" and "three-block wars," anticipating more operations like the one in Somalia, as well as the protocols of humanitarian missions and working with the media.

Fick joins the First Battalion of the First Marine Regiment, commanding a weapons platoon in Bravo Company that will eventually be attached to an Expeditionary Unit and sent to cruise the Indian Ocean and Persian Gulf.

In August 2001, they sail on the USS *Dubuque* past Guadalcanal, where Fick thinks about 1942, when the First Marine Division wrested control of the island from the Japanese. "History," he notes, "is the Marine Corp's religion" (72). Then, while the platoon stops over in Australia, news reaches them of the September 11 World Trade Center attacks. The world has changed, and so has their place in it. "Fellas," his friend Jim remarks, "history just bent us over" (74). If history is the Corps' religion, and the Corps also worships and embodies hardness, then that same phallic notion of history has just feminized Fick and his fellow recruits—it has made them vulnerable, the very state against which all that hardness is supposed to protect. In placing these two statements so close together, Fick seems at least moderately aware of this irony.

He responds by buckling down. First in Afghanistan, his weapons platoon transports a load of materiel on foot while other soldiers ride in a convoy, and he feels the kind of pure exhilaration that he wanted from the beginning. He loves it:

> Now, as I had as OCS, I sensed an outpouring of grit, pride, and raw desire to live up to the traditions we'd inherited.... Television commentators could pontificate from their climate-controlled studios about technology and the "revolution in military affairs," but out on the battlefield that night, long history marched unchanged into the twenty-first century. Strong men hauled heavy loads over rough ground. There was nothing relative about it—no second changes and no excuses. It was elemental and dangerous. It was exactly why I'd joined the Marines. (133, 134)

Thus far, Fick has wanted something like a gym in extremis, and he got it. Whether or not history will in fact bend him over, in the words of his friend, remains to be seen. Fick has enjoyed what was literally grunt work, but he has yet to be shot at or, more crucially, kill. Back on the *Dubuque,* he and his friend Patrick wonder if their experiences were, in fact, "real" war. As I discussed in chapter 1, Colby Buzzell went overseas with an appreciation for and comfort with technology, but Fick describes his comrades considering those developments with suspicion. With JDAMs (Joint Direct

Attack Munitions, or guidance kits for bombs) and Tomahawks and lasers, Patrick wonders—echoing Swofford—"does that mean Americans won't be in combat ever again?" (140)

Fick doesn't answer, but before he has a chance to find out, he reports stateside to yet another training program, this time the fabled Recon Indoctrination Program and Basic Reconnaissance Course. Recon is unapologetically, openly phallic. Hardness is once again Fick's goal, and this time he articulates it as such—not just the physicality of strong muscles and a powerful physique, but mental impermeability, the inability to be penetrated:

> "Hardness," I was learning, was the supreme virtue among recon Marines. The greatest compliment one could pay to another was to say he was hard. Hardness wasn't toughness, nor was it courage, although both were part of it. Hardness was the ability to face an overwhelming situation with aplomb, smile calmly at it, and then triumph through sheer professional pride. (145)

He goes through SERE training, where again the goal is to avoid penetration, to stay hard: "On the instructor staff were men who'd spent more time in foreign prisons than I had in the Marine Corps. The purpose of the course, they said, was 'to learn to overcome the mind-fuck of captivity'" (149). When he completes the course and checks back into his battalion, his colonel tells him in no uncertain terms what his job will be: "to be the hardest motherfucker in your platoon" (155). And as 2002 draws to a close, he readies himself for Iraq.

Despite all of his physical and mental training, the multiple rites of passage he has put himself through, the thought of fighting in Iraq simply doesn't compute. The idea of American tanks in Baghdad is "too far removed from any point of reference in my life. That I would be among those troops was simply unthinkable. I could intellectualize my way through how the war would unfold, but I couldn't feel it. It wasn't real" (167). Likewise, Fick's carefully constructed identity becomes unknowable as well. In San Diego when he receives his summons, he watches other people eating dinner and living normal lives. He imagines the inevitable and unknowable rupture in the narrative of his life:

> These people looked forward to Saturday, and Sunday, and the coming months and years of their lives. Mine felt as if it had ended. I didn't have a

future. Trying to conjure up a mental image of myself after Iraq, I found that I couldn't. Iraq loomed like a black hole into which all the thoughts and acts and hopes and dreams of twenty-five years were being sucked. I couldn't imagine what might come out the other side. (168)

Later, the troops prepare to enter Iraq from Kuwait, and Fick continues to reflect on the blank that is his future. "We try to control what comes next and shape it to meet our will," he notes, but this is "too big for me to shape…Strangely, I tried to conjure up images of what I might see and how I might react, but all was blank" (194). In that absence, however, he does find something to shape his intentions: "I was absolved of responsibility for my future. It was replaced with responsibility for twenty-two other futures." His own identity, his own future, will literally become that of his men, the objects of all those leadership skills he has worked so hard to inculcate in himself.

At this point the men are joined by Wright, the *Rolling Stone* reporter. Wright's portrait of Fick is generally positive, and reflects the deep respect he and his men have for one another, as well as their similar love for hardness. Recon Marines, Wright notes, is one of the few fields in the military that is still closed to women, one of the last "all-male adventures" in America. And hardness is key: "having stronger muscles, being a better fighter, being more able to withstand pain and privation" (21). The men are defiantly male, as reflected in their profanity, scratching, fighting, their quest for dominance. They are also a diverse group, and Wright notes that one is as likely to meet a Marine who joined to escape a street gang or an alcoholic father as a Marine who went to prep school or turned down scholarships for the opportunity to join the military (24). "What unites them," Wright notes, "is an almost reckless desire to test themselves in the most extreme circumstances" (24).

Fick defines himself in reference to the classics, to Thucydides and the Spartans and the purity of a timeless tradition, but Wright has a different view of today's military, as Marines who would be "virtually unrecognizable to their forebears in the 'Greatest Generation.'" They may have a shared love for hardness, but beyond that, this masculine collective is a varied one:

They are kids raised on hip-hop, Marilyn Manson and Jerry Springer. For them, "motherfucker" is a term of endearment. For some, slain rapper

Tupac is an American patriot whose writings are better known than the speeches of Abraham Lincoln. There are tough guys who pray to Buddha and quote Eastern philosophies and New Age precepts gleaned from watching Oprah and old kung fu movies. There are former gangbangers, a sprinkling of born-again Christians and quite a few guys who before entering the Corps were daily dope smokers; many of them dream of the day when they get out and are once again united with their beloved bud. (5)

The men in the platoon represent a range of masculinities. One of the most striking is Sergeant Rudy Reyes, who has "the insanely muscled body of a fantasy Hollywood action hero" and who has competed nationally in kung fu and tai chi. Reyes is the battalion's best martial artist and one of the strongest Marines, and is also, in Wright's words, the "gayest." "Though he is not gay in the sense of sexual orientation—Reyes, after all, is married—he is at least a highly evolved tough guy in touch with a well-developed feminine side...His fellow Marines call him 'Fruity Rudy,' because he is so beautiful" (42). As one Marine explains, finding Rudy hot doesn't make you gay. "He's just so beautiful," the Marine says, showing an openness one would perhaps not expect from a group that values hardness to such an extent. "We all think he's hot." Wright conveys, in a way that Fick doesn't, the variety of masculinities to be found in the military, including a consideration of the male body as beautiful and sexual, and the male soldier as "gay"—though not homosexual. Wright is admittedly not a soldier, but his description here is one of the more telling instances of the relative acceptance of different masculine performances. In fact, "Fruity Rudy," as he's called, will go on to perform *himself* in the HBO adaptation of *Generation Kill*. In the miniseries, the audience is introduced to Rudy in the opening episode, with a shot of the back of Rudy's beautiful, "hot," and nude body ("Get Some").

Fick and Reyes have different interests, backgrounds, and pursuits, and the masculinities they model are also quite different. Each is both acceptable and admired—one based on Western notions of Spartan toughness and duty, the other on Eastern martial arts and a celebration of physical beauty. As long as you perform well, you can play a variety of roles as a military man. Another soldier, however, offers an example of a bad performance. Wright calls him Captain America, and notes that the group dislikes and distrusts him as much as they adore Fick. Captain America is "prone to hysterics," and tends to respond to stimuli with an excess of aggression (68). Twice in Wright's telling he attempts to bayonet a prisoner who is well under control, and also misdirects a Humvee carrying critically injured Marines. Wright condemns Captain America as a soldier whose hyper-performance of masculinity mistakes a kind of severe toughness for hardness, and thus takes hardness to an inappropriate extreme. This reflects Fick's own painful conclusions about what it means to finally be "too hard."

Fick continues his memoir with descriptions of moving into and through Iraq, the unknown that is this foreign country and his presence in it. Driving in Humvee convoys, watching for ambushes and seeing the bloody, burnt remains of other Humvees that fell victim to attack, he thinks about what he is supposed to feel in combat:

> Everything seemed to pass in a blur. I thought of war stories that talked about hyperclarity in combat, seeing every blade of grass and feeling colors more intensely than ever before. But for me, whole city blocks faded into a gray fuzz. I feared I was processing information too slowly, seeing only one of every ten things I should. I felt short-changed. I wanted hyperclarity, too. (204)

As part of the Humvee convoy, Fick *is* moving faster than most soldiers have in the past, and has to process information more quickly than if he were on foot. A few pages later, when the convoy is ambushed, the blurring becomes a sensation of excess: "Sensory overload paralyzed me... There was no fear, but no bravado either. I felt nothing. I was a passive observer watching this ambush unfold on a movie screen" (214). Finally, the "long-sought hyperclarity kicked in" as he fires grenades at the attackers. He watches one young man slump over his rifle after a grenade explodes near him, and the final veil is lifted: he has killed in combat. At last, he thinks, he can see.

That clarity, however, disintegrates a short time later, after the ambush is over and the platoon settles in for the night. The men "refight" the fight, telling stories about what happened. Fick, appropriately, encourages the activity, considering it "as psychological unburdening and as improvised classrooms where we sharpened our blades for the next fight" (219). But this time, what he hears unnerves him. His memory of the firefight, he finds, is only his. "Afterward, five Marines told five different stories" (219).

He remembers distances, the location of armed men, and even a domed mosque differently than all the other soldiers. "I was trained to thrive on chaos," he remarks, "but nothing prepared me for the fear of doubting my own senses" (219).

Doubt emerges as a central motif in the latter half of the book, as Fick recounts more ambushes and firefights. Being the hardest motherfucker in the platoon doesn't prevent the world around him from sliding into a hall of mirrors. While on reconnaissance in Qalat Sukkar, feeling the effects of fatigue and stress, Fick catches "a blurred glimpse of people, cars, and camels running through the brush. Men carried long sticks, maybe rifles" (237). After the assault, the Marines see several villagers carrying bundles, which turn out to be two young boys with gunshot wounds. Fick is horrified when he realizes their mistake: "The pieces fell into place. Those weren't rifles we had seen but shepherds' canes, not muzzle flashes but the sun reflecting on a windshield. The running camels belonged to these boys. We'd shot two children" (239). Fick successfully fights to get the boys American medical treatment, but the experience is deeply traumatic. Afterward, he tells his men to compartmentalize, to put the experience "way back" in their brains, and mourns for the self he was before war (243).

When the Marines and the Army converge on Baghdad, Fick looks forward to settling in, developing personal relationships with the locals and "deliver[ing] on our promises" (316). His faith in the postwar planning cracks a bit, however, when his men are moved repeatedly and looters take over the city. He worries about the young Iraqi males, who have been emasculated by the takeover and resent the American presence. And he makes more difficult choices, "rarely between good and bad, but rather between bad and worse," such as medically treating a young Iraqi girl instead of completing a search for an enemy weapons storehouse. When another recon platoon discovers signs that surface-to-air missiles had been removed from that storehouse, Fick wonders if the American casualties he hears about in the coming months came at the cost of the young girl's life (339). The doubt that began with his inability to imagine himself in Iraq and continued with his uncertainty about his own sensory impressions and decision-making skills continues to accrue. For Fick, masculinity has been about performance and the power to prevail under duress. Here, however, he can't perform. Circumstances are such that hardness is simply not enough.

Fick goes home in June 2003. Like Colby Buzzell, at times he thinks that his four-month stint in Iraq was a dream, something to be forgotten (362). But he feels the effects: he remains hyper-alert when in public spaces, imagines slitting the throat of a man who cuts him off in traffic, and cries for no reason (363). Fick wonders if he might be losing his sanity. He is promoted to captain, but ultimately decides to leave the Corps. He explains the reason behind his decision with some care:

> I left the Corps because I had become a reluctant warrior. Many Marines reminded me of gladiators. They had that mysterious quality that allows some men to strap on greaves and a breastplate and wade into the gore. I respected, admired, and emulated them, but I could never be like them. I could kill when killing was called for, and I got hooked on the rush of combat as much as any man did. But I couldn't make the conscious choice to put myself in that position again and again throughout my professional life. Great Marine commanders, like all great warriors, are able to kill that which they love most—their men. It's a fundamental law of warfare. Twice I had cheated it. I couldn't tempt fate again. (364)

Unlike his beloved Spartans, Fick will no longer wade into the gore. Hardness does, it seem, have a limit. Fick sees the paradox of the masculine collective here. The collective is timeless, aesthetic, and seductive, but it is also characterized by the necessity of its own internal acts of sacrifice, what Fick calls killing your own men. He can no longer perform, because to do that is, in both senses, "too hard." Fick ultimately has to abandon the masculine collective because he sees it as unsustainable.

And so, leaving that through which he has defined himself in every possible way, he drifts. Fick further reflects after leaving the Corps that combat had nearly unhinged him (368). A year after his return to the States, he drags a friend to the Antietam battlefield and thinks about the costs and benefits of war. "You helped do so much good for so many people," his friend says. "Why can't you take comfort in that?" Fick wonders. "The good was abstract. The good didn't feel as good as the bad felt bad. It wasn't the good that kept me up at night." His friend asks about pride. Why not be proud of what was accomplished? Fick's answer ends the book:

> I took sixty-five men to war and brought sixty-five home. I gave them everything I had. Together, we passed the test. Fear didn't beat us. I hope life

improves for the people of Afghanistan and Iraq, but that's not why we did it. We fought for each other.

I am proud. (369)

Fick's answer is ambiguous and unsettling. He reasserts the value of the collective here, not as an ongoing entity but as a unity achieved in a particular moment in time. The significance is in the successful performance, the passed test. For him, this has to suffice. It can at least tell him who he *was,* if not who he *is.* The people of Afghanistan and Iraq, pointedly, are largely irrelevant. "I *am* proud," he says, though one detects the implicit defensiveness in that final statement. And like the Thucydides quotation that opens the book, it is probably not beyond Fick's notice that he sets this last moment at Antietam, where more Americans died in battle on 17 September 1862 than on any other day of military engagement. In "That Is My Life," Iraqi poet Adam Hatem writes of a strange voice, singing:

> Beware of this drunken youth—
> he who has not spared himself
> can cause you harm.

Fick chooses to spare himself and, in so doing, perhaps spares the lives of his comrades, at least in his understanding. What effect that decision has on Iraqis like Hatem, however, is left unclear.

How hard is too hard? For Fick, the hardness that draws his masculine community together cannot forge in him a willingness to sacrifice that community for the purposes of war, or for the good of those "Others" who are outside the circle, props if not participants in this old ritual. Killing them is acceptable, if unpleasant, but watching a hard man die—watching him succumb, fall down instead of rise up as a figure of phallic mastery—is beyond the pale, or at least beyond the conception of this hard pale man.

Women, Weapons, and War

> When a woman has masculine virtues, you feel like running away; and when
> she doesn't have masculine virtues, she runs away herself.
>
> —NIETZSCHE, *Twilight of the Idols*

Like Turnipseed and Fick, Kayla Williams also begins her memoir of life in the military with an epigraph that introduces the book's main thematic concerns and its particular way of understanding the experience of war. Turnipseed espouses the portability of philosophy, and Fick draws us to a consideration of severe training, both through the use of quotations from renowned writers and thinkers. Williams's, too, is a classic of sorts:

> Cindy, Cindy, Cindy Lou
> Love my rifle more than you
> You used to be my beauty queen
> Now I love my M-16.

Williams's memoir also takes its title from this Army marching cadence which, as is common in military training, encourages the transference of a young recruit's affection from women to weapons. But the cover features Williams herself under the title, grinning broadly in camouflage while brandishing an M-16. Williams would seem to delight in the upending of gender norms. If the Cindy Lou of song has been rejected in favor of war and its fetishes, and relegated to a space beyond the collective of military masculinity, then Williams, in using the line "Love my rifle more than you" as the title, reclaims that space. This is *my* sphere, she seems to say, and "you," the would-be object of my affections (lover? reader? world?) are not exactly welcome.

The title is cocky and self-aware, though the subtitle *Young and Female in the U.S. Army* indicates that this will *not* be the reflections of "Just Another Soldier," as one popular (and male-authored) milblog is known. Williams points out very early in the book that her story has nothing to do with the stories of other female soldiers who inadvertently found fame in Iraq. "Don't count Jessica Lynch. Her story meant nothing to us," she rather boldly commands. "The same goes for Lynndie England. I'm not either one of them, and neither are any of the real women I know in the service" (15). Her subtitle, however, betrays something like the same sentiment as the title of Lynch's story as written by Rick Bragg: *I Am a Soldier, Too.* Williams is indeed a young woman in the military, and she presents that central conceit of her book as something that is both natural and strange.

In contrast to Williams, Jessica Lynch—as presented by Rick Bragg—is a small, fragile, feminine country girl from West Virginia. She is a "five-foot three, hundred pound waif," "doll-like" as a child and called princess by her siblings, a former beauty queen with perfect blond hair (11, 24, 14). Though it was reported in the aftermath of her capture that Lynch went

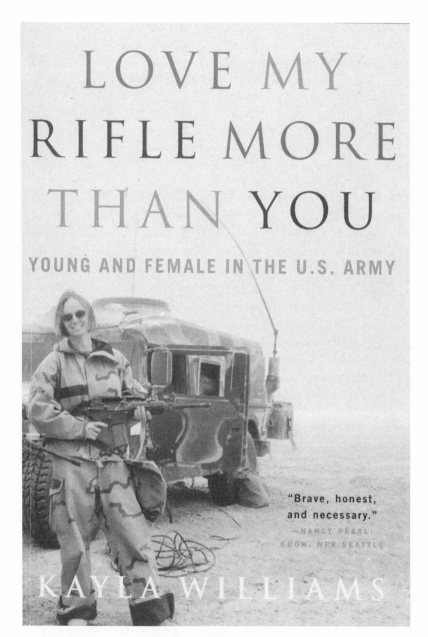

Figure 4. Kayla Williams, competent and confident on the cover of her memoir. From *Love My Rifle More Than You: Young and Female in the U.S. Army* by Kayla Williams with Michael E. Staub. Copyright © 2005 by Kayla Williams and Michael E. Staub. Used by permission of W. W. Norton.

down "guns blazing," that myth was quickly dispelled by Lynch herself. The bravery that Lynch displays and is celebrated for is that of an enduring victim rather than an inspired aggressor. That endurance and her recovery from a collection of traumatic injuries are significant and worthy of the intense attention she received. The way that attention was directed and the architecture of Lynch's story, however, hews closely to traditional gender norms, and is not sufficient to break down the gender barriers inherent in conceptions of soldiers and war.

Lynndie England is the other polarity that Williams invokes. England was one of several soldiers at the center of the Abu Ghraib scandal when photos emerged of them abusing and humiliating prisoners. England appeared in one widely circulated photo holding a naked prisoner on a leash. If Lynch has been celebrated—accurately or not—as an iconic damsel in distress, England has been vilified as a persecutor. In interviews, she has shown little regret for her participation in abuses that earned her a three-year prison sentence and a dishonorable discharge. "[W]hat happens in war, happens," she told the *Guardian* in 2009. "They were the enemy. I don't want to say they deserved what they got, but they . . . um" (Brockes). In statements like this, England would seem to be the epitome of hardness, yet she has expressed regret over her relationship with Charles Graner, another soldier ten years her senior who was sentenced to ten years for his actions at Abu Ghraib. It was Graner, England claims, who manipulated her into participating in those actions. "When you join the military," she notes, "no matter what anybody says, it's a man's world. You have to either equal a man or be controlled by men" (*Standard Operating Procedure*). England attempted to do the first as a result of the second. She loved Graner, who in her description is both charismatic and dangerous. Later revelations of her pregnancy and Graner's ongoing involvement and eventual marriage to Megan Ambuhl, another soldier stationed at the prison, have amplified that regret. Thus the persecutor frames herself as the persecuted, blinded by love and intimidated by authority. England may be tough, but in her own telling she's not that different from Jessica Lynch after all.

And so Kayla Williams may indeed be telling another kind of story. She is closer to what Judith Halberstam has called the female masculine, although Halberstam does not include a discussion of women in the military in her book *Female Masculinity*. Halberstam draws our attention to female masculinity because, as she argues, it "affords us a glimpse of how masculinity is constructed" as such, because masculinity becomes legible "where and when it leaves the white male middle-class body" (1, 2). Halberstam examines a number of hybrid spaces such as transsexuality and drag king performances, where, she claims, "the breakdown of gender as a signifying system in these arenas can be exploited to hasten the proliferation of alternate gender regimes in other locations" (41). Halberstam is most interested in homosexual female masculinity, because though heterosexual female masculinity can "menace gender conformity in its own way," it too often represents a level of masculinity that is "acceptable" in a woman, as compared to the "excessive masculinity of the dyke." Here she is thinking of the female protagonists in films like *Terminator 2* or *Aliens* (28).

Although this may be true in many categories of representation, the situation of Williams—the female soldier operating in a real-life combat zone—is more loaded, both literally and figuratively. A female action hero battling aliens can be titillating, if initially unsettling, but a real woman firing real bullets (among, it must be noted, what are often conceived of as "real men") is a different story. "When women pick up a gun and engage in struggle, violence, and death, ambivalence is generated," note Susan Owen, Sarah Stein, and Leah Berg. "In other words, ambivalence is endemic to any narrative vehicle that positions heroic women to struggle violently and face brutal death" (200–201). Owen, Stein, and Berg are specifically addressing films about female soldiers like *G. I. Jane* and *Courage under Fire*. When a woman enters the "most masculine" sphere of war, the result is a kind of cultural trauma:

> In a broadly cultural sense, each film expresses anxieties about female bodies in the geo-political public sphere as soldiers engaged with male cohorts and enemies. In that sense, the films explore the fluid intersections of gendered performance space and embodied performance in the context of nation states at war. To varying extents, each film expresses deep cultural anxieties specific to changing gender norms and soldiering. (210)

The presence of a woman in the field of war would appear to be far from a fully "acceptable" form of female masculinity, whether her sexuality is "alternative" or not. In the films Owen, Stein, and Berg examine, the woman's embodied presence is figured as a problem to be solved, as it "disrupts the homosocial bond between men that is and has been the foundation of the

American military" (216). To that end, in a film like *Courage under Fire,* the female soldier is acknowledged, sanctified, and removed (218).

Courage under Fire (1996) is about the man as much as, or more than, the woman: Denzel Washington's character, a lieutenant colonel investigating the death of Meg Ryan's character, Capt. Karen Walden. His perceptions of her personality and her service guide the film. She is presented through the other's eyes, in the same way that Bragg provides us with the portrait of Jessica Lynch—who she is and what she means to a nation at war. But what of a female soldier telling her own story, fully aware of its potentially unsettling status? Moments of cultural anxiety can, in some cases, give way to spaces of hybridity and potential, as Halberstam chronicles. Williams's narrative reveals a great deal about the status of military masculinity, the masculine collective that is comradeship in war, and the potential—or lack thereof—for a more fluid notion of gender performance in that arena and more generally.

At the same time, the woman warrior is nothing new, and Williams has a number of predecessors. Many cultures have stories like those of Athena and the Amazons, Queen Boudicca, Joan of Arc, and Vishpala, a female warrior in the *Rig Veda* who loses her leg in battle but then fights on with an iron prosthesis. Even Calamity Jane cuts a memorable figure in the history of the American West, and has been featured in such various narratives as dime novels, a 1953 musical starring Doris Day, and the HBO series *Deadwood.* These women warriors are known as women, but there are others whose female status is only discovered or revealed after the fact. One ancient example is Hua Mulan, the Chinese girl who disguised herself as a man in order to fight in the army. (Her story has been more recently taken up by Maxine Hong Kingston in *The Woman Warrior* [1975], as well as by Disney in the 1998 movie *Mulan.*) In the eighteenth century Anne Bonny did the same in order to become a pirate on a ship captained by her lover. On that ship Bonny famously met another woman in disguise, Mary Read, and according to some accounts the two became lovers. Bonny and Read, as cross-dressing women fighters, are not as exceptional as one might think. As Julie Wheelwright notes:

> Although there is mounting evidence of women donning men's clothes to enter a wide range of occupations, the best-documented cases are those of women soldiers and sailors. The long years of war in the eighteenth century

when naval press gangs roamed Britain produced more than 100 female warriors who surfaced in more than 1,000 variations of Anglo-American ballads. (8)

As figures of transgression, these women are both fascinating and threatening. At times, however, the fire of patriotism proves an acceptable explanation for such radical behavior. In 1917, the Russian Maria "Yashka" Bochkareva commanded a battalion in World War I, known as the Women's Legion of Death and consisting of hundreds of volunteers. In July the Legion saw combat against the Germans during what was called the Kerensky Offensive, and stayed at the front until they were dissolved in December. The Legion inspired the creation of the Petrograd Women's Battalion, some 1,200 soldiers, many of whom helped defend the Winter Palace during the October Revolution.[5] As Wheelwright notes, these women's desire to fight was often attributed not to sickness or "gender inversion," but to a love of fatherland (or perhaps motherland) so strong that even women were moved to pick up a gun:

> Such accounts neatly tied together the ideals of female devotion to husband and country. The women's more complex, less sanguine reasons—the desire for escape, the longing for independence and excitement that a masculine identity seemed to offer—were overlooked. (33)

When a woman dons the soldier's attire that is more typically worn by a man, in one sense she is always engaging in female-to-male cross-dressing, whether or not she is actively trying to be mistaken for a man. Male-to-female cross-dressing is something of a military institution in the twentieth century and especially World War II, note Marjorie Garber and others, as a form of comic relief in an all-male atmosphere. This is represented in films like *This Is the Army* (1943), *South Pacific* (1958, adapted from Michener's 1948 novel and the 1949 Rodgers and Hammerstein musical), and even *Bridge on the River Kwai* (1957). Garber argues that these kind of shows and impersonations "often seem related to the trope of the world-turned-upside-down," which perhaps offers a different reading of the cultural context of World War II than what Susan Jeffords claims about Vietnam (59). That is, if these male-to-female drag shows offer a site of hybridization, then perhaps the staunchness of the gender binary that Jeffords sees in and around Vietnam doesn't apply here. But Garber goes on, and claims that though gender may be put into some kind of play, the primacy of masculinity and maleness is then quickly reestablished:

> To cross-dress on the stage in an all-male context like the army or the navy is a way of asserting the common privilege of maleness. Borderlines like officers/"men" or gay/straight are both put into question and redrawn or affirmed: "woman"—the artifact made of wig, makeup, coconut breasts, and grass skirt or sailor's "frock"—offers a space for fantasies that are at once erotic and misogynistic. (60)

In these military contexts, men cross-dress as a self-conscious and finite act of performance that is intended to assert the ridiculousness of blurring gender boundaries. It's funny to "be" female, at least for an hour or so. But, as Garber argues, cross-dressing has the power to "unsettle assumptions, structures, and hierarchies," and the liminal possibilities that male-to-female performance opens, if only to shut them down again, are more completely taken up by women assuming the sartorial markers of military men (37).

The first American woman known to serve in the military was Deborah Sampson, who disguised herself as Robert Shurtlieff in order to fight in the American Revolution. In 1782 she was shot in the thigh, but removed the musket ball herself rather than reveal her true sex. After the war, she gave talks (as a woman, also something of a rarity) about her military experiences, and fought, finally successfully, to receive a war pension (Wheelwright 132–35). In 1797 Herman Mann published the story of her life, the full title of which reveals some of the ways Sampson's transgression is made more palatable for the public:

> The female review; or, Memoirs of an American young lady; whose life and character are peculiarly distinguished—being a continental soldier, for nearly three years, in the late war. During which time, she performed the duties of every department, into which she was called, with punctual exactness, fidelity and honor, and preserved her chastity inviolate, by the most artful concealment of her sex. With an appendix, containing characteristic traits, by different hands; her taste for economy, principles of domestic education, &c. By a citizen of Massachusetts.

Later American history saw the creation of the Women's Army Auxiliary Corps in 1941, as well as the Women's Naval Reserve, Women Accepted for Volunteer Emergency Service (WAVES), and Marine Corps Women's Reserve, also during World War II. But the Gulf War of 1991 was the real turning point in American women's military history. During that war, approximately 41,000 female soldiers served in or near combat zones; this was the first time in the American military such a significant number of women served in such a capacity. Today, women constitute approximately 15 percent of the military's active duty force. Most military positions are open to women, although a 1994 policy restricts women from serving in units that engage in direct ground combat (Tyson). Many believe, however, that conditions in Iraq have effectively rendered that policy moot. "As American women in uniform patrol bomb-ridden highways, stand duty at checkpoints shouldering M-16s and raid houses in insurgent-contested towns, many have come to believe this 360-degree war has rendered obsolete a decade-old Pentagon policy," notes *Washington Post* reporter Ann Tyson. Instead of being assigned to battalions, women are "attached in direct support of" them, but the result is often the same. "There is no rear area," notes Maj. Mary Prophit, an Army reservist who handles security duties (qtd. in Tyson).

The experience of war puts a great deal of pressure on the soldier's identity. Among all the other aspects of being a soldier, directly or indirectly inflicting violence on others and becoming the object of similarly targeted violence can greatly change a person's sense of self, or, in some cases, forge that sense into greater certainty. Williams feels this pressure, and writes about it. But Williams's experience of war is colored more primarily by an incessant awareness of her sex and sexuality. She finds herself defined by both of these things, even as she defines herself as a tough soldier and as part of the masculine collective of the war effort. Like Turnipseed's, Williams's narrative is in part an unsuccessful attempt to reconcile two seemingly opposed definitions of the self.

Williams's opening gets right to the point, as she sees it:

> Sometimes, even now, I wake up before dawn and forget I am not a slut. The air is not quite dark, not quite light, and I lie absolutely still, trying to will myself to remember that that is *not* what I am. Sometimes, on better mornings, it comes to me right away. And then there are all those other times.

Slut.
     The only other choice is bitch. If you're a woman and a soldier, these are
the choices you get. (13)

She goes to explain the difference between being a slut and a bitch, as
the "old joke" has it: "A slut will fuck you, a bitch will fuck anyone but
you" (13).

     This is the lesson that Williams uses to begin her story: to be a woman
in the military is to be perpetually defined by your sexuality. Regardless
of whether you choose to fuck or not to fuck, as Anthony Swofford
might put it, you're fucked either way. But Williams's story as a whole
is not quite this simple. This lesson doesn't function for her the way one
might expect—the book is not an indictment of the military, of her experiences in it, or even of the men who objectify her. As Williams admits in
this opening section, there is something appealing about this situation as
well, or at least something "more complicated" (14). Existing as the object
of the gaze may be shaming, but it confers a kind of power. "I don't like
to say it—it cuts inside—but the attention, the admiration, the *need:* they
make you powerful." She elaborates on this point in the second chapter,
"Queen for a Year," the term, she says, "we've called American women
at war since nurses traveled to Vietnam in the sixties" (19). "A woman at
war," she explains; "you're automatically a desirable commodity, and a
scarce one at that." Williams goes even further to say that this heightened
awareness of sexual appeal is "key" to any woman soldier's experience in
the American military, and that the experience carries a "strange sexual
allure" (18). What Williams does not note here is the irony that this power
can *only* come from a commodified sexual identity, or that the designation
of royalty only lasts for a year.

     The other complicating factor, she says, is the female soldier's familial
relationships with the men she works with. "They're *yours,*" she asserts.
"Fuck, you left your husband to be with them, you walked out on him for
them. These guys, they're your husband, they're your father, your brother,
your lover—your life" (14). Presumably Williams means to assert her participation in a kind of "brotherhood," and as noted with regard to Swofford
and Buzzell, her casual use of obscenity as amplification would certainly
qualify. She frames that participation, however, as a woman's traditional
subservient relation to the patriarchy—a woman gives up what she wants

in order to serve the father, the husband, the brother, the lover. Their life is your life. Within the circle of comradeship, soldiers do take responsibility and care for one another, but as Williams's memoir reveals, it's not at all certain that that is the case for her and the men who surround her.

This question exists at the center of *Love My Rifle More Than You*. To what extent, if at all, is Williams a part of this masculine military community, and what are the implications for her own identity? Her answers are both troubled and troubling. Like Turnipseed's and Fick's, Williams's exploration of masculine comradeship reveals that the ideal of a "brotherhood of arms" is not entirely attainable, and that the freedom to achieve masculine status through performance is complicated or limited by war.

Williams writes when she is twenty-eight, after serving in Military Intelligence for five years, in the United States and in Iraq. The brief snapshot she offers of her previous history indicates an awareness of and ability to exist in different social contexts. After her parents' divorce, she lives in a bad neighborhood but attends an excellent private school, and so moves between "these two worlds—privileged and poor" (27). The school is multicultural, and encourages the study of foreign languages. After dabbling in the punk and alternative scene in high school—wearing combat boots, striving to look tough and intimidating—she graduates from college and dates a Muslim man named Tariq, who speaks a variety of languages and begins to teach her Arabic. Though the relationship ends after two years, Williams credits her decision to enlist to the respect he had for her and his confidence in her abilities: "[That] helped me believe that I was capable of doing something I never thought I could do" (39).

She joins the Army Reserves to do something "hard," as Fick would put it, and in order to prove her worth (25). Pre-9/11, the economic incentives are appealing as well. Drawing on her interest in languages and her previous experience with Tariq, she trains as an Arabic interpreter. Williams sees the Army as an escape from the looming threat of domesticity and the traditional feminine role: "I was at a point in my life when I felt that if I didn't do something drastic, I was going to wake up in a house with a white picket fence and a minivan and kids who hated me" (32). In her description of basic training, Williams further clarifies her identification with masculine rather than feminine qualities. She enjoys discovering her endurance, stamina, and willpower (46). She does not bond with the other women in basic, criticizing one for crying constantly and others for fixating on their appearance. Forced into close quarters, she explains, women are catty. "I really hated living with females," she adds (46). Notably, Williams never seems to question her ability to cross boundaries: to date outside her own race and religion, to learn about different languages, cultures, and countercultures, or to act like a man rather than a woman. For Williams, unfortunately, acting like a man also entails defining herself against the negative qualities associated with women.

At the Defense Language Institute, where she trains after basic, she does meet another woman who becomes a long-time friend. "It's unusual for me to pursue a friendship with another woman," she qualifies, "but I really liked Zoe" (49). She goes on to describe Zoe in perfect patriarchal style, apparently unironically: "Beautiful and amazing Zoe. Crazy and wild. Small tits. Great ass." Around the same time, she is briefly married to a man she describes as "the anti-Army" (50). She is drawn to his kindness, but finds him effeminate and shameful for the same reason:

> A sweet and sensitive civilian who began to urge me to end my Army life. (Especially after we were married and we saw *Black Hawk Down:* I had been assigned to an air assault division, and when we saw the helicopter crash in the movie my husband freaked over what might happen to me in a combat zone. *I* was freaked because the movie made him cry—in public. There were people I knew in the audience. It made him look like a big pussy.) (51)

Williams praises people who "have balls," like her friend Lauren, a five-foot-tall Korean linguist who yells at and threatens a male soldier who throws a football at her face, but derides others for being "pussies." She also consistently criticizes her female leaders in Iraq. One of these, Staff Sergeant Moss, makes "critical errors in judgment," but compounds those problems by crying in front of Williams. "The bitch," Williams says. "You *never* cry in front of a subordinate. Especially if you're a woman in a position of authority. The guys already think we can't handle this. It just isn't done" (88, 91). Likewise, she derides Staff Sergeant Simmons's "cluelessness and lack of motivation," but what really gets her is Simmons's reaction to being chastised for losing track of her night vision goggles:

> Simmons sits on her cot and cries. In front of everyone.
> And in front of everyone, she blames her crying on PMS. Yet another thing that is absolutely not acceptable in the Army. It encourages men to

think what most men think already: that PMS makes girls do incompetent things. Which I prefer to think is not true. Because you still hear a lot of stuff like, Women should never be president because they're too emotional to handle it. What if she got PMS, she'd start a nuclear war!

...This woman's incompetence makes all women in the Army look incompetent. (268–69)

Williams's anger here is something of a turning point, and reveals her suspicion that the masculine ideal, both individual and collective, for which she strives may not be attainable after all. "Most men," after all, already believe that women are weak and incompetent; you hear things like this all the time, she says. The contrast with Simmons, however, allows Williams to implicitly assert her own competence and her commitment to the team. After all, this is the reason she is in Iraq: "I was here because of my loyalty to my unit and my fellow soldiers. That was the beginning and the middle and the end of my sense of loyalty at the moment" (70).

In the summer, Williams is assigned to assist a combat observation and lasing team (COLT). These men are chosen from a larger group, a fire support team. They call themselves FISTers, "an acronym they love" (159). (One assumes they enjoy being associated with the more extreme or aggressive heterosexual practice rather than the homosexual, although it's also possible that they like the ambiguity. Either way, their use of the acronym is another way of making frequent reference to sexuality and aggression.) This group is the central masculine collective in Williams's narrative, and the struggles she describes are—more often than not—to be accepted or at least respected by these men.

In some ways, the FISTers do accept her. When she drives a Humvee up a dangerously steep incline, she berates the men who refuse to ride with her, calling them "fucking pussies" (160). After she makes it up the mountain without flipping the vehicle, one FISTer alters his vocabulary in order to praise her. Instead of saying she has balls, he comments: "Look, this one's got *boobs*" (161). Although it would seem positive that the man has created new slang to commend a brave performance that takes the female body, rather than the male, as its standard, the sexual body is still front and center here. And if the sexual body is still front and center, then Williams is still different, regardless of her bravery. "Look at *this* one," as the man says.

But Williams is encouraged. She joins the FISTers for banter and jokes, which are often insulting and blatantly sexist. Williams can go them one better, however. She cuts off one man who asks about the difference between a hooker and an onion: "'Ah, that's my joke,' I complain, passing the can to him. 'No one ever cried when they cut a hooker'" (168). That joke is hers, as she says, and the next one is as well. "What's the first thing a woman does when she gets back from a battered women's shelter?" No one knows the answer. "The dishes, if she's smart" (168). Williams appropriates the sexist jokes as her own, and uses them as an entrée into the group. She presents herself as masculine—tough, blunt, hardworking, and aggressively opposed to the feminine. But acceptance is a struggle, and Williams wonders if it has been—or ever will be—accomplished:

> Maybe it sounds like they were jerks who hated girls and liked to talk us down. And I would say to that: They were, but they weren't.
>
> In the real world, guys bond through competition. They play football games. They play video games. They verbally spar. They throw rocks at one another. Guys like to try and establish a hierarchy. They jockey for who's on top.
>
> Now, I can play that game...I can play it with guys who value intelligence. But I can only sort of play it with guys like the FISTers. It's not the same with them.
>
> The FISTers would talk trash with me to bond with me.
>
> They wouldn't talk trash with me if they didn't like me. If we weren't friends. (181)

Like Turnipseed's claim that his banter with the Dog Pound is "difficult to capture," Williams wants to play it both ways here, and her statement is remarkably ambivalent. Masculinity, in her estimation, is expressed through competitive bonding, in which she can participate if intelligence, rather than mere physical aggression, is accepted as currency. She can play that game, and she wants to. She can perform. Like Fick, she defines masculinity by what you can do. But the others don't operate on the same terms, and ultimately her status as female—regardless of that convincing performance—excludes her from the group, and that exclusion leads her to question both the military and her own identity.

Kim Ponders has written a novel based on her experience as an Air Force pilot during the Persian Gulf War titled *The Art of Uncontrolled Flight,* published the same year as Williams's memoir. Though the reconciliation of gender and military identity doesn't emerge as a central concern of the narrative the way it does in *Love My Rifle,* Ponders does indicate similar challenges in attempting that reconciliation. At the Academy, she writes, one learns "how not to be like a woman, how not to be weak, how not to cry, how not to have PMS or even periods, as if to be female meant to put forth a constant effusion of unpleasant secretions, as if to be a man was to withhold" (62). One learns, but the difference is still there. Three days after Iraq invades Kuwait, the protagonist Annie Shaw is in Nevada awaiting orders when she visits a strip club with her fellow pilots. One of them buys her a lap dance, and she accepts it, wanting to be part of the group. "In any case, I'm one of them now," she tells her husband later. "Oh, bullshit," he responds. "You're different, all right. You really think you're just another guy? Tell me something, which one of those boys wants you? Is it Jago? Or is it all of them? And don't tell me you don't know" (69). In fact, her husband is dead on—the growing attraction between Annie and Jago will soon blossom into an affair, which becomes the focus of much of the rest of the book. In Ponders's story, Annie's body and sexuality make her different despite her competence, skill, and toughness.

Annie has an affair that is both thrilling and devastating. The intrusion of sexuality on Williams's wartime experience, however, is much less pleasant. The "banter" she enjoys with her comrades grows unsettling. One of the FISTers calls her "hatchet wound," which gives her "a nasty shiver," even if she does respond to that Freudian bon mot with "Fuck off, peanut prick" (167–68). A few pages later, she and the men are drinking vodka, and one of them pretends to stumble into her, groping her breasts. She pushes him away as the others look on; they don't encourage him, but they don't help her, either. She leaves, and doesn't comment on the incident again until she reports that the FISTers offer a kind of apology, which consists of cases of vegetarian food, the kind she has so much trouble finding in Iraq. Around the same time, she asks a friend why the men in her regular platoon have consistently shunned her. He answers that they think she is a whore and a slut, because of a brief sexual relationship she had at Fort Campbell before deployment. The response hits a nerve, and Williams is angry. She reveals that she was sexually assaulted at thirteen, and made bad choices in high school, but has distanced herself from that time. "Now here I am in Iraq," she fumes, "being made to feel crappy all over again...Because at Fort Campbell I was basically responsible. I was basically good. And here these guys are treating me like I'm some dirty slut. It is very upsetting. It brings back a lot of unpleasant memories" (176).

Even with what she sees as a reasonably good relationship with most of the FISTers, Williams begins to feel increasingly isolated. She may be contributing to the larger mission and interacting closely with the other soldiers, but on a fundamental level, she simply doesn't belong. That belonging is denied both by the soldiers who sexually assault her (in two separate instances), and, paradoxically, by the ones who treat her with respect:

> The Army puts out an informal policy against physical contact. Even though the Army is one of the few environments in the States in which men can touch each other and it's okay. Guys pat each other on the ass all the time in the Army. It's called a "good game." Guys can also half hug each other; not front hug, but a little side shoulder hug. That's perfectly manly and acceptable. If two men in civilian clothes hugged like this it might be considered gay. But Army guys can do it whenever they want—because they're Army. Real tough guys.
>
> But physical contact was more or less something I did not have during my deployment. Guys were extra careful not to touch me. As a female I was not really a part of the "good game." (188)

This is quite significant. If war is considered a place where the ideal masculine collective can at last be achieved, without concern for race or class or the strictly gendered expectations for behavior of civilian life, then here it is still a collective that is both masculine as well as male. This seemingly utopian community—perhaps one of the last available to contemporary American men—is still off-limits to Williams. She has proved herself to be perfectly capable of meeting the standards for this military masculinity: she is brave, she is stoic, she can handle a weapon, she is dedicated to the group. But she is not male. The men Williams describes presumably want to treat her with respect, but it is that very form of respect—that dictates *not* touching her body, *not* treating her as an object—that also isolates her, excludes her from the all-male community of the good game.

What finally pushes Williams over the edge is a second, more intense sexual assault. After verbally propositioning her, a soldier named Rivers waits for her when she gets off shift in the middle of the night. He grabs her, and they struggle. Williams's description of what happens is somewhat elided: "The shame of being in a position where you might have to do that. Yell for help. Like some damn damsel in distress. Knowing that you would have to explain what just happened here. But eventually Rivers drops his grip on my arm. He lets me go. I leave and go back to my vehicle" (208). For Williams, being in distress makes you a damsel, which makes you damned; she cannot bear the thought of conforming to this gender norm after all of her efforts as a soldier. The next day, Rivers apologizes, and Williams wonders if she should report the incident. Her doubt is crippling, and Williams is torn between resenting the collective that does not accept her and wanting to preserve the group that she still values and, in contradictory fashion, still feels a part of. "[T]he guys would all back him," she thinks, and explains that making a report is "risky" because "girls who file EO (equal opportunity) complaints are treated badly" (208, 209). Williams talks herself out of filing an official complaint, however, by invoking the spirit of the group:

> I can and will put up with a lot. I *do* put up with a lot. I am very understanding about a lot of male behavior. I know these guys are under tremendous pressure. They are in a rough environment. They are away from their lover, their family, and everything they know—for a long time. So am I, and I know it isn't easy on any of us. And I don't want to pursue an investigation and risk ruining someone's career under these circumstances. Plus, to be honest, I am afraid that if I do file a complaint, Rivers would tell on me for drinking alcohol. Turn it around. Get me in trouble if I get him in trouble. (209–10)

After some time, she speaks about the incident to a Sergeant First Class, off the record, and Rivers is reassigned. The problem is thus addressed outside of the official channels that she dreaded. About a month later, however, one of Rivers's friends approaches her and gives Rivers's account of the incident: that Williams initiated the sexual contact, that Rivers wanted none of it. For Williams, this is a betrayal, and a breaking point. Her attempt to defend herself while also protecting the group proves to be a failure, and this final act of rejection is more than she can take. "Everything shifted," she says. Now her blood freezes when she hears some of the guys telling rape jokes, and she wonders if rape jokes are ever funny (212). The disturbances continue: "After Rivers's friend confronted me, and I withdrew from the COLT guys, things got a little freaky for me. I began to lose it" (212). She describes experiencing intrusive images, seeing things that aren't there, and she even contemplates suicide. She considers eating less and less, getting "thinner and thinner," until she just disappears (215). This contemplation of anorexia, apparently not undertaken, is sadly appropriate to her feelings. Her body as signifier of sex and sexuality just won't go away, and so she wants to erase it. Williams's exile from the masculine community—or the realization that she was never really a part of that community in the first place—plays a significant role in the fracturing of her identity and sense of self:

> And now the guys I considered my friends were treating me like a *girl*. I was tits, a piece of ass, a bitch or a slut or whatever, but never really a *person*. *Bros before hos.* (214)

Williams realizes, in essence, that despite her proper performance of masculinity, she is still considered an object, a girl. She finds the feminine identity undesirable, and the masculine identity—fully realized here only as part of the masculine collective—unattainable. Despite all this, Williams fights to stay in Iraq after undergoing foot surgery because of her "deep commitment to my fellow soldiers. My brothers in arms." But she also "started to pay attention to how females were getting treated," and finds that treatment rather lacking (231, 259). Owen, Stein, and Berg write about the ambivalence generated in representations of women at war. What is remarkable here is Williams's ambivalence about her *own* identity and place in the military community, and the way that ambivalence is expressed as a kind of vacillation in Williams's representation of her own life.

Williams returns home to the States in February 2004, and like other memoirists, feels at first as though Iraq was "a sick dream...this gap in the normal passage of time" (273). She decides, post-Iraq, to stop apologizing. "That's what being in the Army has taught me when all is said and done," she notes. "I used to be this girl, like so many girls...we *qualify* everything we say" (278). The combat zone cured her of that, she says. This happens despite the military's inherent sexism, its characterization of competent or assertive women as bitches or ballbusters. "This is a struggle that is magnified in the military," she notes, "because it is still such a male environment—a weird little microcosm of society on steroids." She used to be "this girl," she says, and no longer wants to act or be treated like "so many girls." But what is she now?

After her return, Williams struggles with depression, hyperalertness, difficulty sleeping. She continues a relationship with Shane Kelly, the FISTers' platoon sergeant, whom earlier in the book she describes as someone who "could often be an asshole. A real cocksucker" (171). Her account of how the relationship begins is telling:

> So we'd talk about music, ideas, politics, books—things like that. We would have interesting conversations even though at the same time Kelly could be a real jackass. Literally, he'd say to me: "Fix me some eggs, bitch." And I'd fix him eggs. Because I'm retarded. Or nice. Or whatever. (171)

Here, Williams describes being valued for her intellect at the same time that she is "retarded," assuming the role of a subservient female, even while realizing that "historically I've dated a lot of guys who treated me like shit" (172). Her relationship with Kelly, however, then changes drastically. His convoy is attacked in Iraq, and he sustains serious wounds, including a traumatic brain injury. When he moves into Williams's house after their return to the States, he has undergone several operations and suffers from headaches, depression, and memory loss. His attempts to get the proper medical care are frustrated by bureaucracy and backlogs. "Everything was fucked up," Williams says. "Does the Army expect a man with a traumatic brain injury to advocate on his own behalf for the care and treatment he deserves? There are days he can hardly get out of bed in the morning, the pain is so intense. Watching how shabbily the Army treats Shane—not to mention so many other seriously wounded veterans of this war—has been the deepest disillusionment for me" (287).

Shane appears to be a pseudonym. Williams notes that she has changed some identifying names, and the book's dedication is "For Brian—Who gives me hope." Williams also thanks him in the acknowledgments "most of all—I cannot imagine having done this without you" (290). In the body of the book, Williams gives him the first name of an iconic American male and paragon of individualist masculinity—Shane. The Shane of literature and film never asked Marian Starrett to "fix me some eggs, bitch." But neither did he end his adventures with shrapnel in his brain.

Williams ends her own narrative wondering if the Army will call her back, as she is to be classified as inactive ready reserve until 2005. "And the letter could come," she notes ominously. "Tomorrow. Next week. Next month. Next year. No, it's not over. Not for a long while yet" (288). Buzzell's experience of being recalled in 2008 comes to mind. Williams's time in the service may not be over, just as America's involvement in Iraq will not be over "for a long while yet." And her identification with or against the masculine collective of the military is unresolved as well. Other than her decision to stop apologizing, she makes no move to fight against the patriarchy of the Army or of society as a whole. Her final acknowledgments to her "brothers in arms," as she calls them, are strikingly ironic. Apparently unintentionally, her statement of thanks also reads as a threat: "All you soldiers are better than anyone gives you credit for...I could never name all of those who touched me, but I will not forget" (289).

Finally, it is worth noting that Williams's memoir is mediated by a male ghostwriter, Michael Staub, whose name is not included on the cover. Staub is a professor of English at Baruch College-CUNY, and has written scholarly books on postwar Jewish liberalism and the politics of representation in 1930s America. In the acknowledgements, Williams credits Staub with "coming to me with the idea of this book and working so hard to keep it as accurate as possible" (289). Though it's difficult to determine precisely how much of a hand Staub played in the way her story is told, Staub himself emphasizes that "the book really is Kayla's," and advertises his work with it much less than, for instance, Rick Bragg with Lynch's *I Am a Soldier, Too.*

Jennifer Guay is not unlike Kayla Williams. Guay is an Army specialist who was the first woman assigned as an infantry combat medic. The 170-pound former bartender enlisted in 2002, and went to work providing medical care to troops during and after firefights. She took pride in the fact that she could out-bench some of the men she worked with. "I wanted to be as grunt as possible," she says (Tyson). How possible is that, and how grunt can a female soldier be? Guay reports being accepted by the men in the 82nd Airborne, who called her "Doc," their own "kick-ass medic" (Tyson). In their 2009 "Women at Arms" series, the *New York Times* published articles that made this same point, with titles like "G.I. Jane Breaks the Combat Barrier" and "Living and Fighting Alongside Men, and Fitting In." In the same series, however, the *Times* also ran pieces that emphasized the difficulties faced by female soldiers: the challenges of balancing motherhood and a military career, the threat of sexual abuse by one's fellow soldiers, and the isolation of female veterans with PTSD.[6] Williams's story reveals a similar ambivalence—she indeed breaks the combat barrier, but she suffers because of it.

In some ways, Williams's book seems to indicate her ability to move seamlessly between different performances, from feminine to military masculine. The section of black and white pictures in the book includes shots of her in camouflage outside of the Defense Language Institute barracks, posing with rifles with another woman, rock climbing, and playing with a puppy. The final page of photos shows two images: one of Williams in camouflage gear after arriving home in 2004, and one of her dressed up for a "big night out" in Tennessee. Here, she wears a strapless evening gown, necklace, and makeup. The photos reveal a variety of gendered identities, and the confidence to display them side by side. If one just looks at the images, Williams would seem to inhabit a hybrid space, one that contains different expressions of gender, sexuality, and self in the same linear narrative. She can be butch, and she can be femme.

But the story reveals Williams's experience of war to be less a hybrid space than a site of vacillation. Williams is a part of the masculine community, but she is excluded in fundamental ways. She praises her brothers in arms, and serves for them, but never gets to feel quite like a brother. She is masculine, but not male. She is reminded that she is still, as she says so bitterly, a *girl,* and to be a girl is to be excluded. For Williams, the distinction of gender—and its corollary here, sexuality— never really goes away. This is true even given an excellent or excessive performance of toughness, as is the case with Lynndie England's story— defined, in the end, by the dictates of male authority. Dunya Mikhail writes about England in "An Urgent Call," imploring her to return to America and hide "those terrible pictures," lest her child see the nakedness of the prisoners. Mikhail's diagnosis of England's problem is similar to England's own:

> She is pregnant
> and is sinking in deep mud.
> She sinks deeper and deeper
> as she hears: "Good job!" (13)

For Mikhail, England's pregnancy and impending motherhood make her actions at Abu Ghraib that much more regrettable, and certainly that was the case for the general public as well. For these female soldiers, the ability to perform as well as a man either doesn't count, as in Williams's story, or counts against them, as in England's.

This chapter opened with the claim that these three writers, Williams included, experience ruptures in their sense of masculine identity and a corollary failure of the masculine collective—hence the contrast with Jeffords's thesis about the Vietnam and post-Vietnam years. One might object, however, and note that in Williams's narrative, the collective in fact seems to succeed. The men do, after all, isolate her and deny her masculinity because she is not male. One could argue that because she fails, the collective succeeds and is reasserted. Certainly to see the failure of the male masculine collective, one needs also to consider Turnipseed and Fick, but Williams's notion of comradeship—which is *not* exclusively male—fails as well. She is not accepted in the ways that she wants to be. But in this story of failed potential for a new way of conceiving comradeship, one can see see exactly that: potential. Her very presence in Iraq speaks to that, and she does put pressure on the old and accepted notions of what makes a military man.

That potential is also visible in the language of another soldier who writes about the presence of women in the military. As Colby Buzzell does, Jason Christopher Hartley publishes his milblog "Just Another Soldier" in book form in 2005. Hartley served as Army National Guard in Iraq, beginning his blog in 2003. The Army ordered his blog shut down after five months, though Hartley continued writing privately. Like Buzzell's *My War,* Hartley's book contains his original posts as well as additional material. Notably with regard to this section of the chapter, Hartley is the only male writer covered in this project who comments explicitly on the status of women in the military. In an entry dated 25 April 2004, he argues that "women cannot be in the infantry," though he acknowledges that the issue is "tricky" and that it is "the one thing in my personal philosophy that I am sexist about" (93). He notes the primal attitudes of the average grunt who "finds meaning through fucking," and observes that job discipline goes "straight to hell" in the presence of a female. Hartley also argues that most men are "dumb" enough to push themselves to ridiculous lengths to accomplish a physical task, whereas women are less likely to do so, and that men are generally physically stronger (94). He also briefly notes potential problems with hygiene, pregnancy, the threat of rape if captured, and the way that breasts can interfere with the proper functioning of body armor and other gear (95).

Hartley addresses these issues bluntly, although the fact that he addresses them at all makes him something of an exception. He calls himself "sexist," yet his apologetic tone speaks to the ways cultural attitudes toward gender have changed in the years since World War II and the Vietnam War. "Women deserve equal opportunity," Hartley is careful to say in the concluding statement of this entry, "but equality in certain combat jobs may not make the best tactical sense" (95). And he acknowledges that conditions in Iraq blur the distinctions between infantry and non-infantry anyway, making his recommended prohibition superfluous. Women "can always join the MPs," he notes, who, after all, "end up doing most of the same stuff as the infantry, at least in Iraq."

In Iraq, then, the extreme conditions of war make boundary crossing difficult, as Williams's experience demonstrates. In circumstances in which order is so aggressively enforced, experimentation with hybrid identities is seen to be inappropriate. Yet in Iraq, the circumstances of *this* war are such that soldiers are needed, translators like Williams are needed—and that need places people like Williams in an environment where, in the past, she wouldn't have been allowed to go. Williams may feel rejected, but she is *present,* and she survives.

Fighting for a New Community

In the years since Vietnam and its cultural aftermath, the masculine collective seems to have taken a hit, at least as seen and understood in these contemporary American memoirs of war. That collective no longer functions effectively as the frame for a master narrative about war and the self. According to Turnipseed, Fick, and Williams, the master narrative has become a blur—unknown figures advancing on a convoy, a child holding what might or might not be a rifle, a fierce storm that cloaks everything in uniformly colored sand. The circle of one's fellow soldiers is not immune, as it turns out, to the doubts and second-guessing that all of these situations engender.

Joel Turnipseed struggles with the proper performance of masculinity, not because it's "too hard," but because he sees it as just that—a show. It's a show for which he has not a small amount of talent, but which role is the right one? Is it the drama of the struggling intellectual, searching for truth, or the comedy of the Marine Corps smart-ass, cynical asides at the ready? The pipe-smoking, port-drinking white man with precise elocution, or the chain-smoking, rapping, honorary black man? Turnipseed's awareness that his identity is really just a performance creates a fragility in the connections he has with other people. If it's all just a show, then what's a friendship made of? The Dog Pound may be a delightful distraction from the labor of war, but when the opportunity comes to leave, Turnipseed jumps at the chance.

For Nathaniel Fick, the logic of military masculinity is a reductio ad absurdum. Hardness is key to being a real man, he learns, and he gets harder and harder until he realizes that the leadership role he has undertaken requires him not just to protect and guide his fellow soldiers, but also to sacrifice them if necessary. The hardness that brings the group together—the tests they all pass, the impossible tasks they all complete, the stoicism they all inculcate within themselves—is the same hardness that can potentially lead to the group's annihilation. That, as he concludes, is too hard.

Finally, Williams, who struggles so mightily to be accepted only to fail in the end. She can hardly be called a pioneer—there have been too many women serving in too many capacities for that—but her story does mark what is perhaps a crucial point in the history of gender and the American military. She sees and acts on the potential for crossing boundaries—as a female soldier and as a scholar of Arabic. But Williams is denied true acceptance into the tight circle of military comradeship, and that sense of personal betrayal leads to a recognition of larger, political betrayals as well, like Shane's inability to secure proper medical care.

Though Williams does include this description of her disillusion with the military near the end of her book, neither she, nor Turnipseed, nor Fick include an extended consideration of the political motivations and justifications for war in their narratives, and the absence is telling. America's notion of national hardness is also failing, as the war in Iraq drags on and, as all three writers note, is fraught with moral complexities. Fick begins as perhaps the most gung-ho and patriotic of the group, and believes that, given the chance, the Marines in particular could do good work and community building in Iraq. That belief makes his subsequent orders to keep moving—rather than staying in one place and "digging in"—all the more devastating, ultimately contributing to his decision to leave the Corps. In his final statements, he dismisses any humanitarian or liberation goals as immaterial to his reasons for fighting, which as he says were focused instead on his troops, his men. Turnipseed and Williams are more flippant. Turnipseed wrestles with his desire to see the worst of war even as he feels strongly that the Gulf War is "stupid" and "avoidable," while Williams writes that "we all knew there was no connection between the war in Iraq and 9/11" despite "what our fearless leaders wanted us to think about why we are here" (193). Williams even jokes about the weapons of mass destruction that everyone is supposedly fighting to find and contain. For Turnipseed and Williams, the idea that these wars could be politically and nationally justifiable is not even a question, dismissed before it is posed at all. As in Fick's case, the identity he and his soldiers are ultimately concerned with is their own, not America's. America would seem to have problems beyond their capacity to address.

When the national cause for war is tainted or, as Williams frames it, an outright lie, one would perhaps expect to see that realization play a more central role in memoirs like these, as it often does in memoirs of Vietnam. But the collective these more recent writers are interested and invested in is a smaller one, at least as they see it. Yes, these are stories about "bad wars," but that judgment does not constitute the whole of the story, or even a very significant part of it. Nor are they stories of personal triumph against the odds, the eking out of a "good war" in a bad situation. Instead they are stories of ambivalence generated by the seductive power and the capacity for rejection and failure inherent in these conceptions of the masculine collective. The group of hard men doing hard tasks in hard circumstances ultimately exists in the world of myth rather than in sustainable reality— but everyone seems to keep pursuing this ideal.

When masculinity becomes so visible, when it becomes a subject for self-conscious nostalgia, parody, even camp, as it has in the decades since Vietnam, the staunchly structured and binary notions of sex, gender, and identity may be losing their cultural grip just a bit. In the particular theater of war, Turnipseed, Fick, and Williams are each disillusioned by their experiences and find that their performances, so energetically undertaken and executed, don't quite work. But in telling their war stories, they each find a different kind of performance that does, and a corollary community that is, perhaps, more sustainable.

3

Consuming the Other

Blinding Absence in The Last True Story I'll Ever Tell *and* Here, Bullet

In the early nineteenth century, the military theorist Karl von Clausewitz famously called war the continuation of politics by other means. Other means, indeed. Whether one thinks of war as an extension of politics, business, natural human aggression, or any other motivating factor, war is fundamentally one community's marshalling of force against another. It is, with very rare exceptions, characterized by those communities', or their representatives', attempts to kill one another. ("To subdue the enemy without fighting," argues Sun Tzu in *The Art of War,* "is the acme of skill" [77]. This circumstance, however, does not constitute the bulk of Sun Tzu's advice on the subject, as it is clearly not the norm.)

And so for soldiers, at the heart of war is the anticipation, experience, and aftermath of the lethal confrontation with the enemy, one who is defined by his oppositional politics, ideology, cultural practices, or simply by the direction his weapon is pointed. In any war story, this confrontation is a crucial moment, even when the moment's force is due to the absence of killing, as in *Jarhead.* But war entails more than encountering the enemy on the battlefield. In war generally, and certainly for American soldiers in the twentieth and twenty-first centuries, war also means traveling abroad, often for the first time, and seeing places, hearing languages, and interacting with the civilians of other cultures, about which soldiers often have little or no prior knowledge. All these encounters affect the central confrontation with the enemy soldier, which in turn affects how soldiers work with and relate to the civilians of the war zone. At least initially, everything is Other.

In two very different accounts of the Iraq War, John Crawford in *The Last True Story I'll Ever Tell* (2005) and Brian Turner in his poetry collection *Here, Bullet* (2005) narrate their encounters with peoples and landscapes that are overwhelmingly foreign. Crawford and Turner frame those encounters, however, in very different ways. Crawford is raw and unapologetically racist, as he takes pains to define himself against the grubby, less-than-human Iraqis who are so easily dismissed from his consciousness and his story. Turner, however, is fascinated with Iraqi culture and history, and makes an obvious effort to "earn his right to speak" about such matters, as he puts it in his opening poem. Turner's desire—thwarted as it may be—to reach across the cultural and political divide is all the more striking when set against Crawford's reactionary denial. But as different as they are, each writer struggles with the power of language to convey the act of consumption—the obliteration of a home, a nation, a life, or many lives. The result of that consumption is a kind of blinding absence, a trope that figures prominently in each work. In the end, Turner's empathy with the Iraqis may be as personally devastating as Crawford's coldness turns out to be. Neither a humane nor a dehumanizing mindset is adequate protection against the effects of encountering the final Other, death. Turner, like other writers on Iraq, recognizes and revels in the potential for productive cultural contact, but finally sees that potential as stunted or failed.

A number of writers have addressed the soldier's encounter with the Other in the specific context of war, an encounter that occurs primarily as engagement with the enemy, and secondarily as interaction with civilians of the local communities. With regard to the former, soldiers are encouraged to depersonalize the enemy in order to facilitate combat; the enemy *must* become the Other for most soldiers to overcome their resistance to killing. "Without the creation of abstract images of the enemy during training," argues Richard Holmes, "battle would become impossible to sustain" (361). Those images can be created by mass propaganda ("Halt the Hun! Buy War Bonds"), methods of combat training (such as the cultivation of instinctive rather than considered response), and the use of language ("Target has been neutralized").

Language is particularly effective in veiling the real business of war, and can be employed artistically, institutionally, or by soldiers themselves. Paul Fussell has written about the romantic terms used to describe war before World War I, when a general and widespread innocence was supported by what he calls a "curious prophylaxis of language" (23). In *The Great War and Modern Memory,* he provides a chart of some forty "translations" in order to detail this prophylactic quality. "Obedient soldiers" are referred to as *"the brave,"* he explains. "Warfare is *strife,"* "The dead on the battlefield are *the fallen,"* and "The blood of young men is *'the red / Sweet wine of youth'"* (22). The ugliness and atrocity of raw killing are glossed over by lovely phrases that emphasize instead the glory and honor of this ancient and institutionalized pursuit, during which bodies are simply "fallen" rather than unrecognizable, mangled, or putrescent. In the stories Fussell discusses, soldiers maintain their dignity and their individuality, even as they fight as part of a whole. Most important, no one ever dies an anonymous, painful death.

In real war, of course, it can be as frightening and messy to shoot at others as to be shot at yourself, and often soldiers instinctively try and avoid both activities. In 1947, S. L. A. Marshall alerted the military to exactly this phenomenon, which he discovered based on surveys of soldiers fighting in World War II. Throughout the war, he observed, only about 15 percent of soldiers actually fired at the enemy, even when they were under fire themselves. "We are reluctant to admit," he observed, "that essentially war is the business of killing" (67). The employee, then, is the soldier who kills, but to do so means reversing what "his home, his religion, his schooling, and the moral code and ideals of his society have made him" (78). For those reasons, the fear of killing in war can trump even the fear of being killed as a cause of battle failure. "At the vital point," Marshall notes, "he becomes a conscientious objector" (79). This is clearly a problem if one wants to win a war.

In order to overcome that resistance, Marshall advocated changes in military training as well as changes in the institutional language used to describe military action. Instead of ordering a soldier to shoot at or kill an enemy soldier, one instead would order him to "mass fire" against a stand of trees or a riverbank. It's easier, he noted, to aim your weapon at a feature of the landscape (where, not incidentally, enemy soldiers might be located) than to point it specifically at another human being. Institutional language can make killing easier—by not calling it killing. Marshall's observations and suggestions were a big hit, and today, as Dan Baum writes,

> A regular soldier can serve years in the Army and hardly ever hear the word "kill" outside bayonet practice, a vestigial relic of the days before the use of assault rifles. (No American soldier has participated in an organized bayonet charge since the Korean War.) Army manuals and drill sergeants speak of "suppressing enemy fire," "engaging targets," and "attritting" the enemy. "We attempt to instill reaction," said Captain Tim Dunnigan, who trains infantry in the woods of Fort Benning, Georgia. "Hear a pop, hit the ground, return fire. Act instinctually." Captain Jason Kostal, a twenty-eight-year-old former commander at Fort Benning's sniper school, says that, even in a unit whose motto is "One Shot One Kill," explicit discussion of the subject is avoided. "We don't talk about 'Engage this person,' 'Engage this guy.' It's always 'Engage that target,'" he said. "You're not thinking, I wonder if that guy has three kids." (47)

Soldiers themselves use language to distance themselves from the killing that they inevitably witness in war, as well as the killing that they often participate in themselves. Lawrence Tritle has written about the "contortion of language" that took place in Vietnam, noting soldiers' sardonic responses to violence (like calling napalm victims "crispy critters") as well as the paradoxically expressive phrase "It don't mean nothin'." As Jonathan Shay and William Broyles have also noted, in denying meaning, the phrase encompasses all the wartime experiences "so brutal and extreme that they lie outside normative language and represent events that run counter to every principle, value, and right one has been taught" (Tritle 131–32). Attacking others and being attacked by others can defy one's powers of expression—and so what soldiers say can reflect that defiance. Tim O'Brien identifies a similar phrase that shows how soldiers in Vietnam struggle to represent their experiences by saying everything and nothing at the same time:

> There it is, they'd say. Over and over—there it is, my friend, there it is—as if the repetition itself were an act of poise, a balance between crazy and almost crazy, knowing without going, there it is, which meant be cool, let it

ride, because Oh yeah, man, you can't change what can't be changed, there
it is, there it absolutely and positively and fucking well *is*. (21)

All these different modes of language provide a kind of distance, a delicate psychological buffer between the soldier and the brutal acts that war
necessitates. Language can help depersonalize the killing that one has to
do. Joanna Bourke notes, in fact, that early in the twentieth century soldiers were taught not just to depersonalize but actively hate the enemy,
because "virulent hatred was believed to stimulate pugnacity, which was
the most effective antidote to fear and anxiety (the chief obstacles to combat effectiveness)" (139). Yet hatred, perhaps obviously, has its drawbacks,
chiefly that it is hard to control. When control breaks down in the self and
in the ranks, soldiers become "little better than an armed mob" who, among
other things, no longer distinguish between soldiers and civilians (156).
Thus encounters with the Other on the battlefield and in non-combat situations begin, literally, to bleed together. Holmes argues that the "road to
My Lai was paved, first and foremost, by the dehumanisation of the Vietnamese and the 'mere gook rule,' which declared that killing a Vietnamese
civilian did not really count" (391).

Depersonalization, then, is a delicate process to use and maintain. Holmes notes the problem: "[I]f the abstract image [of the enemy] is overdrawn
or depersonalization is stretched into hatred, the restraints on human be-
haviour in war are easily swept aside. If, on the other hand, men reflect too
deeply upon their enemy's common humanity, then they risk being unable
to proceed with a task whose aims may be eminently just and legitimate"
(361). Deficient or excessive identification with the enemy hurts the soldier's ability to do his job, as well as to recover after the fact. When one has
not only gone to war but killed someone there, then the perceptions about
that someone greatly affect how the memory of the killing will be assimilated (or not assimilated) into one's sense of self. For Dave Grossman, there
is no undamaging way to do this. He calls this a soldier's "tragic Catch-22.
If he overcomes his resistance to killing and kills an enemy soldier in close
combat, he will be forever burdened with blood guilt, and if he elects not to
kill, then the blood guilt of his fallen comrades and the same of his profession, nation, and cause lie upon him. He is damned if he does, and damned
if he doesn't" (87). Crawford and Turner's opposing reactions to the Other
reflect Holmes's articulation of the soldier's problem. Crawford's reaction

is marked by depersonalization so extreme that it could be called hatred if that much emotion could be attributed to it, and Turner's by a deep reflection on common humanity that leads to an understanding of war—and the author's role in it—as correspondingly inhuman.

Popular representations tend to simplify this problem. In many cases the only real effect of a cinematic good guy killing a bad guy is the elimination of evil, narrative denouement, and the satisfaction of the audience. The extremely popular films *300* (2007) and *Avatar* (2009) have each been understood as allegories of the Iraq War, though they assume opposing political perspectives. *300* is a highly stylized film based on Frank Miller's 1998 graphic novel that depicts the heroic last stand of a small group of Spartan warriors against hordes of attacking Persians at Thermopylae in 480 BCE. The battle is fought against the wishes of the Spartan Council—representative to some of the United Nations. The Spartans define themselves as courageous, hard, and independent, and the film highlights their sculpted, phallic physiques and graceful fighting skills. The Persians, however, are epitomized by their leader, Xerxes, who is dark-skinned, bejeweled, effeminate, and monstrously cruel. The Spartans lose, but that loss is figured as the victory of humanity and of masculinity. The "bad guys" here—Persians, or, to some, Iraqis—are so bad that they're not even really "guys" anymore, but rather ogres, trolls, and freakish combat drones. Killing them is like zapping aliens in a video game, at least until they have you surrounded.

Avatar reverses the allegory. Paralyzed Marine Jake Sully (Sam Worthington) inhabits the body of a Na'vi male, one of the native beings of Pandora. The security forces of a mining corporation that wants access to the resources of the Edenic Pandora send in Na'vi-Jake to gain intelligence on how to best facilitate that access. The Na'vi are skilled, gentle creatures who live in harmony with their environment; the contrast with the greedy, violent "security" forces couldn't be more stark, and Jake defects, fighting valiantly with the Na'vi against the encroaching Americans. Audiences cheer when the evil Colonel Quaritch (Stephen Lang) is finally done in by Jake's Na'vi girlfriend, and the anti-imperialist, eco-friendly message could hardly be more clear—or simplistic. In *300* and *Avatar,* the bad guys are easy to identify—they are hypermasculine in the latter and not masculine enough in the former—and their deaths leave no unpleasant aftertaste. There is little "blood guilt," to use Grossman's term, for the enemy or for one's comrades. There is only moral triumph.

But in more realistic depictions of combat, encounters with the enemy make a greater impression. They include all the weight of other cross-cultural encounters as well as the variously traumatizing burden of participating in the killing of other people. As *Avatar* demonstrates (and *300* proudly defies), soldiers who have fought in the Persian Gulf and Iraq wars have done so at a time when ideas of multiculturalism and cultural awareness have been widely championed, more so than ever before. (Certainly the years of the Vietnam War, for instance, the most recent full-scale engagement to pre-date the Persian Gulf War, were hardly marked by widespread racial toler-ance within the United States.) Turner embodies those ideals while Crawford rejects them, yet neither attitude is an inoculation against suffering.

In some ways Crawford sees himself as a cinematic Spartan, though Iraq in 2005 is not Thermopylae in 480 BCE. In Crawford's narrative, the Iraqis are mere shadows who are hardly acknowledged at all. Reading the book is almost like reading a nineteenth-century colonial text, though he presents this attitude as bracingly "old school." Crawford's story consumes the Other, and presents Iraq as a landscape and a people that are empty and in-ferior. Yet Crawford also narrates the story of his own consumption. By the end of the book, his identity and indeed his whole life have effectively been obliterated, and Crawford's cocky presence has eroded into nothing. In the end, Crawford expresses grief and even hatred for himself in the wake of these obliterating encounters, a sudden expressive turn that, though not fully developed, implies his awareness of the consequences of such extreme dehumanization.

Turner, like Jake Sully, may also consider the devastating effects of an American military presence in a place rich with history, culture, and re-sources, but for him there is no escape route from the burdens of being an American soldier, and defecting is not an option. Turner is a different kind of writer than Crawford, yet his often sensual descriptions of Iraq and Iraqis might give the reader pause as well. In the context of contem-porary American cultural production, bell hooks has written about the phenomenon of "eating the Other." This commodification of Otherness reveals how a "contemporary longing for the primitive is expressed by the projection onto the Other of a sense of plenty, bounty, a field of dreams" (369). Getting oneself "a bit of the Other," which, as hooks points out, is slang for sex, enhances "the blank landscape of whiteness" while also af-firming the white male's own dominant place in the power structure (372).

hooks describes eavesdropping on a group of young white men talking about their plans to have sex with women from as many non-white racial/ ethnic groups as possible. "To these young males and their buddies," she reflects, "fucking was a way to confront the Other, as well as a way to make themselves over, to leave behind white 'innocence' and enter the world of 'experience'" (368). They might themselves frame their attitude as a celebration of diversity, but hooks argues that this approach—which has parallels in many contemporary American films, commercials, and other forms of cultural production—merely commodifies non-white culture and offers it up "as new dishes to enhance the white palate," ensuring that the Other will be "eaten, consumed, and forgotten" (380).

And so what of Turner? His imagery and his frequent assumption of the Iraqi point of view might be just a more poetic version of those boys that hooks describes. But Turner goes much further in his literary journey. His studied references to the Qur'an and Arab writers suggest this, as do his careful notes at the back of the book, explaining his use of various transla- tions and the histories of works to which he makes reference. If the boys in hooks's essay want "a bit of the Other," the sexual pleasure found in eating, consuming, and forgetting the object of one's desire, Turner is haunted by a different kind of consumption that he can neither forget nor justify. He wants to show how war forces people on both sides of the conflict to eat the Other—but for Turner, this means internalizing the reality of suffer- ing and death. hooks makes the connection between sex and "a bit of the Other." Sexual climax is also a moment of personal obliteration, of the loss of the self in pleasure, *la petite mort.* Thus the irony inherent in the use of sex as domination—a moment characterized by the loss of control becomes, in hindsight, the assertion of it. For Turner, the consumption of the Other is not the exploitative use of an object of pleasure, but rather the taking in of loss. The pleasure he takes in Iraq is inseparable from obliteration. Turner real- izes, in a way that Crawford experiences but doesn't fully articulate, the way that this Other then resides permanently within, and is never forgotten.

Hometown Boy Makes Bad

John Crawford is not happy about his experiences fighting the war in Iraq. He wants to explain those experiences as something that happened to him, like getting caught in a bad rainstorm or finding himself in the path of a tornado, and his book *The Last True Story I'll Ever Tell* is subtitled *An Accidental Soldier's Account of the War in Iraq*. His dedication and acknowledgment indicate his sense of himself as a lone voice crying in the wilderness, a truth-teller, as the title suggests, whose news will be harsh and unwelcomed by many. Crawford dedicates the book "To the soldiers who, having scouted ahead, stand alone knocking dust from their boots and waiting patiently for their comrades," and acknowledges the author and journalist Christian Parenti for his support. He writes to Parenti,

> It's the same in skanky oil towns the world throughout:
> Few people will vouch for you.
> Thanks for doing so.

These opening pages prepare us for an account of the war from a hard cynic, a trailblazer, someone who will tell it like it is and who has clearly suffered consequences for doing so. Someone who will call a spade a spade, and Iraq a collection of skanky oil towns full of backbiters and traitors. Someone who didn't ask for war, but got it anyway.

Crawford did get a war. What, then, do we get as readers? His preface further defines his approach. This will be a story of initiation, he says, a story of quiet optimism "replaced by something darker, a kind of hatred—of what, I cannot even grasp or imagine" (xi). He will describe "innocence not lost but stolen, of lies and blackness—a story not of the insanity of war but of the insanity of men" (xiv). Crawford frames his narrative as one that moves from innocence to experience and even, possibly, to insanity, and the weight of that transformation as all the more crushing because the catalyst, the war, was thrust upon him. "This book is the story," he says again, "of a group of college students, American boys who wanted nothing to do with someone else's war. It is *our* story" (xiii).

Crawford's perspective is clear here. His story is about "us," the clean-cut, all-American college boys who were sent overseas to some skanky oil towns. Iraq almost destroys him, he intimates, but it also gives him the experience he needs to write and to assert his own agency. He didn't want to fight the Iraq War, but after three years in the 101st Airborne Division he enlists in the Florida National Guard in order to pay for his education at Florida State University. In his last year of college, he is sent to Kuwait and then to Iraq (xii). Crawford's bitter complaints about his unit's drastically extended tours in Iraq are well founded, though calling himself an "accidental soldier" despite his many years as part of the military organization is perhaps less so. He doesn't ask to be sent to Iraq, but then soldiers rarely have the privilege of determining where they will serve.

This is *our* story, he insists: American college boys who didn't want this. Crawford's take on the military's demographics and motivation is remarkably constricted by his personal views, and he continues by stating that he intends to be the voice for that collective. The book is not intended to assuage pain, or bring back the dead, but "simply make people aware, if only for one glimmering moment, of what war is really like" (xiii–xiv). Crawford has staked his claim, and the reader turns the page to see what he can do—and to see what portrait of the wartime experience emerges from his work.

Crawford begins his story proper with a detailed description of a desert sandstorm, a metaphor for the obliteration of everything familiar and the loss of orientation that he associates with Iraq. He titles the chapter "Empty Breath," another reference to absence, and in the first paragraph rattles off a list of things that are lacking. Here, there is no visibility, no means to escape, and no time to prepare. The perimeter quickly disappears into the swirling sand, as do the men sitting next to you. "You're alone," Crawford says, "no war, no home, just you and desert" (1–2). That complete absence, the desert's consumption of everything, provides Crawford a way to talk about this war as a kind of black hole, sucking in and negating everything but his own voice.

He says that unlike many veterans from other wars, he understands the political causes of this war in Iraq, though he emphasizes that he disagrees with those politics. He frames his participation as both contractual and unfair, a kind of legal screwing-over:

> I recognized the importance of Middle Eastern oil to European and Asian powers. This was a war I didn't believe in, but no one had asked my opinion. I had signed a contract, reaped the benefits of a cheap college education, and now it was time to pay it back. Two credits from graduating, recently married, and with less than a year left in my contract, I was going to Iraq. (8)

Crawford says he understands that this war isn't being fought for any "higher" purpose—he doesn't acknowledge claims that America is bringing democracy to a fraught nation or stabilizing the region. He believes the war is being fought over turf and wealth, and he distances himself from those motivations. Neither does Crawford trust his weapons or support, which he describes as "a light machine gun, *no* air cover, *no* heavy weapons, *no* naval gunfire" (11, emphasis added). He also dislikes his leaders, who attempt to act like "one of us" but merely give vague answers about missions and announce more extensions of their tours (19–20). Tensions divide his own unit and the units from one another. Crawford, it would seem, likes almost no one, and his isolation is reminiscent of that depicted in Jones's *The Thin Red Line* and Mailer's *The Naked and the Dead*. In those World War II novels, the authors take pains to emphasize the soldiers' alienation from one another, and thus avoid a standard genre element: deeply felt (if hard won) comradeship between soldiers fighting together. Crawford, too, is on his own.

Given his disdain for the military, his comrades, and the Iraqi landscape, Crawford's negative attitude toward the Iraqis, friend or foe, is not surprising. His first impression of Baghdad is of an "unfathomable" labyrinth of alleys, permeated with an unbearable stench, and populated by enemies "behind every corner and in every window, their dark eyes plotting our demise" (22). Crawford seems to revel in the deliberately racist cant of his descriptions, enjoying the opportunity to be both "honest" and politically incorrect. The Other here is dark, plotting, and fetid, living in a place that is literally unfathomable—both illogical and unilluminated.

Early in the book, Crawford participates in an illegal raid in which he and other soldiers take six Iraqis into custody while also looting a house for money and valuables. He "makes conversation" with the prisoners, talking to the uncomprehending men in English with a machine gun resting in his lap, casually pointed at them. "It wasn't that we were particularly nasty to our prisoners," he explains, "we just didn't really care about their final destination. It wasn't our concern, nor were the politics involved" (50). As another soldier announces, "the whole country is stupid" (45). When the unauthorized spree is investigated by the CIA, blame is initially placed on a soldier named Ramirez instead of Crawford's superior, Staff Sergeant Connel. Despite his hatred of Connel, Crawford is unwilling to explain what really happened, preferring to see the investigation and ensuing consequences as another situation that is beyond his control: "It's their decision, I guess. I'm just glad I'm not part of it" (55). But of course he *is* part of it. He finally talks when his platoon sergeant questions him directly, and only then because he dislikes Connel so much. "I would have lied my ass off for a friend," as he says (58). His primary motivation is antipathy rather than a desire to clear Ramirez's name or come clean about the unethical raid. Crawford may claim that he doesn't support what he sees as the war's real purpose—the seizure of Middle Eastern resources—but he is content enough to participate in this smaller-scale version of the same thing.

Later, Crawford develops what one might generously call "relationships" with other Iraqis, and seems to take pains to emphasize his own callousness, perhaps as a kind of self-castigation. He describes in turn his interaction with a young boy, that boy's older sister, and an older man who runs a local shop, all of whom are dehumanized and presented as variously substandard foils to his own white male logic, power, cleanliness, and agency. Crawford is first befriended by a young Iraqi boy, a "grubby little bastard," and because he doesn't know the child's name, takes to calling him Cum (102). Like he did with the prisoners, Crawford has one-sided conversations with Cum, who speaks little English. (Crawford does not note that he speaks little Arabic.) His dominance over the child is complete—he bestows on him a humiliating name, both delights in and wearies of the child's perceived imitation of him, and describes him as pitiful, dirty, homeless, and lice-ridden. He eventually meets the boy's sister, a beautiful young woman who, he is told, wants to marry an American and leave Iraq. But once more, Crawford doesn't care: "I knew she was aglow with dreams of an American husband and an American lifestyle. I, on the other hand, had no intentions of marriage, but I did enjoy the conversations" (110). Shortly thereafter, Crawford discovers that the young woman's house has been burned down, and that both the boy and his sister are gone. This happened, most likely, because the sister was rumored to be involved with American soldiers. Crawford's amusing conversations, then, appear to have taken a serious toll. But his feelings of remorse or responsibility are, once again, absent:

> "Where's Leena?" The woman didn't answer. She just fearfully slammed her gate and fled into her house.
> "Fuck, man. That sucks." Fucking Sellers, but no one had anything else to say. We walked back to the station and went back to work. (114)

In the absence of more compelling entertainment, getting to know Leena and her brother was fun. Ultimately, however, it amounts to nothing. Her disappearance is an absence that no one bothers to comment on. These Others have no hold on Crawford, other than the mild pressure of something that sucks when it is no longer there to entertain him. Crawford is slightly more demonstrative about the owner of a small auto-parts shop named Whalee, which the soldiers pronounce "Wall-Lee" (148). Something about him was likeable, Crawford says, though of course that doesn't make him human. "He was the closest thing we had to a hajji friend," he notes, perhaps unaware that his use of *hajji,* a pejorative American term for anyone Iraqi and/or Arab, as a modifier for "friend" is rather oxymoronic. "That is to say," he clarifies, "we almost considered him to be a real person" (148). Whalee is an adult male engaged in commerce, unlike the boy and his sister, and those qualities are perhaps more easily recognized by Crawford. Whalee becomes used to the semi-preferential treatment, and when another American soldier orders him out of his own store, Whalee refuses. In the ensuing argument, he is apparently killed, although Crawford only says that his head "was crashed through the same window that he had once shot looters from" and that without him, the store wasn't a fun place to be. After the incident "we no longer manned it at all" (154). Whalee's death is mentioned but not lingered on, another thing that "sucks" because it takes away from Crawford's fun. Whalee is absent from the store, and thus from the story. Like Leena and her brother, Whalee just disappears. In her review of Crawford's book, Janet Maslin notes that this sudden sucking of characters into nothingness, this consumption of the Other, "is the book's single most potent effect."

Crawford's dehumanization of the Iraqis is repeatedly made apparent in these and similar episodes throughout the book. In Baghdad, the soldiers make an empty building their temporary residence. When the building is attacked, Crawford is outraged at the imposition:

> We were Americans, of this there was no doubt; most of us were from Florida, a few from Georgia, all Southern boys, some with roots tracing back to the last time the Florida militia was really called up, in what we jokingly referred to as the war of northern oppression. We had names like John, and Steven, and Terry. We didn't eat dried lamb's heads or pay any heed to the five-times-daily call to prayer, but things had changed. We might not have

belonged, but it became our town, our block, our home, and we got to feeling that it wasn't right that some fucker could come in and blow up our
house. (61–62)

The elements here are unmistakably characteristic of a group that views
itself as superior to a foreign culture. Who are "we," according to Crawford? Southern Americans with "normal" names who simply don't belong
in a place full of strangely named, faceless people who eat strange things
and pray strangely often. The "war of northern oppression" is mentioned
as a joke, but it's no joke that these boys take pains to identify their dominant place in a similarly racist hierarchy. Crawford may have disagreed
with the reasons for invading Iraq, but once there he is happy to appropriate the foreign soil as his own. He hates it, but it is still *his* town, *his* block,
his house, and certainly not available for penetration by "some fucker."

Near the end of his time in Iraq, Crawford helps guard a group of
refugees, a tired and hungry collection of people devastated by the war.
But sympathy is impossible, in the same way it was when Joel Turnipseed encountered a similar situation. "[W]e had already lived too many of
those moments," Crawford asserts, "to give a fuck about anything except
ourselves" (200). Crawford may be representing his callousness here—and
perhaps in the whole book—as a symptom of his and the other soldiers'
trauma, the inevitable numbing that results from an overexposure to the
horrors of war. If so, it doesn't quite work. This reads less like trauma
than simple laziness or selfishness. The Other is not even the exotic, the
savage, the mysterious, something to be fucked and learned from. If hooks
laments white culture's "eating, consuming, and forgetting" of the Other,
then Crawford couldn't be bothered with the first two steps. He just for-
gets. His story consumes the Other, but this happens as a result of Crawford's passivity rather than his active enjoyment or sensualized use of the
Iraqis.

Yet the story doesn't end here, leaving Crawford alone on a stage full
of nothingness. That same consumption eats at him as well. If Iraq is all
absence for Crawford, something to make him more confident of his own
presence and identity ("We were *Americans*," he says, "of this there was no
doubt") then that absence nevertheless grates on Crawford's mental state.
The obliterating emptiness of the desert that Crawford sees drives him to
want to obliterate himself as well. He likes Valium and Prozac, Turkish

whiskey, cases of beer confiscated from Iraqi men, and goes to some length
to attain a dose of morphine (63, 129). Crawford's sense of the place, the
mission, and the people are all empty. In response, he seeks to empty *himself* out into the blurred and dark haziness of drunkenness or drug-induced
stupor. And he succeeds, as his own life and identity begin to disintegrate
and become sucked into this consuming nothingness. "I wanted to go to
my home and my wife," he says, "but I didn't have either a home or a wife
anymore. Twenty-five years old and nothing to live for" (156). He even
considers suicide, but is too afraid to do it. There is no solace: "I wanted to
believe that when I got to America things would be all right. I was wrong;
you can never go back home" (157).

In the absurdity and bleakness of the situation, surrounded, as he sees
it, by nothing, but unable to consider suicide as a viable option, Crawford
deals with these difficulties by doing "something incredibly stupid" (160).
He doesn't mean that he makes a mistake, or botches an otherwise reasonable task, but that he deliberately seeks out a dangerous and also pointless
task to perform. While manning a watch station, Crawford and another
soldier decide to commandeer an old motorcycle from an Iraqi man. Despite the man's protests, they climb on—Crawford in the sidecar—and
take it for a joyride late at night. They zoom along, and then discover
that they are unable to steer or turn the vehicle. As a result, they end up
far outside their safety zone and out of gas. They have to run back to the
station while wearing full gear, dodging the threatening Iraqi "phantoms"
that appear out of the gloom (166). When they finally return, the owner of
the bike asks about its whereabouts. Crawford only says, "Ali Baba," and
breaks into laughter.

This may be Crawford's only real reference to Arab culture, and so it
is appropriate that the reference is neither the product of his seeking understanding about the culture nor actually Arab in origin. His gloss on the
situation refers to *The Thousand and One Nights,* or *The Arabian Nights,*
the collection of ancient stories that became widely popular in Europe in
the nineteenth century. "Ali Baba and the Forty Thieves," while one of the
best-known stories, was not a part of the original Arabic collection and was
actually added by European translators. For many in the West, "Ali Baba"
has represented the East in all its exotic, Oriental glory, though it is an
imitation that, through its commodification, has become an "authentic" ar-
tifact. In contemporary Iraq, "Ali Baba" has become an equal opportunity

slang term originally used by American soldiers for Iraqi thieves, but that has been picked up and used within the Iraqi communities as well as a general term for suspected robbers—including the American military presence and government. Ironically, as Jerry Levin has noted in his exploration of the term's wartime use, the Ali Baba of *The Arabian Nights* fame was not actually a thief, but a poor man who seizes the opportunity to take from thieves what wasn't theirs in the first place (96). So Ali Baba is an Arab character (who wasn't really of Arab origin), a thief (who didn't really steal), and in Iraq, a faceless, small-time criminal (and sometimes the most powerful nation in the world.) It is appropriate for Crawford's general stylistic approach that he uses this term here with no understanding of these layers of history and ironic meaning. For him, it's simply another way to denote a disappearance. He takes someone else's property and loses it, but in his explanation, the motorcycle is eaten by the desert. "Yeah, it was stupid and we could have died," he explains to his squad leader. "I know that, but it's fucking funny and you know it" (170). As Chris Bray remarks in his review of the book, "[a]n entire set of absent values is neatly conveyed in those two short sentences." If, Bray notes, Army officers have called the reservists at Abu Ghraib "the seven idiots who lost the war," then after reading Crawford's book, "[w]e can add another one to the list."

It's difficult, when reading Crawford's book, to encounter episode after episode showcasing his self-pity, indifference, and inability to take responsibility for his actions. Yet in addition to his figurative negation of the Iraqis and their nation, of his comrades, and of the military, he finally negates himself as well. "Nothing was gonna work out," he says. "Our lives were crumbling so that we could pretend to help people who pretended to appreciate it" (178). Crawford sees his own presence in Iraq (and perhaps his presence generally) as deeply inauthentic, not unlike his use of the term Ali Baba. Everything is simply more layers of make-believe. Statements like this one, as well as the final section of the book, may be intended as a kind of veiled confession. As he does when describing his reaction to the refugees, Crawford may want to portray his callousness as the result of the trauma of war. He writes in his preface that in Iraq, his native optimism is replaced by "a kind of hatred," though he cannot "grasp or imagine" what the object of that hatred could be (xi). In the closing section of the book, Crawford suggests that what he has grown to hate so much isn't so much the Iraqis, their nation, his comrades, or the military, but himself.

The last chapter works as one final, obliterating stroke. "The Last True Story I'll Ever Tell," from which the book takes its title, relates Crawford's return home to Palatka, Florida, with his wife for the Blue Crab Festival on Memorial Day. Over beer and good food, his friends ask him to tell a war story, and he proceeds to tell about killing a child who appeared to have a rifle. He stops, overcome and unable to continue, and his friends and wife comfort him—he can finish the story another time. Crawford's final move here is an obvious nod to Tim O'Brien; in an article by Christian Parenti about the National Guard unit, he notes that Crawford is a fan of O'Brien's work, "particularly *The Things They Carried*," and that at the time of Parenti's visit Crawford was working on writing this "last true story." In *The Things They Carried*, O'Brien subtly undermines his own truth claims, and signals his intentions to do so before his narrative even begins. His book is subtitled *A Work of Fiction* yet it is dedicated to Jimmy Cross, Norman Bowker, Rat Kiley, Michell Sanders, Henry Dobbins, and Kiowa—all characters in the stories he tells. O'Brien's epigraph is taken from John Ransom's *Andersonville Diary,* and reads in part "Those have had any such experience as the author will see its truthfulness at once." "This is true," "Is it true?" "That's a true war story that never happened," "It's all made up," he says variously in "How to Tell a True War Story" (67, 83, 84, 85). O'Brien's book is as much about concepts of truth, memory, trauma, and grief as it is about war, much less one particular war, and these concepts are engaged throughout all the stories. In contrast, Crawford waits to address the notion of truth and war until the final pages of his book, and does so in a way that is sudden and stark.

In the middle of Crawford's story about a comforting reunion, he abruptly shifts the scene. He awakens back in Iraq, and realizes he was dreaming. The trip to Palatka didn't really happen, and the supportive friends and family weren't really there. "What I'm about to write is true," he claims, and proceeds to say that the story he just told was a fictional short story he wrote while in Iraq, that it was a dream of how he would like things to be. When he returned to the States, he actually stayed in a few friends' houses and was evicted from several apartments. The final passage of the book is brief and blunt:

> Most days I was sick. It was a lingering, wasting sickness that comes only when you have nothing left. There are people out there who really don't

know why they get up in the morning; it's sad, and that's how you know it's true.

In my dream, my wife never told me things would have been better off if I had just never come home. In reality, I agree with her.

This is a true story. You can tell because it makes your stomach turn. I am home now, and I will never again write a true story. (219)

Crawford glosses O'Brien's statement in "How to Tell a True War Story" that a true war story, "if truly told, makes the stomach believe" (78). What turns Crawford's stomach here is perhaps the turning of the tables. His story begins with his depiction of the steady consumption of the Other. Iraqis appear as less than human, occasionally amusing creatures who then disappear into nothingness, consumed by the desert, the stinking alleyways, and the forward motion of Crawford's narrative. But by the end, Crawford finds that he has been eaten away as well, with nothing left but the bile of an empty life. Ultimately, all that's left is the blinding absence of everything—of home, self, truth, and meaning.

Ironically, Crawford's central theme appears more poignantly in Betool Khedairi's *Absent* (2005), a novel about a young Iraqi woman living in Baghdad during the sanctions that followed the Persian Gulf War. When she was an infant, her parents were killed by a landmine left over from the Six Day War of 1967. Custom dictated that parents be named after their firstborn child, but when her aunt and uncle decide to raise her, her uncle refused to be named after his dead sister-in-law's child. "Instead, he insisted that he should be called Abu Ghayeb, the father of the absent one" (1–2). This child, Dalal, grows up amid the losses caused by war—for more years and in more extreme ways than Crawford—and never seems to fully inhabit her life. Using lipstick, she would draw herself in the mirror, outlining her body on the glass. "Suddenly the electricity is cut off," Khedairi writes, and the resulting image says more about war, trauma, and identity than any of Crawford's: "The red oily frame goes out. I abandon my pose, leaving behind me a map tracing out my figure hanging in the middle of a mirror in a darkened room" (12).

The Afterimage of a Dream on Fire

The cover of Brian Turner's *Here, Bullet* provides another image of absence. The almost faceless figure of a soldier stands in the middle of brown desert and white-blue sky, alone, with a faint suggestion of tire tracks beside him. This first impression is very similar to the one Crawford gives in his opening passages—a lone soldier, surrounded by emptiness and sand. For Crawford, that emptiness results in part from his refusal to see and to acknowledge the culture and the people around him. Turner's cover evokes something like the same feeling, especially if the reader discovers that the original photograph was altered to exclude a military vehicle and a number of captured insurgents (Mahler 99).

In the book proper, however, Turner takes a very different approach than Crawford in telling his story, and weaves in it a deep curiosity and appreciation for Iraqi people and Arab heritage. Turner's interest, in fact, reflects the deeply conflicted way he understands himself as both a soldier and a poet. The book begins with Turner's poem "A Soldier's Arabic," which notes and comments on *habib* and *maut,* the words for love and death, and ends with the claim that for this language to be spoken, "it must be earned" (1). The epigraph for the poem is from Hemingway—"This is a strange new kind of war where you learn just as much as you are able to believe"— and the following page features a quotation from the Qur'an: "Who brings forth the living from the dead, and the dead from the living?"

Turner effectively introduces himself here, and does so in radically different terms than does Crawford. He indicates a grounding in American writers like Hemingway as well as a deep respect for the language and culture of Iraq, the knowledge and the use of which must be earned. By what, he doesn't say, although the epigraph to this first poem would indicate perhaps the cultivation of or capacity for belief. "There is so much poetry in that land," he comments in an interview. "You know how as a poet you want to honor the tradition, so I studied to give respect to the culture that's there too" (Mahler 97). At the same time, he is always aware of his job as a soldier, and the very different mindset that often entails. Much of the energy of his poetry derives from the clashing of those two projects. "I was writing the poems as a response to what was happening and what we were doing," he explains, "but at the same time, I was trying to learn as much about the place as possible." In another interview, he makes it clear that he privileged his project as a poet over his job as a soldier: "I was surrounded by an amazing and storied humanity…I did not want to give in to the process of de-humanizing the Iraqi people so that I could get on with the job at hand" (Hammond and Bagley). Turner is well aware that that process has been presented to him as a necessary part of the training for and experience of being a soldier. He resists that process, but he still has a job to do, and an often horrific one at that. Perhaps because of this division within himself, this poet-soldier dwells more and more on the idea of division generally, within selves and between cultures and nations, regardless of their common humanity. As he notes in "A Soldier's Arabic," the word for love is written from right to left, "starting where we would end it and ending where we might begin."

After this opening poem, which sets the stage for the collection as a whole, *Here, Bullet* is divided into four sections. The sections feature epigraphs from Arab writers and texts, and Turner also incorporates considerations of ancient and modern Arab writers into his poetry. Two of the epigraphs are drawn from the Qur'an, one from a poem "Every Morning the War Gets Up from Sleep," by the contemporary Iraqi poet Fadhil al-Azzawi, and one from Abdul 'Ala' al-Ma'arri (973–1057), an Arab philosopher and poet who, though natively Syrian, longed to return to Baghdad after leaving there. The four sections of Turner's book follow an arc of disillusion, or more precisely, an arc of dis-illumination. In Section I, Turner offers an introduction to Iraq and the soldier's experience there, and educates the reader about communication, weaponry, landscape, and the ubiquitous presence of death, the absence of life. If one learns one's lessons with care, these poems suggest, one can achieve a kind of understanding, if not control, of this experience. The poems in Section II begin to explore and complicate the less tangible factors of war, and show that knowledge held within the self can be both illuminating and utterly devastating. Understanding, it seems, has its difficulties. In Section III Turner explores the possibilities for transcendence, or ultimate and total illumination, but finds that they are coupled, seemingly irrevocably, with moments of destruction. Finally, Section IV dwells on the failure of that possibility, and figures that failure as a kind of afterimage, the blinding absence of a mode of communication that might salve the ruptures that war brings.

The poems in Section I are arranged in such a way as to introduce the reader to Iraq from a soldier's perspective, albeit a particularly observant and articulate one. In "Hwy 1," Turner takes the reader through vignettes of Iraq, from the ghosts of the Highway of Death to the "spice road of old," Babylon and Sumer, the land of Gilgamesh, "where the minarets / sound the muezzin's prayer, resonant and deep" (6). "In the Leupold Scope" gives us a view of the surroundings as seen through a rifle scope, including the sight

of a woman hanging laundry on her rooftop. Turner is most consciously di-
dactic in the centerpiece poem of this section, "What Every Soldier Should
Know."[1] Here, Turner offers instructions and hints about the soldier's life
in Iraq. Some are cultural: you should enter a home with your right foot;
guns are often fired into the air at weddings. Some emphasize the linguis-
tic: "*O-guf*! *Tera armeek* is rarely useful. / It means *Stop! Or I'll shoot*" (9).
The rest are warnings. You will hear the Rocket-Propelled Grenade (RPG)
as it approaches, but you won't hear a roadside bomb. Explosives can be
anywhere. There are many different kinds of people, but "any one of them /
may dance over your body tomorrow." Remember, Turner urges, that for a
soldier in Iraq, death is a constant presence and possibility. In "Here, Bullet," the title poem that also appears in this opening section, he renders that
possibility in sensual and horrific detail. He addresses the personified Bullet and offers it his body, "the clavicle-snapped wish, / the aorta's opened
valves" (13). The Bullet craves adrenaline and flight, and Turner taunts it
sadly: "I dare you to finish / what you've started." Death as delivered by
this thrill- and heat-seeking missile is complete and inescapable: "because
here, Bullet, / here is where the world ends, every time." Every soldier must
contemplate the possibility of his own death, and Turner infuses this contemplation with a poignant and self-conscious bravado.

Indeed, many of these poems linger on the various vignettes of death in
war. "Body Bags" imagines the questions corpses would ask the soldiers
standing over them,

> wondering who these strangers are
> who would kick their hard feet, saying
> *Last call, motherfucker. Last call.* (14)

"AB Negative (The Surgeon's Poem)" describes the fruitless efforts of a
surgeon to save a woman named Thalia Fields, who cannot feel the surgeon's hands or hear his voice. He cries when she dies, in a plane above
Iraq. His grief and tears are inaudible,

> because nothing can be heard
> where pilots fly in blackout, the plane
> like a shadow guiding the rain, here
> in the droning engines of midnight. (16)

That negation of the senses and the final negation of death are described literally here, but the trope of nothingness that Turner explores in more complex variations in later poems is evident in this beginning, explanatory section. "The Hurt Locker," where Turner shuts away the sights and sensations of war, is both full and empty.

> Nothing but hurt left here.
> Nothing but bullets and pain
> and the bled-out slumping
> and all the *fucks* and *goddamns*
> and *Jesus Christs* of the wounded.
> Nothing left here but the hurt. (11)

Jesus Christ may be inside, but so is the damning of God. Open it, he urges, and learn "how rough men come hunting for souls."

In this opening section, Turner's lessons are common ones that are seen frequently in the tradition of war writing. Be aware of the culture and the language, so that you can communicate, especially when you have a gun in your hand. War is the business of death, and you will see death on all sides and in all varieties. It will be ugly. It will be painful. This is not unlike the message Crawford offers, although Turner writes more eloquently. But Turner wants to illuminate other, less tangible factors as well. The poem "*Ashbah,*" Arabic for "ghosts," describes the ghosts of American soldiers wandering the streets at night, "unsure of their way home, exhausted" (18). A voice from the minaret reminds them "how alone they are, / how lost." "Into the Elephant Grass" portrays a woman washing clothes at dawn, carving fruit at noon, and bathing in the river at dusk. The details are domestic and sensually described; Turner notes the mangy dogs stretching, the dull heat in the middle of the day, and the relief of the water as she

> undresses, loosening her *hejab*
> and laying it down, easing her body
> out into the dark water, cooling her
> better than she ever imagined it would. (19)

Turner invests the image with a deep longing, and one senses how much a soldier would like to put his uniform aside and seek the relief of dusk, cool water, and rest. The image here is less one of eroticization than it is of envy. How nice it must be, he reflects, to put away the clothes that make us who we are, and find shelter in the consuming darkness.

In the last poem in this section, "Eulogy," a soldier seeks and finds this same kind of relief by a method more extreme and final. The poem is dedicated to PFC B. Miller, who committed suicide on 22 March 2003. "It happens on a Monday, at 11:20 a.m.," Turner begins, at a moment when tower guards are eating their sandwiches and seagulls are in flight. The sound of the shot reverberates when Miller "pulls the trigger / to take brass and fire into his mouth" (20). The latter half of the poem describes how Miller finds stillness in the midst of motion:

> and nothing can stop it now, no matter what
> blur of motion surrounds him, no matter what voices
> crackle over the radio in static confusion,
> because if only for this moment the earth is stilled,
> and Private Miller has found what low hush there is
> down in the eucalyptus shade, there by the river.

This poem serves as a transition into the next section, in which Turner begins to complicate the basic lessons of war that he has laid out in the opening section. Yes, enemy soldiers can kill you, a roadside bomb can cripple your body, bullets are longing to pierce your flesh—but death can also come from within, a desire for stillness and the low hush of the riverside. As in "Into the Elephant Grass," Miller finds relief down by the river, but he never walks back up the bank to start a new day. Stillness can be found in the midst of motion, and yet for Miller, that discovery also means the end of *all* motion.

"This is war, then," reads the epigraph for Section II. "All is well." The quote is taken from Fadhil al-Azzawi's poem "Every Morning the War Gets Up from Sleep," and echoes Turner's interest in the paradoxical truths of war, like Miller discovering a low hush in the loud shot of a gun. In this section, understanding is not so easy. Reflections on war can enlighten, but that illumination can reveal ghosts and bombs that go off internally as well as externally. In "Kirkuk Oilfield, 1927," an old man tells a boy named Ahmed, the subject of the poem, that the gas flares and flooding oil are *"the roof of Hell,"* but that nevertheless *"you must learn how to live here,"* in this place

> where the dead are buried deep in the mind
> of God, manifest in man and woman,
> given to earth in dark blood,
> given to earth in fire. (23)

The dead exist everywhere, in God, man, and woman, and are given to the earth as a sacrifice after the flood—of oil rather than water. Death may be a negation, but the dead are ever present in a world of dark blood and fire. The dead even speak when two people make love, as in "Where the Telemetries End," and will have to be told "to wait, to be patient" (25). But at other times, one might *want* to be with the dead, as in "Repatriation Day," set in Shalamcheh, at the Iran–Iraq border. "I want to lie down among them," says the speaker of the twenty-year-old skeletons resting there, "to be wrapped in sheets like the flags / of nations, banded in light and shadow" (27). Flags may be made of both light and dark swaths intertwined, but in paradise the illumination is unequivocal. When the gates of paradise open, they do so in "unbanded light," as described in "Najaf, 1820" (28). This is a place where all darkness is taken away, where "the blood [is] washed clean / from their bodies." And so in the next poem, "For Vultures: A Dystopia," Turner offers the birds

> the remorse of flesh,
> unflowered and darkening, my life
> a gift of heat and steam. (29)

His body is dark, but the sun is high and bright, "as high / as the arc of the heavens will carry it," and the vultures will rise as well. "[L]et the vultures feed on me," he implores, "let them tear me apart."

    In these poems, Turner describes how one can take death in the self, how one can "eat this Other" characterized by loss, pain, and absence. In response, one longs for light out of darkness, to be consumed and cleansed, to be taken into a different existence. The brightness of paradise follows the remorse and darkness of life. But for those still at war, that Manichean deliverance is not forthcoming. Instead, there is force, noise, and confusion. In "16 Iraqi Policemen," an explosion rips apart a road and the surrounding community, destroying storefronts, cars, people. This poem is a set piece of destruction that is echoed by the longer poems "2000 lbs" in Section III and "9 Line Medevac" in Section IV. Here, "[t]he shocking blood of the men / forms an obscene art," as a moustache is separated from its owner, and Doc Lopez struggles to bandage a girl's face back together (30). "Allah must wander in the crowd / as I do," the speaker notes, "dazed by the pure concussion / of the blast." In this poem, light and sound are transforming, but not transporting—they bring dazedness and confusion, but no relief. The violence of war is a rupture that occurs both externally and, as the next poem indicates, internally. "Dreams from the Malaria Pills (Barefoot)" describes a man coughing up shrapnel and wondering about the need for so much blood. The metal is removed by someone named Ibn Khaldun, who advises him that

> *You carry the pearls of war within you, bombs*
> *swallowed whole and saved for later.*
> *Give them to your children. Give them to your love.* (31)

In an endnote, Turner explains that Khaldun (1332–1406) is the author of the classic Islamic history of the world *The Muqaddimah*. The poem's epigraph reads *"Tamaghis ba'dan yaswadda waghdas nawfana ghadis,"* which are magical words that Khaldun explains should be "mentioned on falling asleep so as to cause the dream vision to be about the things one desires." This is according to the *Ghayat al-hakim* by the tenth-century Spanish scientist Maslamah b. Ahmad al-Majriti and other "practitioners of magic," says Khaldun (70). William S. Burroughs' 1981 novel *Cities of the Red Night* makes reference to the same words. Burroughs figures the words as "Tamaghis, Ba'dan, Yass-Waddah, Waghdas, Naufana, Ghadis," and explains that they refer to the six "cities of the red night," which were located roughly in the area of the Gobi Desert (153). "The traveler must start in Tamaghis and make his way through the other cities in the order named. This pilgrimage may take many lifetimes" (159).

What are the things that Turner desires? His poems do read like dream visions, though the object of his desire is understanding, a metaphysical rather than physical satiation. He grapples with the realization that the physical remnants of war can be removed, but the emotional remnants are far more deeply rooted within the self. These remnants, the pearls of war, may go off at any time. Give them to your loved ones, Khaldun urges, yet that would seem less a recipe for healing than a warning about further damage to come.

The next few poems continue in this vein, giving details of the war within, how violence can consume you inside and out. In "Katyusha Rockets," 107s crackle over the rooftops of Hamman al Alil, pinwheeling all the way to a Fresno, California veteran's day parade. "Rockets often fall / in the night sky of the skull," he explains,

> down long avenues
> of the brain's myelin sheathing, over synapses
> and the rough structures of thought, they fall
> into the hippocampus, into the seat of memory...(32)

The brain traps war inside you, snug up against your fondest and most comforting memories, as in the next poem, "R&R." The speaker lingers "ten thousand miles off in the future somewhere...deep in the landscape of the brain" (33). Here, he has all the resources he needs:

> I have a lover with hair that falls
> like autumn leaves on my skin.
> Water that rolls in smooth and cool
> as anesthesia. Birds that carry
> all my bullets into the barrel of the sun.

Paradise, Turner has revealed, is bathed in unbanded light, just as here the light of the sun can figuratively consume the destructive power of bullets. For soldiers in Iraq, however, the actual light can be so bright as to be overwhelming. In "Dreams from the Malaria Pills (Bosch)," the sun rises "like the opened mouth of a flamethrower, 140 degrees." In response, the man in this poem (presumably Bosch) dreams that he soaks his skin in lighter fluid and consumes his forearms, legs, chest, head in fire. Likewise, "How Bright It Is" shows how soldiers don't notice the dryness of the air, or the scratching of grasshoppers in the dirt, because they see only wreckage, bodies, and the "hard and flat and white" sun (35).

Light can be blinding and obliterating, and can prohibit a viewer from seeing other things, like those grasshoppers or, as the epigraph from Section III asks, "Do they not see the birds above their heads, / spreading their

wings and closing them?—Qur'an, 67:19." Light here is so overpowering as
to reduce clarity rather than heighten it. In "Easel," Nathere paints the landscape, but "pauses, unsure. / There is too much heat." Figures fade and blur:

> All burns in light here,
> all rises in heat as colored tongues
> lift in flame, brushstroke by brushstroke,
> an erasure the sky washes out in blue. (40)

Light actually creates an absence, an erasure. Yet Turner still dreams of
that tantalizing possibility of transcendence. In "Alhazen of Basra," the
speaker imagines being able to ask the eminent physicist Abu Ali Hasan
Ibn al-Haitham (965–1040) about

> the light within us,
> what shines in the mind's great repository
> of dreams, and whether he's studied the deep shadows
> daylight brings, how light defines us. (39)

As the central conflict in the collection continues to develop, Turner wonders whether it is possible to reconcile the blinding light outside (which defines his life as a soldier) with the desire for illumination within (which he
seeks as a poet).

One of the key poems in this third section is "2000 lbs," a story about
the effects of an explosion that echoes Yehuda Amichai's "The Diameter of
the Bomb." Amichai shows how a bomb's detonation includes "the entire
world in the circle," and Turner does the same without saying so explicitly.
Instead he creates a series of affecting portraits. Throughout the collection,
Turner frequently assumes both American and Iraqi points of view to tell
his stories, and here he uses that device to describe a bomb detonating in
Ashur Square, Mosul. Six people immediately affected by the blast experience the confluence of light and clarity with force, heat, and confusion. A
man named Sefwan thinks of a summer spent with a lost love, and how
the years go by

> light as grain, bright
> as the streets concussion of metal, shrapnel

> traveling at the speed of sound to open him up
> in blood and shock, a man whose last thoughts
> are of love and wreckage, with no one there
> to whisper him gone. (42)

Sgt. Ledouix of the National Guard, who will "bleed to death in minutes" rather than die instantly, is struck by the "strange / beauty, the shine of light on the broken," and finds that the silence after his eardrums rupture "lends the world a certain calm" (43). Rasheed, who bicycles by a bridal shop with Sefa,

> glimpses the sidewalk reflections
> in the storefront glass, men and women
> walking and talking, or not, an instant
> of clarity, just before each of them shatters
> under the detonation's wave. (43)

Lt. Jackson stares at his missing hands before he blacks out; an old woman cradles her dying grandson. And the man who triggers the bomb "is obliterated at the epicenter, / he is everywhere, he is of all things," and is "the surge of blood / searching for light and color" (45). The survivors wander the wreckage, confused and comforting one another, "speaking *habib* softly." Moments of clarity and calm are possible here, but they occur immediately before or simultaneously with moments of extreme destruction and death. The light and concussion are so strong and sudden as to be obliterating. Love and wreckage are intertwined, each made sharper by the other.

Turner's depiction of the pain of both American soldiers and Iraqis is evenhanded—everyone is vulnerable to force. That force is unpredictable, and in this way Turner reflects the nature of the war in Iraq. There is no easily identifiable enemy, nor even a single enemy fighting as a guerrilla force and blending in with the civilian population, as there was in the Vietnam War. Here, a complex web of factions fight the Americans and each other, using both conventional weapons as well as IEDs and suicide bombers. Turner doesn't pretend to explain the political or social motivations of the people in his poems, but he does emphasize the universal experience of emotions like loss, love, and pain in such an environment.

Hooks describes the young men she watches consuming and forgetting their "exotic" sexual partners, but though Turner seems to enjoy taking Iraq in, he does so with respect rather than the carelessness hooks describes—he watches, studies, considers, empathizes. The clarity of his writing comes from this desire to cross boundaries between people, nations, and ways of seeing. That possibility is truly illuminating. Yet as the collection progresses, the viability of boundary crossing as a sustainable or even productive practice becomes increasingly suspect. Moments of clarity are inextricable from moments of destruction, and light that illuminates can also blind. The penultimate poem in Section III foreshadows the exploration of this failure of possibility that Turner continues in the final section of the book. In "Dreams from the Malaria Pills (Turner)," the speaker dreams of bombs, bandages, and limbs washing up on shore, along with pages from the Qur'an and the Bible, "their bindings stripped loose, their ink / blurred into the sea" (46). If there are people crying, "wading out into the surf to carry it all / back in, then he hasn't seen them yet."

Turner notes in one of his interviews that all the dreams he writes about really happened, and are written down "nearly verbatim" (Mahler 98). If so, it is telling that in this third and final dream induced by malaria pills, a dream he ascribes to himself, Turner laments the cultural wreckage of war, and grieves over the lack of concern that wreckage creates. Turner assumes so many different perspectives and points of view in his poems that he would seem to highlight how easy it is to step into someone else's shoes, to see the thoughts and feelings that everyone has in common. But he assumes those different perspectives as a poet. As a soldier, he wears the uniform of one nation at war with another. One part of his identity mourns the work of the other, and the two are perhaps irreconcilable. Beginning in 2007, Turner has participated in a blog project for the *New York Times* called "Home Fires," which follows a number of Iraq War veterans as they return to life in the States. He writes there that he thinks often and painfully about the civilians in Iraq. "I have passed by so many on the streets of Baghdad and the streets of Mosul," he remembers. "I wonder where they are now. I wonder if I'll ever be able to walk those same streets without desert fatigues and an M-4 in my hands. There is culpability in my hands that I can never remove" ("Mountains of the Moon").

The first poem in Section IV makes clear this sense of loss and failed possibility. *"Mihrab"* (Arabic for "gateway to paradise") notes that long ago, the Garden of Eden blossomed in this place,

> and this is all that remains,
> wind scorpions and dust, crow-like jays
> cawing their raspy throats in memory
> of a song. (51)

What was once sustaining is now "a ghost of beauty," though it does linger on in memory and afterimage. That loss is present, as something that once was:

> If I say the desert is an afterimage,
> that birds serenade us, that the moon
> is the heart of God shining in heaven,
> that if there is a heaven it is
> so deep within us we are overgrown,
> that the day brings only a stripping of leaves
> and by sundown we are exhausted,
> then let it be, because if there is a definition
> in the absence of light,
> and if a ghost can wander amazed
> through the days of its life, then it is me,
> here in the Garden of Eden,
> where it is impossible to let go
> of what we love and what we've lost,
> here, where the breath of God is our own.

This stanza of the poem is a conditional statement about the speaker's own claims. If he says that what he sees is an afterimage—a blinding absence, seared upon the eye—and if heaven exists as something buried and impossible to excavate, then, he urges, "let it be." This is perhaps less a godlike order to make things the way he demands than a plea for a sympathetic audience, a patient listener who will let him continue the story. Do this, he says, because if there can be such a thing as a present absence—light that is not light, a wandering ghost—then that present absence is the speaker himself, in the Garden of Eden that is also gone. Turner's conflicting identities are collapsing in on themselves. He is made too much of what he loves and what he has lost.

The American and Iraqi texts in which Turner roots his poetry may be lovely, but in the end, he questions humanity's ability to hear and act on what those texts have to say. "Gilgamesh, in Fossil Relief" asserts that history is "a cloudy mirror made of dirt / and bone and ruin" (53). Questions about the love and loss that one is made of must be answered

> by war and famine and pestilence, and again
> by touch and kiss, because each age must learn
> *This is the path of the sun's journey by night.*

This truth cannot be effectively communicated and thus must be always rediscovered in dark and unseen places. The sun is real—it exists—but it travels through darkness, and will not consistently offer illumination. Likewise, "Ferris Wheel" insists that the "history books will get it wrong" about the search for survivors and bodies from a boat accident (54, 55). As light fails, so does language and communication. In this last section, things fall apart. It should "nightmare you" to kill, reads "Sadiq," should render you desolate and despairing, regardless of your beliefs or the rightness of your anger. "It should break your heart to kill" (56). The implication, of course, is that it doesn't, at least not always. Even as "Last Night's Dream" features a lover kissing "Arabic into my skin and I understand / every word of it," this "geography of pleasure" is also marked by destruction, grenades that mark the moment of penetration and an orgasm that "destroys a nation" (58).

Like "16 Iraqi Policemen" and "2000 lbs.," "9-Line Medevac" describes the wreckage of an explosive encounter, and dwells on the inability of language to capture and communicate the truths of such destruction. The speaker is calling in a medical evacuation for those injured in the blast, and "9-line medevac" refers to the standard procedure for doing so. One submits nine pieces of information, each one a different fact needed to facilitate the pickup, such as the exact location of the site and its security level, the number of patients and the severity of their injuries, and any special equipment that is required. In the poem, the voice on the radio asks for these pieces of information in sequence, and Turner gives us both the speaker's brief verbal responses as well as the words he would like to say, but can't.

The voice asks for the location of the blast, and the speaker responds with a ten-digit grid. He thinks, however, that although he can "name this spot" he "cannot make it real," perhaps because he is "too eager to romanticize the land and maybe even what's happening, though there's nothing romantic about this" (61). His statement that there are two patients *"urgent surgical"* doesn't communicate the particulars of these individuals or their injuries. Neither does his answer about required special equipment reflect the need for someone who knows how to treat "that drifting of the mind into the fizzling lights." Security? "No one knows who the enemy is" (63). Method of marking the site? "How best do you mark a place of loss and pain?" Patient's nationality? Does that matter? If they die here, "this land of confluence and heat will become their nation." Turner would wish for a common nation defined by love, perhaps, but the reality is very different.

How *do* you mark a site of loss and pain? All war writers ask and answer this question, and Turner answers as paradoxically as many others. The speaker who returns to America in "Night in Blue" asserts that "I have no words to speak of war" (64). In the end, everything goes "To Sand," the final poem in the book. To sand go "[e]ach finned mortar, spinning in light, / Each star cluster, bursting above" along with the reticles of the brain, minarets, sludge from sewers.

> To sand
> each head of cabbage unravels its leaves
> the way dreams burn in the oilfires of night. (66)

Turner's reactions to the consequences of war are intriguing and complex, though even so his poetry echoes phrases like "There it is" and "It don't mean nothin'"—in content if not form—in its struggle to convey an absence or lack that is paradoxically full and rich with pain and lost potential.

Turner's book ends on an unmistakable note of loss. Dreams are burning, and the light they give off is unearthly and dreadful. Everything is consumed by war. If Crawford takes in nothing of Iraq and empties himself out until he is a hollow shell, Turner takes in so much that he is full to bursting. The light and concussion of roadside bombs and the pressure of desert heat are blinding and destructive outside, but those explosions also detonate internally. Turner, more than almost any other war writer, appreciates the beauty and history of the country to which he has been sent, and not merely as a site for exoticized desire. He does give us sensual vignettes of local life, but his earnest curiosity is obvious—his is not a condescending interest. Yet his understanding and empathy, enacted on both the cultural and individual levels, make his role as a soldier fighting a war unbearable. It renders him both humane and inhuman.

The guilt that Turner feels may be individually unbearable but, he argues, it is also nationally necessary. In "Home Fires," he echoes Holmes: "If we learn who the dead are and what they were like, if we allow the dead their own unique humanity, we risk the possibility of being overwhelmed by loss. I believe that, as a country which has initiated war, we have no right to do otherwise" ("Verses in Wartime, Part 2"). War consumers lives, communities, property, security, and the individuals fighting the war. The loss, on all sides, is overwhelming. Even when pushed down deep, it returns. Turner describes receiving an e-mail from his former rifleman, on his second tour in Iraq, who tells him about a grenade that exploded directly in front of him. "They tell him the shrapnel now lodged in his hand will be absorbed by his body," Turner says. "But late some night years from now, he may realize it has worked its way up through the surface of his skin—that grenade might reveal itself once more" ("The War in Present Tense"). Grenades of all kinds often do.

Dying from Consumption

Encountering the Other is a dangerous business. And the real danger, as hinted at by Crawford and more explicitly stated by Turner, lies in the recognition of the loss, death, and destruction that is the inevitable result of war and of the soldier's presence. In the end, Crawford mourns only his own life, too far beyond considerations of the Iraqis to even really see them. Turner, in contrast, delights in and takes in the history, landscape, and artistic culture of Iraq, but he also takes in that destruction, the final Other that is the loss of all things in death. Then, like Crawford, he watches as the self is also consumed. The final image in each book is of dreams burning up and disappearing into nothing.

But those dreams still exist, if only on the page. Crawford begins by stating his intention to "make people aware, if only for one glimmering moment, of what war is really like" (xiii–xiv). Crawford can tell a good story, but of all the literary works that have thus far taken the Persian Gulf War or the Iraq War as their subject, Turner's *Here, Bullet* perhaps has the best chance to become a classic, a representative artistic work of the period. Since its publication in 2005 Turner has won a number of literary awards and become known as a "war poet," a designation either validating or irksome, depending on how you look at it. Turner writes in "Home Fires" that after *Here, Bullet* was published, he intended to go on and write about subjects other than war, to "focus on expanding my own possibilities on the page" ("Verses in Wartime, Part 2"). Then his old unit returned to Iraq, and sent him e-mails about their experiences during the fifteen-month deployment. "This war felt as if it were surfacing in my everyday life," he explains. "I was slow to recognize it at first." The Iraq War, he thinks, "doesn't often seem to exist in America." And so he sets himself a new project, to create an "imaginative bridgework" that will link America and Iraq by "bring[ing] Americans into the dusty streets of Iraq [and bringing] Iraqis into American cities and into our homes." His second book of poetry, *Phantom Noise,* was published in April 2010, and offers vignettes of the war like "Al-A'imma Bridge," where hundreds of Iraqis died or were injured when panic over a possible suicide bomber broke out among a crowd of worshippers in 2005. Other poems portray experiences of an American childhood or of postwar trauma and recovery, evidence of Turner's wish to make connections between different human lives.[2] Turner also provides a positive blurb for the excellent poetry collection titled *Flowers of Flame: Unheard Voices of Iraq* (ed. Billy Collins), in which several poets mentioned in this study appear. "We need the poetry of the Iraqi people," he writes. "Through war our two countries have become intimately wedded."

Turner, it seems, can't give up the desire—or, perhaps, the imperative— to cross boundaries, to blur the categorizations of nation and ethnicity in order to facilitate simple human awareness. He calls the idea "a surreal move," and "one that I'm still working on," but work he does. In late 2007, he writes a "Requiem for the Last American Soldier to Die in Iraq." "What will the name be?" he wonders. "Anthony. Lynette. Fernando. Paula. Joshua. Letitia. Roger." He wants other Americans to wonder too, to care. That last soldier's death will be both a devastation and a triumph, a moment of destruction that also marks the end of conflict, a loss that means there will be no more loss. This mourning for a death that signals the end of a war evokes the elusive transcendence that lurks in all of Turner's work—seductive, just out of reach, and costly. Once again, he writes about the merging of life and death, lightness and weight, past and future—of transcendence and inevitable obliteration:

> Maybe, just maybe, as I stand here in the quiet moonlight of Vermont, the American who will one day be the very last American soldier to die in Iraq—maybe that soldier is doing a night jump in Ft. Bragg, N.C. Each parachute opens its canopy over the darkness below—the wind an exhilaration, a cold rush of adrenaline, the jump an exercise in being fully alive and in the moment, a way of learning how it feels to fall within the rain, the way rain itself falls, to be a part of it all, the earth's gravity pulling with its inexorable embrace.

One of U.S.

Combat Trauma on Film in Alive Day Memories *and* In the Valley of Elah

The experience of war doesn't always end after the soldier returns home. The life of a veteran is different both from the life of a soldier and from that of a civilian, although the social and political acknowledgement of that difference is by no means a given. The years during and after the Vietnam War brought the figure of the veteran, and in particular the physically disabled veteran, into the public eye in new ways. Popular representations like *Coming Home* (1978), *The Deer Hunter* (1978), and Ron Kovic's best-selling autobiography *Born on the Fourth of July* (1976), which was adapted for the screen in 1989, told stories about disabled vets that were both compelling and sympathetic. Since that time our understanding of the physically and mentally traumatic effects of war has continued to grow, yet the result of that understanding is not always the appropriate or even adequate availability of treatment. Physically disabled veterans, for instance, have become much more socially and politically visible, yet during the Iraq War the resources for their rehabilitation have been revealed to be scandalously lacking. In February 2007 Dana Priest and Ann

Hull of the *Washington Post* published a special report on the Walter Reed Army Medical Center that described the facility as overcrowded and bureaucratically bogged down, as critically injured veterans struggled for even the most basic medical care. Psychological care for veterans is also much needed but often deficient. A study by the RAND Corporation, released in April 2008, revealed that nearly 20 percent of soldiers returning from Iraq or Afghanistan suffered from Post-Traumatic Stress Disorder or major depression. Slightly more than half of those soldiers seek help for their symptoms; others fear that acknowledging the problem would hurt their careers. But even among those who do, only about half of that number receive help that researchers consider "minimally adequate" for their illnesses ("One in Five").

Trauma generally, and physical disability in particular, are often discussed with reference to the tropes of vision or visibility. How much damage is or is not seen? What exists in or out of the "public eye"? How do these bodies and identities function as objects of the non-traumatized and non-disabled gaze? Appropriately, given this connection to vision, these aspects of the war (and post-war) experience have been explored on-screen. Among a number of films in 2007 dealing with the Iraq War, HBO's documentary *Alive Day Memories: Home From Iraq* and Paul Haggis's *In the Valley of Elah* both place physical and mental trauma and the homecomings they engender in the glare of the spotlight. In *Alive Day,* this glare is literal, as James Gandolfini interviews ten veterans whose disabilities range from triple amputation to severe traumatic brain injury and are shown unveiled by dim lighting, camera angles, or concealing clothing. *Elah* follows a father's quest to uncover the circumstances of the death of his son, who was killed while AWOL in America. As the film progresses, the father pieces together fragments of a portrait of combat trauma and its aftermath that is finally rendered tragically clear.

These soldiers' stories emphasize their access to technology both during and after war, in the form of sophisticated prostheses as well as digital media. These technologies carry the promise of transcendence—theoretically, one can communicate easily with loved ones by sending messages, pictures, and e-mail, thus bridging the long distance between the war front and the home front, or make oneself whole again with artificial limbs that allow for mobility and independence. (The idea that anyone, traumatized or not, can ever achieve "wholeness" or "normality" has been critiqued by disability scholars like Lennard Davis; nonetheless, the desire for that status is still a common element in these kinds of personal narratives.) These two films, however, demonstrate the inevitable difficulties of healing minds and bodies that have been fragmented by war. Technology isn't always the answer for the self—though it may be, as it turns out, for the story. In both films soldiers' use of digital technologies is a prominent narrative element, and those soldiers' images and videos of the war experience "fill in the gaps," so to speak, in these stories of trauma, allowing the audience to see what might have been previously hidden.

For these filmmakers, purporting to tell the whole story, to be able to show us everything, is a necessary device that serves their larger purpose. *Alive Day* and *Elah* suggest that the causes and effects of wartime trauma not only *can* be seen, but *must* be seen—not cloaked, veiled, or suppressed, as they so often are. We have to look at the whole story here so that we can see that *we* are not whole, individually or collectively. War shatters us, and leaves the national body and mind in fragments.

Although film and digital media have certainly changed the way we see the consequences of war, the representation of those consequences has a long history. Soldiers in Homer's *Iliad* and *Odyssey* tend to die quickly from their wounds (unless healed by the balm of a god or goddess), but Homer does give us one memorable portrait of a wounded warrior. Book II of the *Iliad* briefly mentions Philoctetes in the catalog of ships. This "great archer" now

> lay in pain on an island,
> Sacred Lemnos, where the Achaeans stranded him,
> Afflicted with a wound from a deadly snake.
> He lay there in anguish. (II.830–35)

In his tragedy *Philoctetes,* Sophocles tells the story of this warrior, who is bitten on the foot by a snake, a wound that becomes infected and thus hurts terribly and smells even worse. Odysseus leaves him on the island so that the army may travel on to fight the Trojan War. Nine years later, Odysseus learns that the Greeks will not win the war without the arrows bestowed upon Philoctetes by Heracles, and so returns to Lemnos to find him. They both go back to Troy, where Philoctetes's wound is finally healed. His story is taken up in other ancient and modern representations as well; Ovid includes Philoctetes in the *Metamorphoses,* and artists such as Pierre-Paul Prud'hon and James Barry depict the wounded warrior in portraits. Martha Edwards has argued that the myth illustrates "several realities of the plight of the disabled veteran in the ancient world," particularly the lack of "codified practice" (55). That is, it's important to remember that the Greeks didn't have Veterans Administration hospitals, a Department of Veterans' Affairs, or a Veterans Day holiday.

Clearly, the status of the veteran has changed a great deal, most dramatically in the twentieth century. David Gerber notes that especially during the years of World War I, World War II, and the Vietnam War, large numbers of civilians were conscripted into the military, which made the realities of military service and the effects of battle more widely known. Medical breakthroughs also made it easier to save lives on the battlefield, which resulted in more veterans coming home with severe injuries. Perhaps the most significant development, however, is that physically disabled veterans became "a major project of the modern state." That project, as well as veterans' activism to create and enhance the attendant programs, brought the veterans increasingly into the public gaze, a spotlight from which they were often previously shunned. "If the visibility of the disabled generally, and for our purposes disabled veterans specifically, has increased in this century," says Gerber, "so, too, has our ability to *see* them—to conceive of the meanings and consequences of disability and to understand the lived experiences of people with disabilities in the context of both war and peace" ("Introduction" 3). In Gerber's view, seeing the effects of trauma is a necessary precedent for understanding and ultimately supporting disabled veterans' efforts to gain equal treatment.

Although stereotypes certainly remain, disabled veterans have indeed been more widely and variously represented both politically and artistically in the years since the Vietnam War, and as Gerber notes, both that visibility and veterans' activism has had positive and significant effects on the disabled population generally. Lennard Davis has argued that this growing awareness of disability has changed the way we think about the human body and identity overall. According to Davis, we are now more likely to realize that "difference is what all of us have in common. That identity is not fixed but malleable. That technology is not separate but part of the body. That dependence, not individual independence, is the rule. There is no single clockmaker who made the uniform clock on the human body" (26–27).

And so the status of disability in recent years as both visible and *seen* has led to encouraging developments in social policy, public attitudes, and even critical notions of the body and identity, according to Gerber and Davis. *Alive Day* and *In the Valley of Elah* also emphasize this need to see the traumatic physical and mental effects of war. But what we are invited to see—in fact, what the films insist we see—does not constitute progress. Often "the disabled veteran as heroic symbol has been a necessary ideological tool of the modern state in advancing its interests and goals" (Gerber, "Disabled Veterans" 18). These films, however, criticize the state's engagement in the Iraq War, and depict the soldiers' trauma as an unnecessary rather than necessary sacrifice. And in the aftermath of trauma, the most sophisticated technology in the world can't always reverse the effects of that fragmentation.

The Total Gaze

On 19 June 2004, First Lieutenant Dawn Halfaker was in Baqubah, Iraq, when she took a direct hit from an RPG. She knew the injury was serious, and tried not to look. "If I didn't see it, if I didn't think about it," she says, "then it didn't exist." Halfaker's right arm and shoulder were amputated as a result of her injuries, and she appears as one of the ten veterans in *Alive Day*. It's hard for her to look, because looking means acknowledging the reality of a serious injury and the resulting changes in her life and sense of herself. It is perhaps easier for the audience to look. David Hevey has argued that representations of the disabled body become the "voyeuristic property of the non-disabled gaze" (377), and Lennard Davis has noted how disabled characters in narratives often exist "for" the non-disabled, "to help them develop sympathy, empathy, or as a counterbalance to some issue in the life of the 'normal' character'" (45). And yet Ginia Bellafante, in reviewing the film, says that *Alive Day* "permits a voyeurism that never feels exploitative," perhaps because it avoids presenting the veterans as uncomplicated or stereotypical. Looking here is not supposed to be titillating, nor does *Alive Day* encourage a uniform response to the stories of these quite different lives.

In his book *Freaks: Myths and Images of the Secret Self,* Leslie Fiedler says that the non-normative body "stirs both supernatural terror and natural sympathy," because unlike storybook monsters, he is "one of us, the human child of human parents, however altered by forces we do not quite understand into something mythic and mysterious" (24). Fiedler, however, adds that this is true of "no mere cripple"—rather, freaks by birth, not accident. I wonder, though, what Fiedler would think of *Alive Day*, which in several cases invites us to watch insurgent-released video of the very IED explosions and roadside bombs that caused the disabilities set in the spotlight. No myth, certainly, but these forces can be as capricious and incomprehensible—if not more so—than those Fiedler has in mind. *Alive Day* presents disability as a permeable category. "[A]nyone can become disabled," Davis notes reasonably, "and in fact, most people will develop impairments with age" (36). For combat soldiers, the risk is simply higher. If the spectacle of these veterans evokes sympathy as well as terror, it is perhaps a terror that is less supernatural than uncomfortably real.

Halfaker felt that if she didn't look at her injury, then it wouldn't be real. Not seeing it meant not having to acknowledge its existence. In a sense, her comment provides a conceit for *Alive Day* as a whole. The film insists that we shouldn't feel guilty for looking, but for *refusing* to look—that we should look and see what is so often hidden, and stop pretending that the Iraq War hasn't caused devastating losses. The film brings to bear a number of narrative resources, including pre-traumatic self-representations in photos and home videos, stories and accompanying video of the violent event that caused the injury or injuries, photos of hospitals and recovery centers, filmed comments about the choice and use of a prosthesis, and final assessments of life and identity as they are now experienced. *Alive Day* begins by immediately alerting the viewer to these resources: "The following film includes personal video, news coverage and footage released by insurgents." The intertitles that follow provide the historical, military, and medical context of the documentary:

> A new generation
> of veterans is
> returning from Iraq
> For the first time
> in American history,
> 90% of the wounded

survive their injuries
But a greater percentage
of these men and women
are coming home from Iraq
with amputations,
traumatic brain injuries
and severe
post-traumatic stress

Finally, the opening intertitles claim that these veterans' lives are defined by two days: their birthday and their alive day. One's alive day, the film explains, is the day a soldier experienced—and survived—a potentially or nearly fatal incident in Iraq.

The next shots literally set the stage, and show the spare set in which the interviews will be conducted. We see the lights, cameras, and a clapboard, and hear the voices of the crew in the background. We are reminded that we are watching—because watching is, after all, the point. Intercut with shots of James Gandolfini welcoming, shaking hands with, and hugging some of the veterans are short clips of wounded soldiers being evacuated from combat and comments from those veterans about the experience of

Figure 5. In the stripped-down set of *Alive Day Memories: Home from Iraq* (HBO Films, 2007), Bryan Anderson speaks with James Gandolfini.

almost dying. The intertitles then continue, formally marking the film's beginning and emphasizing these veterans' status as survivors:

> James Gandolfini
> spoke with ten
> young men and women
> who have survived
> the war in Iraq
> These are their stories
> ALIVE DAY MEMORIES
> Home from Iraq

The first interview segment is illustrative of the approach the film takes to telling these stories, and a good example generally of a soldier's thwarted desire for technological transcendence. An intertitle introduces Army Sgt. Bryan Anderson, lists his age (25), his military affiliation, and the date of his alive day. First, we see a clip from a home video showing him in an Army boxing match some time before he was injured. An announcer calls him into the ring, noting that he is "standing about five foot four, 125 pounds soaking wet." We root for the little guy, as he gets in a few good punches and then reacts to the cheering of the crowd. The film cuts from this glimpse of his life before his disability to his interview. "Why don't you tell me what happened?" Gandolfini asks from offscreen. (As he is for much of the film, Gandolfini as host and interviewer is only minimally seen and heard. His popular and critically lauded HBO series *The Sopranos* ended in June 2007, and *Alive Day* premiered on the heels of that acclaim in September of the same year. Gandolfini's celebrity enabled him to produce *Alive Day,* yet during the film he is quiet and mostly offscreen, presumably to prevent his fame and his imposing physical presence from distracting our gaze from its intended object, the veterans.)

Anderson, framed in a close-up of his head and shoulders, then tells the story of his alive day. He was driving a Humvee and making idle chatter with his team leader, joking together so that they wouldn't have to be scared. We see a clip of this chatter, courtesy of a digital camera that was embedded in the Humvee. Anderson continues: "I was smoking, I had my left hand on the steering wheel, and then the bomb went off." The film cuts again to what is labeled as an "insurgent released video" that shows a wide shot of a busy road, Humvees coming and going. Then, in the center of the screen, a large explosion lights everything up, so bright that it washes out the image.

Anderson returns, describing his reaction to the blast, and as he speaks, the film cuts to the first long shot of Anderson. We see him and Gandolfini speaking, framed by boom mikes and a few crew members, and we see for the first time that both of his legs have been amputated above the knee. He continues his story, further describing the aftermath of his injury, and his eventual realization that he was missing his left hand and both his legs. We see still photos of Anderson in the hospital and walking on prosthetic legs, and then Anderson moves the material of his cargo shorts aside to allow the camera an extreme close-up of his amputations, which he describes. He also shows and describes his prosthetic hand, before an intertitle announces that Anderson underwent forty operations and spent thirteen months in the Walter Reed Army Medical Center. Anderson remarks that if he had lost his right hand as well, he would consider his situation to be much worse, but emphasizes that he still has the ability to perform basic functions. As if to counter the optimism of this claim, the clip that follows is a 1999 video of Anderson performing a difficult gymnastics floor routine and receiving a score of 9.0. Finally, Anderson returns in close-up remarking on the perversity of celebrating one's alive day, as is standard at Walter Reed. "I can see their point," he notes generously, "but we're sitting here celebrating the worst day of my life." At that, the film once again shows the video of the explosive blast filling up the screen before moving on to introduce the next veteran.

The audience is privy to Anderson's "complete" narrative. In a combination of moving and still images, supplemented by his narration, we get to see Anderson's life before, after, and even during the traumatic injury that resulted in his disability. This is, of course, hardly a truly complete portrait of Anderson, or even a terribly detailed one, but in its ability to present this unprecedented variety of visual material *Alive Day* claims a kind of 360-degree gaze, a seemingly total view of the costs of war. The camera is everywhere, and it is not shy—though the segment delays revealing Anderson's amputations, it then lingers on them closely. The shock of seeing the effects of such an extreme injury is ameliorated somewhat by Anderson's plucky attitude, but the placement of the gymnastics clip reminds viewers not to take his loss lightly.

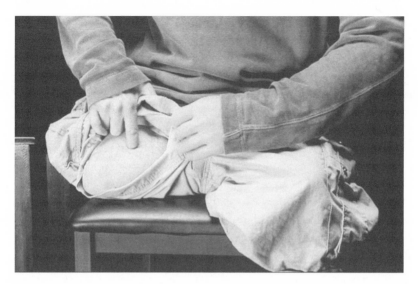

Figure 6. During his interview with James Gandolfini in *Alive Day Memories: Home from Iraq* (HBO Films, 2007) Bryan Anderson reveals his amputations.

In addition to his appearance in *Alive Day,* Anderson has been featured twice in *Esquire.* He appears on the January 2007 cover, holding his Purple Heart, and is interviewed by Brian Mockenhaupt for a story called "What I've Learned." Then in March 2008, Mockenhaupt revisited his subject for the feature "Rebuilding Bryan Anderson." "Bryan Anderson's legs keep falling off," notes that article's teaser, striking a different tone than the title (186). Veterans like Anderson are pushing prosthetics technology to greater and greater advances, but despite the incredible leaps in science and engineering, living life with a prosthetic—let alone three—is no cakewalk. "[N]ormalcy remains elusive," writes Mockenhaupt, in part because the "performance [of the technology] lags far behind expectation" (186, 189). As driven as Anderson is to skateboard, jet ski, golf, and rock climb, he also often feels like "half a person" who complains that currently available wheelchairs look "so handicapped, it's ridiculous" (198, 190). The best artificial limbs in the world, ones with powerful motors and processors that are light and responsive, aren't much help if they won't stay on.

The story of the second soldier interviewed in *Alive Day* is different, and reminds the audience of the variety of disabilities possible for those in war. "Especially traumatic, visible injuries have tended to become the primary way in which the general population of disabled veterans often seems to have been conceived in the minds of experts, artists, and the general citizenry," notes Gerber ("Introduction" 2). Amputees like Anderson have historically received much more attention than veterans with other disabilities, and have tended to become representative of all disabled veterans. "The drama of their injury crowds out everything else about them, and about others, with different, less visible injuries or illnesses" (2). And so *Alive Day* urges us to look more closely at people like Anderson, but also at people like Sgt. Eddie Ryan. Ryan was shot twice in the head while in Iraq and sustained a severe traumatic brain injury. Because of his difficulties communicating, he appears with his mother, who tells his story emotionally. We are invited to consider the contrast between a home video of Ryan in Iraq, dancing wildly and comically with a fellow soldier, and the physically and communicatively challenged young man in the interview with severe scarring visible on his shorn scalp.

Lest this lead us to assume that women like Ryan's mother will only appear in auxiliary capacities here, the two veterans who follow Ryan are, in fact, women. Disabled female veterans are seldom seen in popular representations or otherwise, and Gerber notes that they have been neglected both by the governments they have served and by historians, who have written very little about their experiences ("Introduction" 1). *Alive Day* does not include any intertitles commenting on these soldiers' gender, perhaps because neither woman includes that consideration as part of her narrative. Their interviews are striking, however, precisely because these women constitute a growing number of both the disabled and veteran communities.

First Lt. Dawn Halfaker's segment begins with her reflections on the sky in Iraq, and the sensations of night in the desert. She is somber and articulate as she recounts being shot in the shoulder with an RPG, after which her right arm and shoulder were amputated. As noted above, she strongly resisted seeing her injury and receiving visual confirmation of its severity: "I was very scared to look at my own amputation," she says. "I was very scared to know what it looked like." *Alive Day* validates this fear by showing a still photo of her injury, interrupting her interview just long enough for viewers to take in the gruesome damage. Halfaker continues: "because if I looked at it then I sort of acknowledged it. And for a while initially I didn't want to. You know, if I didn't see it, if I didn't think about

it, then it didn't exist." For Halfaker, vision, rather than sensation or function, is the vehicle of truth here. Seeing is believing, but that belief is one
she's not quite ready for.

Nonetheless, she begins physical therapy, and is adamant in her opinions about what constitutes an appropriate prosthetic. "This arm actually
was one of a kind," she explains, picking up her current prosthesis to show
to Gandolfini and the audience. Her artificial limb is a lifelike mold, in
contrast with Anderson's, which sports a maroon and black pattern on the
arm. "I think there's now a few others," she adds. "But I was not happy
with the prosthesis that they gave me at Walter Reed. I said I don't want
to look like a robot and I don't want to wear a frickin' hook." Halfaker
refused to train on such prostheses, "wanted nothing to do with it." She
has strong opinions, and isn't afraid to voice them. But the shift in her
sense of identity has been a difficult one, and she speaks about worrying
that her artificial limb would be noticed in public, that it wouldn't pass as
real. Halfaker had previously been a soldier who enjoyed leading others
and being "put to the test," but after her injury is forced to realize that she
has become quite different. "I was an amputee from the war," she realizes
with dismay, just like the men with missing legs and other limbs. Even
though she is a young, attractive, and competent woman, she is now "one
of them," as she puts it. For her, it is not a desirable sense of community.
She has become Other.

Near the end of her interview, she reflects on her hopes for marriage
and children, noting in somewhat contradictory fashion that she realizes
"it has nothing to do with whether or not I'm an amputee," but also that
she hopes her children will love her for who she is, despite her injuries.
Then, suddenly, she tears up, and at Gandolfini's prompting, she adds that
she realized she won't be able to pick up a child with both arms. "But I
hope they still love me," she says sadly. "I hope I'll still be a good parent.
What can you do."[1] Her final expression is pensive, followed by an intertitle noting that the percentage of amputees returning from Iraq is the
highest since the Civil War.

Halfaker describes an alienation from the self—seeing the self as Other,
despite being "rebuilt" with a realistic prosthesis—that is echoed by a later
interview with Cpl. Jonathan Bartlett. Bartlett speaks rapidly and cheer-
ily, but his description of what it was like in rehab after having both legs
amputated is a searing one. "Every time I looked into that mirror of what

I used to be, of what I was, I saw somebody trying to stand up," he says. "And there was all this blood and pain and he couldn't stand up, he couldn't *do* anything; he'd just lie there and scream." On *Alive Day*'s website, Bartlett's essay about this experience is titled "Broken Mirror." "I don't even feel like the same man," he writes. "Last I slept I was a soldier but when I awoke I am little more than a cripple." Like Halfaker, despite a naturally positive attitude, Bartlett has great difficulty coming to terms with this startlingly different image of himself, and the painful break from the person he was before. Seeing reveals the truth, and the truth is ugly. "It was bad," he concludes in his interview. Certainly identity is malleable, rather than fixed, as Davis notes, but the experience of such an abrupt and painful change is traumatic.

Anderson, Halfaker, and Bartlett all describe their challenges with bravery and resolution, but an interview with Pvt. Dexter Pitts reveals outright despair. A large African-American man wearing a sleeveless Army T-shirt, dog tags, and with visible scarring on his right arm, Pitts looks physically healthy, but reveals his ongoing struggles with severe Post-Traumatic Stress Disorder. *Alive Day* places Pitts mid-film, and by including him rightly claims PTSD, or mental trauma, as a combat disability as deserving of attention and care as those suffered by the other veterans, even though it is less immediately visible. For Pitts, the world now seems a "dark place," and he can't seem to feel welcome in the civilian world. "I'm a nice, lovable guy," he says, but things have changed for him. "I've done some mean things to kids over there that I had to do." The result is a kind of mental break, and those events keep coming back. "In bed, everything plays over and over," like a movie he can't stop. Mental trauma is often described as a personal narrative that gets stuck, like a skipping record, with intrusive images and traumatic scenes that the mind simply can't let go. As Judith Herman notes in her seminal *Trauma and Recovery,* the healing process often works as narrative reconstruction, as the survivor learns how to tell his or her story once again. Before that happens, the traumatic memory is wordless and static. "It does not develop or progress in time, and it does not reveal the storyteller's feelings or interpretation of events. Another therapist describes traumatic memory as a series of still snapshots or a silent movie; the role of therapy is to provide the music and the words" (175). Pitts describes his own traumatic silent movie playing "over and over" as he lies in bed. As *Alive Day* continues, with veteran after veteran telling stories of trauma tinged with hope or despair, Pitts' individual trauma, his skipping record, mirrors the national trauma of a war that goes on and on, and claims more and more victims as it does.

In telling the whole story, however, and requiring the audience to see, and see everything, *Alive Day* positions itself as a kind of therapy, one that gives meaning to that visual information with "music and words," so to speak. The film's total gaze and complete narratives can perhaps begin the process of recovery. Another veteran, Staff Sgt. Jay Wilkerson, suffers from a closed traumatic brain injury, caused by an exploding Humvee that sent shrapnel into his brain. "If you see me on the street," he notes, "I would look normal, but I'm not." In this case, seeing Wilkerson on the street is not enough, and so *Alive Day* completes the picture—it shows you enough so that you can see the truth. Film here is a kind of "second sight," revealing more than would be apparent at first glance.

As discussed in chapter 1, Anthony Swofford and Colby Buzzell describe dealing with the sense of disillusion and anger they feel as a result of their experience of war by making a display of themselves in various ways. By appearing in *Alive Day,* some of the veterans may be doing the same thing, speaking out about their experiences so that others will understand more about the risks of fighting. Cpl. Michael Jerrigan takes the notion of display a step further. Blinded in Iraq, he wears a prosthetic eye in his right socket. The left has too much scar tissue for a prosthetic, he says. Upon closer examination, the prosthetic eye looks unusual—it sparkles. It does so because it has a carat's worth of diamonds in it, which are the diamonds from his wedding band. His marriage fell apart because of his blindness, he says, and so the evidence of that broken commitment now marks the site of his war injury. The war, he says, also feels like a broken commitment. Because it's a "guerrilla war" and no one wears uniforms, you "can't tell by seeing who's who"—"*If* I could see," he adds. Uniforms would help—they would organize the visual field into more manageable categories. But, as Jerrigan notes, he can no longer see at all, and he signifies that loss (and others) with diamonds that glitter coldly, on display for others' perception and understanding. Jerrigan wants others to see and comprehend the results of his loss. After growing up on "all those Vietnam movies" that glorify war, as so many soldiers did, Jerrigan arrived in Iraq to find that "this is not glory." Now, he has dreams about killing people, which he never had before. As he puts it, "you sit there and you wake up, and you're like, whoa, what's wrong with *me*?" Jerrigan's might not be the most technologically advanced prosthesis featured in the film, but it's certainly the most striking—and it was chosen to signify his feelings of incompletion, his loss rather than his rebuilding.

Alive Day ends with a montage of the veterans thanked by Gandolfini and leaving the set, and a set of intertitles reminds the audience of the war's larger costs:

> As of August 2007,
> 27,104 military men
> and women
> have been injured
> 3,649 American troops
> have been killed on the battlefield

Finally, after a short clip of two soldiers flinching as an explosion goes off right behind them, the scene fades to black, and the images are followed by a sound montage of reporters talking about IEDs, roadside bombs, soldiers killed and wounded. Gradually, the voices are overtaken by the instrumental strains of "America the Beautiful," which increases in volume as the credits continue to roll.

Alive Day celebrates the veterans as survivors while mourning the costs of war, costs that it implies are much too high, despite some of the interview subjects' stoic resolution and access to advanced medical technologies. The series of intertitles note that war always entails loss and sacrifice, but the losses of this war are considerable and in some ways unprecedented—specifically, the numbers of soldiers returning with severe physical injuries and mental trauma. Their bodies, emotions, and narratives are put on full display, emphasizing the need for the audience of uninjured noncombatants to look, to see. And we are privileged to see "everything," the visual story of an individual before, during, and after the traumas of war. If what is most literally traumatic is the inability to put an experience into meaningful words and create an explanatory narrative, then *Alive Day* offers the work of recovery by presenting the total gaze of the disabled veteran from Iraq. Seeing and understanding this whole story, the film implies, can help show both individuals and the nation the way out of and beyond the Iraq War, past a trauma that has cost too much.

The digital images that facilitate these stories are also unprecedented. In watching, we see more than has ever been possible of war and trauma. Of course, this isn't really the whole story of these soldiers, their injuries, and their lives. It is, at best, a moving snapshot, and only the illusion of a truly complete narrative. But it's still a snapshot that challenges us. Lennard Davis has argued that the view of the disabled body can bring about a more sophisticated understanding of all bodies and all identities. "What is universal in life if there are universals," he writes, "is the experience of the limitations of the body" (241). *Alive Day* invites us to challenge our conception of the national body as well. If the national fantasy of normality is one of a nation united in purpose, healthy in body and mind, prosperous, and justified in action—a true city on a hill, a beacon of ideals on display for the world—this film presents us with stories that should also make us critique that vision, and consider the ways that we are all wounded by war.

"I Think He Could *See*"

Alive Day invites us to gaze directly at the physical and emotional costs of war as evidenced by the veterans who have suffered them, and to understand that vision challenges our notions of self and nation by showing things that have previously been veiled or unseen. *In the Valley of Elah*, according to critic A. O. Scott, does something similar. "Underneath its deceptively quiet surface is a raw, angry, earnest attempt to grasp the moral consequences of the war in Iraq, and to stare without blinking into the chasm that divides those who are fighting it from their families, their fellow citizens and one another." Also like *Alive Day*, *Elah* trains its spotlight on the trauma of war. Here, however, the focus is almost completely on emotional trauma rather than physical disability, though the effects, *Elah* suggests, can be just as damaging. War is a shattering force that affects conscience, consciousness, and community just as much as it does flesh and blood.

Alive Day begins by challenging the viewer with portraits of veterans who have been radically, often shockingly, altered by war, and as the film progresses works to make the audience feel intimately and empathetically engaged with those veterans' experience. *Elah* follows a different narrative arc, and begins by presenting a collection of ordinary, all-American characters, both soldiers and civilians. By the end of the film, *Elah* reveals those characters' limitations and the trauma that has devastated each of them. Thus *Alive Day* begins by representing difference, but works to create union and solidarity; *Elah* begins with a portrait of seeming normality, but ends by revealing difference and isolation. Both films end with a national symbol under duress—"America the Beautiful" heard in concert with the sounds of war in *Alive Day,* and in *Elah,* the image of an inverted American flag. Although the films focus on individual stories and make use of different narrative arcs, they both ultimately seek to shift our gaze from individual to national trauma. In *Elah,* the murder mystery that drives the plot ends by revealing not just a single perpetrator, but the Iraq War generally. Again, the emphasis is on being able to *see* this—and the views provided by digital technologies are critical to the story's progression.

In the Valley of Elah is based on the story of Lanny Davis, a retired Army Staff Sergeant whose son, Richard, went AWOL after returning home from a tour in Iraq. As Mark Boal reported in 2004, Davis—who spent sixteen of his twenty years in the service as a military policeman—was unsatisfied with the military's explanation of his son's status and whereabouts, and conducted an investigation himself in order to find his son. Eventually, Davis uncovered evidence of his son's brutal murder. The Lanny Davis character is played by Tommy Lee Jones in the film, a casting choice that emphasizes the character's sense of discipline and traditional masculinity. Jones, perhaps best known for his role as Woodrow Call in the television series *Lonesome Dove* (1989), tends to play characters who are laconic, no-nonsense, and know how to get the job done. His parts in films like *The Fugitive* (1993) and *Men in Black* (1997) clearly traffic in those associations, and his more recent roles in *The Three Burials of Melquiades Estrada* (2005) and *No Country for Old Men* (2007) show Jones portraying men steeped in the masculine traditions of ranching and law enforcement, respectively. In *Elah,* that masculine tradition is the military, and it informs his character deeply.

Jones plays Hank Deerfield as a man of few words but effective action. At home in Munro, Tennessee, he receives a call notifying him that not only is his son Mike back in the States, but that he is AWOL. "Soldier, if my son were back I'd sure as hell know it," he retorts. Hank immediately tries to make contact with his son by checking his e-mail messages and calling Mike's cell phone, but when those previously reliable methods fail, he decides to drive to the military base and inquire about him.

He tells his wife Joan (Susan Sarandon) that he will call her when he arrives the next day. "It's a two-day drive," she protests. His response reveals both his determination and masculine exceptionalism: "For some people." On the way, however, he does make time to stop and correct a worker from El Salvador who has mistakenly raised the United States flag upside down outside a school. Hank's eyes are sharply and critically focused on his environment—he can process information and then follow up with swift, competent action. He has a meticulous sense of propriety that is most prominently evident in his dedication to military and patriotic custom. His confidence rests both in his own abilities and in the larger order that he represents.

After arriving at the military base—the fictional Fort Rudd, New Mexico—he examines Mike's room, looking at the contents of his closet and bureau. In a drawer he finds Mike's cell phone, and despite the military's insistence that nothing be removed from the room, manages to pocket it. During his stay in a local hotel room he is careful to make his bed military style, shine his shoes, and keep his clothes neat and clean. "I *will* find him," he assures his wife on the phone.[2] Despite his efforts, however, both the military and the local police are unwilling to speak to him in any detail about his son. As a character Hank is representative of the military tradition and of law and order, but in good detective-story fashion, he will have to be willing to work outside the system as well if he wants the answers he is looking for.

The first answer he gets is not one he wanted. Mike is indeed found after a few days, though not by Hank. The local police discover pieces of his body lying in a field, scattered and burned. When a young man in uniform arrives at Hank's hotel room to give him the news, Hank stops shaving long enough to blot a cut on his throat, and, knowing all too well what the soldier must be there to say, salutes him with a look of dread and dismay. The soldier tells him that remains have been found that are likely Mike's. "Right," Hank responds tersely, though his devastation is apparent on his face. "Do you need me to identify the body?" The body has already been identified by partial fingerprints, the soldier says, and Hank pounces. "What do you mean, partial?" he asks. The young man refuses to say, and Hank explodes in the only expression of emotion acceptable for a traditional Southern man receiving truly horrible news. "I want to see his body *now*!" he demands angrily.

He wants to see; he *must* see. Lt. Kirklander, the military's representative, advises him against viewing the body, which doesn't even exist as a
body so much as a small collection of mangled, burned pieces. But Hank
is compelled. "It's the way he left this earth so I don't see as I have any
choice," he explains. Later Hank returns to the field where Mike's remains
were found with Detective Emily Sanders (Charlize Theron), in order to
see for himself the place where Mike died. There, Hank's sight is exceptional. He almost immediately sees what other investigators missed—that
Mike was likely killed on the roadside and then dragged into the grass,
thus changing the crime's jurisdiction from the military to the local police.
Witnesses reported a green car at the scene on the night of the murder, but
Hank can also see that they should be looking for a blue car, not a green
one. A blue car, he explains to Emily, would only look green parked under
the sickly yellow street light by the field. If you look carefully, you can see
the truth, and Hank seems to be on a roll.

"That's how you fight monsters," he tells Emily's young son. "You lure
them in close to you, you look them in the eye, you smack 'em down."
With a steady gaze and a strong hand, anything can be accomplished, as his
version of the story of David and Goliath emphasizes. The boy asks why
David didn't "just shoot" Goliath there in the valley of Elah (the location
of their confrontation that gives the film its title). Hank explains that they
didn't have guns back then, but goes on to say that using a gun against
someone who is challenging you to fight with a sword would be wrong.
"There are rules to combat," he insists. The boy is enchanted with this
description of strength and courage, and listens carefully as Hank tells him
how David won the battle.

As a former military man himself, Hank lives by a strict set of rules, and
he assumes those rules hold true for other men like him. When Hank and
Emily discover that Mike was arguing and fighting with his fellow soldiers
Steve Penning, Gordon Bonner, and Ennis Long on the night of his death,
he insists to Emily that the soldiers couldn't be the ones who ultimately
killed Mike. "You have not been to war so you're not going to understand
this," he says impatiently. "You do not fight beside a man and then do *that*
to him." Insults and scuffling, perhaps, but such an extreme violation or
negation of the bonds of comradeship is inconceivable to Hank. He can't
see it happening—but as the surviving soldiers offer hints of what life is

like fighting in Iraq, it becomes evident that in Iraq, seeing clearly is either a challenge or an impossibility.

Even Mike, as it is revealed, had problems. Hank speaks to several of Mike's fellow soldiers who all refer to Mike as "Doc." "It's a nickname we gave him," Steve Penning explains to Hank early in the film, and only much later does he reveal the nickname's origin. In Iraq, they arrested "a hajji who was wounded," he says, and Mike pretended he was a medic. He stuck his hand in the man's wound, and asked, does this hurt? The man screamed that it did, and Mike then put his hand in the same place, and asked again if it hurt, an action he apparently repeated several times. Given this explanation, the nickname makes sense—it refers to Mike's physical abuse of a prisoner. In moral sense, however, it makes no sense at all. A doctor, after all, is supposed to "do no harm," but that's exactly what Mike is doing here. The nickname is one of many indications that Iraq is a world turned upside down. The senselessness of these soldiers' experiences plays more a part in Mike's death than Hank is initially able to see or admit. "I don't understand any of this," Penning says later, after Bonner is found to have committed suicide. "It's fucked up, isn't it?" Speaking about Mike, Bonner himself tells Hank: "They shouldn't send heroes to places like Iraq. Everything there is fucked up." The soldiers speak of Iraq as being an absurd or irrational place, as being fucked up, all wrong.

Hank's detective skills are excellent, but he struggles to make sense of these statements about Iraq. The pieces begin to come together, however, when he decides to examine the digital images and videos Mike took while overseas. These "statements" are more revealing. After the stealing the phone from Mike's room, Hank takes it to a technician working out of the back of a van. Hank wants the phone numbers stored in the cell phone, and is initially confused when the man asks if Hank wants "the media" as well. Noting that the phone is "seriously fried" from being around "some intense heat," the man offers to pull off the videos and e-mail them to Hank for $100.[3] Throughout his search for information, Hank periodically receives and watches the garbled and pixellated videos sent to him by the technician and sifts through old photos that Mike had e-mailed him from Iraq. The film indicates that "making sense" out of the pieces of this visual narrative will be of primary importance in unraveling the mystery of Mike's death—perhaps not its immediate circumstances, but the larger cause that set everything in motion. The videos trickle in, and Hank gazes pensively at a collection of vignettes. The opening scene of *Elah* is from one of these videos. As the film begins, broken images flash onscreen and a voice shouts for Mike to "get back in the fucking vehicle." But more are forthcoming: a crowd of Iraqi children run off with Mike's "real American football," and he curses them; soldiers in a Humvee run over something; someone puts a grisly "calling card" on a burnt body; soldiers laugh while someone screams; Mike asks a wounded man where it hurts. Hank watches. He also thumbs through printouts of Mike's photos, and keeps returning to one showing a street scene in Iraq, a blue van, and some sort of object on the side of the road.

When two soldiers offer confessions of sorts near the end of the film, Hank is finally able to put it all together. The first is Penning, whom Emily forces to speak on the record despite the military's deal with the police to handle things discreetly. He sits with Emily, Hank, and Lt. Kirklander, a tape recorder on the table between them. With his blank, ordinary, all-American face framed in close-up, Penning tells the story of the night Mike died. His story is a horrible one, yet his face reveals no real emotion. The camera holds him steadily in the frame, indicating that as the mystery of Mike's death is solved, the mystery of the psychological effects of the Iraq War on young, vulnerable soldiers only gets bigger. Penning explains that on the night of Mike's death, Bonner was needling Mike about his driving skills when they were all in the car together, and that the remarks led everyone to start yelling at one another. They stopped the car and got out. "And then I look down, and I'm stabbing him," Penning says, affectless. "You? You are?" Emily asks, and Penning affirms. "Yeah...It was Bonner's idea to chop him up," he offers. "We would have buried the parts, but it was getting late and we hadn't eaten." "You were hungry," Emily adds, her face as shocked at the realization as Penning's is blank. "Starving," he emphasizes. "We stopped at the Chicken Shack." Then Penning offers his only real explanation for the crime: "I liked Mike," he insists. "We all did. But I think on another night it would have been Mike with a knife and me in the field. I think he was the smart one. *I think he could see.*" Something in Iraq clouds the vision, Penning implies, and makes life more difficult to navigate. What exactly Mike can see, however, Penning doesn't say.

The second "confession" comes from Robert Ortiz, another of Mike's fellow soldiers. Hank asks him about the photo of the street scene with the blue van, which Hank senses is significant but can't make sense of it on his own. Ortiz fills in the blanks. Soldiers have standing orders, he explains. If something gets in the way of a convoy, you don't stop, or "shitheads pop out with RPGs and kill you all dead." During their first week in Iraq, Doc (as Ortiz calls Mike) was driving, and he hit something. Mike stopped the Humvee and got out for a few moments, then got back in and drove on without a word. "Later some guy said we hit a kid," Ortiz continues. "I don't believe it. You asked me…we hit a dog. We killed a dog." His tortured face reveals barely contained emotion. Ortiz looks at the photo. "I don't know what that is," he says resolutely. "No fucking idea." Ortiz knows the truth, but literally refuses to see it. It's easier to maintain that the image makes no sense, and that there's no information to be had from it.

Yet in his denial, Ortiz has given Hank the information he needs to understand the effects of his son's life in Iraq and the causes of his death in America. In the next scene, Hank sits in his truck, and at last "sees" the incident in Iraq that had apparently haunted his son and his fellow soldiers. The blurred, pixellated, and often unintelligible bits of image and sound that he had watched on his laptop now come together in a complete and coherent narrative that the audience sees as well. Mike and another soldier yell at each other in the front seat of a Humvee. "What do I do?" Mike shouts, and the other answers, "Do not stop. Do not fucking stop!" Mike speeds up and runs over something. Mike then leaves the Humvee, and we hear the soldier shouting the same words we hear as the film begins: "Get back in the fucking vehicle Mike! Mike!" Mike is standing in the street and looking at the scene. A blue van is parked on the left side of the road, and a small inert mass lies on the right. It is, we are now to understand, the body of a child. The camera frames Mike's blank, ordinary, all-American face as he raises his cell phone and snaps the picture that he will later send to his father.

Hank finally sees the truth, even as that truth contradicts what he thought he knew about the experience of war and the bonds between military men. According to Penning, Mike "sees" as well, though here, in the film's climactic revelation, it's not enough for him just to look. He also takes a picture. The photo that he snaps—his personal record of this intense and traumatic moment—is a seemingly mundane image that pulses with significance for him and eventually for his father. Understanding the truth about what the photo depicts, the film suggests, means understanding something about Mike's character and his reaction to war, as well as

Figure 7. In a scene from *In the Valley of Elah* (Warner Independent Pictures, 2007), Mike Deerfield (Jonathan Tucker) snaps a picture of a child struck by his Humvee.

the realities of fighting in Iraq, as distinguished from the experience of fighting in previous U.S. wars. To see an image clearly—in the photo or in the film as a whole—means to recognize the costs and consequences of contemporary war.

In late April 2004, what for many remain the most iconic and searing images from the Iraq War were released to the public. First reported on *60 Minutes II* on April 28 and by Seymour Hersh in the *New Yorker* online on April 30 (printed in the May 10 issue), the photos taken at the Abu Ghraib prison revealed the abuse of prisoners in that facility. The most famous of the photographs—a man in a black hood and cloak, standing on a box; a woman holding a leash attached to a man collapsed on the ground; an ordinary, all-American young woman smiling broadly and giving a thumbs-up while leaning over a corpse—had an immediate effect on the nationwide and worldwide perception of American involvement in Iraq, raising questions about everything from interrogation tactics to the role of women in the military. The images seemed to say something about the war that made people both want to look and to look away. In their book *Standard Operating Procedure* (a companion to the 2008 documentary of the same name) Philip Gourevitch and Errol Morris explore the circumstances surrounding the photographs as well as the compelling nature of the photos themselves. "[T]he power of an image does not necessarily reside in what it depicts," they note, "but in its seeming truth, however inscrutable that truth may be." Gourevitch and Morris discuss the picture of the man in the cloak and hood, who stands on a box with his arms held away from his body and with wires attached to his hands. It is an image, they say, of "carnival weirdness: this upright body shrouded from head to foot; those wires; that pose that recalls, of course, the crucifixion; and the peaked hood that carries so many vague and ghoulish associations...So we seize on the figure of Gilligan [the soldiers' nickname for the man in the photo] as a symbol that stands for all that we know was wrong at Abu Ghraib and all that we cannot—or do not want to—understand about how it came to this" (182–84).

In many ways *In the Valley of Elah* presents the relationship among sight, truth, trauma, and media in the same way. Digital photography and video can reveal searing and compelling images and vignettes that in turn reveal something darkly true about Iraq, though they require supplemental narration and information to finally "come together" as a coherent story. On their own, these media fascinate, but they aren't quite enough—it takes film, the complete narrative that is *In the Valley of Elah,* to show what's really happening. As the film begins, we may not know what to make of these characters and the fragments of their recorded lives, but if we keep watching, we find out. We know—we discover—that the photo of the street scene shows the body of a child, the death of innocence.

Hank, as it turns out, had been awakened by a phone call from Mike sometime after this incident, and his plaintive "Dad? Dad?" is heard at various times throughout the film. Only during the denouement do we see and hear the entire conversation. "You gotta get me out of here...something happened," Mike says tearfully, as Hank tries to reassure him. "That's just nerves talking...Is anybody there with you?" he asks. "No, I'm alone," Mike responds, even though we see him making the call in a phone bank, surrounded by other soldiers. "That's good," Hank replies. By Hank's standards, of course, being obviously upset in public would be something to worry about, but he doesn't realize until much later that Mike's sense of being alone even while among his fellow soldiers is a much more worrying problem. "Okay, Dad, um, I gotta go," Mike says, and ends the call.

These communications technologies that have the potential to bring soldiers together virtually with their loved ones are shown, in *Elah,* to be more revealing of personal and social fragmentation than they are of any kind of union. Mike's cell phone, the technician tells Hank, has been "seriously fried," exposed to the kind of intense heat that can break coherent narratives into pieces. *In the Valley of Elah* implies that this is true of both digital narratives and personal ones. Hank can succeed in putting the digital pieces back together and can finally "see it all," but his family's life has been irrevocably shattered. "I'm alone," Mike says, and he is—even as he can hear his father's voice and send him what turn out to be the most disturbing images of his time in Iraq.

At the end of the film, Hank resorts to an older form of communication. After driving home, he takes a worn American flag that Mike sent him from Iraq back to the same school he visited as he was leaving town. With the help of the same worker, he raises the flag and duct tapes the ropes in place. The camera tracks up the flagpole and finally reveals the tattered flag flying upside down, lingering on the image before the screen goes dark and the credits start to roll. The flag works literally as another signifier of inversion, indicating the upside-down mess that Iraq has become and, as Hank explained earlier, the fact that "we're in a whole lot of trouble so come and save our ass because we don't have a prayer in hell of saving ourselves." In the wake of revelations about his son's life and death, the flag shows the clear truth of the Iraq War's devastating consequences.

Seeing Our Way Clear

In his book *Replaceable You,* David Serlin explores how "physical rehabilitation became an allegory of national rehabilitation" in the years after World War II (2). Serlin cites films like William Wyler's groundbreaking *The Best Years of Our Lives* (1946), in which disabled veteran Harold Russell plays a soldier who loses both hands in the war but faces his new challenges with strength, bravery, and the love of his loyal girlfriend (28). But despite even further medical, psychological, and communications advances, both *Alive Day* and *Elah* would seem to doubt the capacity of the individual and the nation to "get better" quite so easily. A number of films about Iraq have raised the same kind of alarm. Brian De Palma's *Redacted* (2007) takes much the same approach to seeing and truth as the two films discussed here. Like *Elah,* De Palma's film draws its inspiration from true events, in this case the rape and murder of a teenage Iraqi girl by a group of

American soldiers. *Redacted* presents its narrative as a montage of created digital footage from a documentary, a surveillance camera, soldiers' video diaries, and Islamist websites. Like the other filmmakers, De Palma wants audiences to look and see the truth: "The movie attempts to bring the reality of what happened in Iraq to the American people," he explains. "If we get these images in front of a mass audience, maybe we can affect things" (qtd. in Jaafar, "Casualties" 16). Technology may not always help soldiers, but it can help the story—and stories that are truthful and sincere, as De Palma implies, can help everyone.

In addition to *Alive Day,* a number of other documentaries have addressed aspects of the Iraq War. Michael Moore's popular and controversial *Fahrenheit 9/11* (2004) attacks the Bush administration's rationale for the war and criticizes the mainstream media's supportive coverage; it was awarded the Palme d'Or at the Cannes Film Festival. *Gunner Palace* (2005) features soldiers in Baghdad during 2003 and 2004, trying to combat the Iraqi insurgency, while *Iraq in Fragments* (2006) offers three portraits of Iraqis living in a war-torn country. And *No End in Sight* (2007) consists largely of interviews with officials who were in charge of the initial invasion and occupation of Iraq, many of whom have since become disillusioned with the war's justification and execution.

Charles Musser has argued that documentaries about the Iraq War often follow a similar structure: "The [traditional] media has provided a distorted and incomplete picture of the war and the circumstances surrounding it," these films attest, but "this documentary itself reveals a hidden, more truthful side" (22). In many cases, the ultimate goal is "to bring viewers (or the public)—seen as remote from and largely indifferent to the lives of their subjects—into a more intimate and empathetic relationship to them" (30). *Alive Day* clearly shares this goal, and fictional films like *Elah* and *Redacted* heighten their realistic effect with the prominent use of verité elements like digital video. Iraqi films about the war, however, achieve a more immediate realism. *Ahlaam* (2005), a fictional film about three Iraqi citizens whose lives are changed by the 2003 invasion, and *The Dreams of Sparrows* (2006), a documentary about life in Iraq under American occupation, were both shot on location at serious risk to the filmmakers. Mohamed Al-Daradji, the director of *Ahlaam,* reportedly shot the film "with an AK-47 machine gun in one hand and his camera in the other" (Jafaar, "Home Truths" 18). He was kidnapped twice, and shot at by both insurgents and American troops. Saad Fakher, an associate producer of *Dreams,* was killed during filming, while a cameraman on that film was shot in the hand and Hayder Mousa Daffar, the director, was captured three times, twice by American soldiers and once by insurgents (Silverman).

Representations of trauma and disability generally, as discussed by scholars like Davis, ideally function not as titillating spectacles for the "normal" viewer's gaze, but rather as reminders that normality is an elusive concept, and that no body or self is ever indeed truly "complete." As Davis puts it, "difference is what we *all* have in common." War creates real differences in those that experience it—even given the palliative effects of medical technology, the availability of media as a tool for expression and communication, and greater public awareness of the realities of physical and emotional trauma. These films encourage us to see those differences and linger on them, but also to contemplate the differences that war engenders in everyone, soldiers and civilians alike. The disabling effects of war spill over onto parents, children, families, friends, and communities, and both *Alive Day* and *In the Valley of Elah* make this point emphatically. As Hank puts it, *"We're* in a whole lot of trouble." In this way soldiers may be irrevocably changed by war, and thus "different," but that very difference makes the soldiers emblematically "one of U.S."—representatives of a nation that hasn't been able to see its way clear from a devastating war.

Conclusion

Many films about the Vietnam War end in the same striking way—one character asks another to kill him or her. The request may be implicit or explicit, and the deaths occur differently, but in each case the killing provides a climax for the plot and a dramatic representation of the ambiguous moral choices that often confronted soldiers in Vietnam. "Shoot me," the wounded female sniper tells Joker in *Full Metal Jacket,* and he does. "Do it," urges Sergeant Barnes, and Chris Taylor does, only to remark in voice-over at the end of *Platoon* that the murderous Barnes and the martyred Elias will both continue to battle for "possession of his soul." Colonel Kurtz never explicitly tells Willard to kill him in *Apocalypse Now,* but he does deposit the head of the murdered Chef in Willard's lap with a flourish, and on the night the natives sacrifice a caribou, seems to be waiting for Willard when he approaches. "The horror," Kurtz whispers, in some combination of fascination and despair. And in *The Deer Hunter,* Michael finally finds Nick in the Saigon underground, playing Russian roulette for the entertainment of throngs of gamblers. Mike enters the game, trying to break through to Nick, compelling him to remember the days when they used to go hunting in the mountains. Nick's eyes seem to clear. "One shot," he smiles, and then brings the gun to his temple and pulls the trigger.

How should one feel about the death of someone who wants to die, who asks to die? Is causing that death right, because it satisfies an earnest request, or wrong, because there are always other ways? The choice, in many ways, is an impossible one, though these characters do choose, for better or for worse. The expressions on their faces—Joker's twisted expression of grief, Taylor's fury followed by tears, Willard's blankness, and Mike's howl of disbelief—all indicate that these choices will fester, as unresolved as the war itself. The "requested death," then, has emerged as a central vignette in representations of the Vietnam War. It's a moment that provides these war stories with a climax and the means to consider the moral ambiguities of that conflict as well as those ambiguities' effect on the individual soldiers who were compelled, by their conscience or by the government, to fight.

A central trope is emerging from the stories about the Iraq War as well, one that also emphasizes considerations of agency and trauma in the midst of war. These more recent stories repeatedly show the accidental killing of a child. In each instance, the bodies of these children call out as totems of the guilt, helplessness, and frustration felt by soldiers fighting a war in which choices are impossible—not because they are morally ambiguous, but because often there is very little time or leeway to make a choice in the first place. These soldiers have even less agency than their Vietnam counterparts. The death of a child is undeniably a bad thing, but in these circumstances almost impossible to avoid. Afterward, real-life soldiers like Nathaniel Fick and fictional ones like Mike Deerfield are burdened by guilt and shame, even though those events were hardly the result of their careful, deliberate actions. In the earlier Vietnam War films, the individual soldier creates the narrative of the war. The stories are personal, intimate, and centered on young men encountering difficult choices. The choices are made, and the story goes on, changed and shaped by those decisions. But one gets the sense in the more recent war stories that the narrative of Iraq has already been written—by the historical and political circumstances, by the commanders and strategists, by the peoples of Iraq who are in conflict both with the Americans and each other—and that the soldiers fighting there are swept along with it, unable to assert their will to help.

Before Colby Buzzell goes to Iraq in 2003, he listens to a briefing about the rules of engagement. "If your convoy was going under an overpass," a female captain asks the soldiers, "and there were women and children on the overpass throwing rocks down at [you], what should you do? Do you shoot or not?" (60) The soldiers debate the consequences of shooting or not shooting until the battalion commander steps in, apparently impatient with such considerations. "He then told all of us not to worry about doing the right thing, that if we wanted to do the right thing to go out and rent a Spike Lee movie. He then stressed to us that if we felt threatened, pull the trigger. It's better to be safe than sorry, better him dead than you" (61). The commander sets right and wrong aside in service of safety, and particularly avoids the tangled moral considerations of targets who are women and children. "Better *him* dead than you," he says, changing a significant detail of the hypothetical situation that the captain had described. All ages and both genders can be threats, and threats must be dealt with.

To some, the Iraq War in 2003 might have seemed uncomplicated. In March, after the invasion was launched, Secretary of Defense Donald Rumsfeld assured Americans that the weapons of mass destruction that Iraq harbored were in the area near Baghdad and Tikrit ("Secretary Rumsfeld"). "We know where they are," he said, and in early April when U.S. soldiers and Iraqi citizens pulled down Saddam Hussein's statue in Baghdad, there seemed to be reason for such confidence. On 1 May, President Bush declared that the mission had been accomplished, and Paul Bremer disbanded the Iraqi army later that month. But these events turned out to signal the beginning rather than the end of the conflict. The war would continue, and decisions would rarely be as straightforward or as easy as the battalion commander described by Buzzell says they are. Kayla Williams puts the problem succinctly. In Iraq, "[t]he right thing isn't always the right thing" (120).

But Williams is lucky—she narrowly avoids shooting a child when a car rapidly approaches her convoy. She prepares to pull the trigger, and then sees a small boy waving at her from the passenger seat. She lowers her rifle, hesitates—and then waves back (242). Nathaniel Fick is less fortunate. Fick is a leader, and enters military service confident in his ability to make good decisions. "Doing right," he thinks, "wasn't only a moral imperative but also the most expedient way to lead the platoon" (182). But as he discovers, what constitutes "right" can be difficult or impossible to make out. On recon in Qalat Sukkar, Fick and his platoon shoot at the figures of men holding rifles. When Iraqi women later approach them carrying the two badly wounded boys, they realize that the armed men had not, in fact, been armed men. "We'd shot two children," Fick realizes (239). And so he tries to fix the situation. His soldiers begin to give the children medical aid, but realize that the boys need more help than they can provide. He appeals to a major, asking that the boys be evacuated to a field hospital, but the major dismisses the idea—send them home, he says. There's nothing we can do. Fick is appalled. "I wanted to tell the major that we were Americans, that Americans don't shoot kids and let them die, that the men in my platoon had to be able to look at themselves in the mirror for the rest of their lives" (240). Instead of arguing, Fick and his men have the boys moved to a spot directly in front of the major's tent, convincing him to assent to Fick's plan.

Fick wants to do right, but it's getting harder. Later he and his men take the time to medically treat a young Iraqi girl who was wounded by an American bomb, and as a result fail to complete a weapons search in the time allotted, likely allowing a large cache of weapons to remain in the hands of the enemy. Fick is frustrated. All his training, honor, and discernment are no match for these circumstances. He echoes Williams: "I was learning that choices in war are rarely between good and bad, but rather between bad and worse" (359). Near the end of the book, he reflects again on "the good and the bad" of war. Ultimately, he says, "[t]he good didn't feel as good as the bad felt bad" (369).

John Crawford can attest to that as well. For him, the experience feels so bad that it ruptures his entire narrative. Near the end of his book, he describes being back in the States, relaxing at a hometown festival with friends, who entreat him to "[t]ell us a war story" (212). And so he tells about being on patrol in An Nasiriyah when he notices a group of three little boys, eight or nine years old, by the side of the road. One of them has a rifle, and Crawford's Humvee skids to a stop. The boys watch the commotion, eyes wide, while Crawford raises his weapon. "The one holding the rifle slowly turned it toward me...The muzzle was almost on me, and I had already hesitated too long. While they stood on the swelling bloody sun, I applied pressure to the trigger" (217). The boy's rifle, however, isn't a rifle—it's just a piece from one, abandoned and used as a toy. "The trigger was gone, as was the buttstock and the bolt...That kid couldn't have shot spitballs through it even if he had wanted to" (218). Crawford breaks off his story, unable to continue, and his friends reassure him that he can tell it another time. Then Crawford breaks off his larger story, revealing that the reassurance of his friends and his wife was make-believe, and that no such support exists for him anymore. It's unclear if the shooting of the child was something that really happened to Crawford, but either way it functions as the event around which a story both centers and will not cohere.

Dexter Pitts, one of the veterans featured in *Alive Day Memories,* struggles with similarly traumatic memories, telling the audience that although he's a "nice, lovable guy," there were also some "mean things to kids over there that I had to do." At night, he hears the voices of Iraqis, and the scenes of his service replay in his head. Pitts doesn't elaborate on those "mean things," but the memory of them is clearly devastating. Brian Turner writes in "Home Fires" that since his service he has also been haunted by dreams of Iraq and Iraqis—specifically, an Iraqi woman approaching him to tell him that her child is dead. While awake, he wonders if this is the dead infant found on a raid outside of Balad, or one of the boys Turner cuffed and blindfolded during other raids. "Maybe when I go to sleep," he muses, "I'm actually entering a world in which Iraqi mothers search through the landscape of my memory in the vain hope of finding their dead sons. My body a sort of graveyard, a repository of the lost and the dead" ("The Night Visitors"). The dead child—anonymous, his identity unclaimed—lives in his memory, mourned but not saved.

In the Valley of Elah, too, places harm to a child at the secret heart of the story. As Hank Deerfield tries to get to the bottom of his son's disappearance, he sifts through a series of cryptic images and narrative fragments that eventually come together in searing focus. The viewer doesn't see what Mike and his fellow soldier saw through the windshield of their Humvee, but does see that the two young men have to make a decision—once again, with little information and less time. Mike panics. "What do I do?" he yells, and the answer is urgent: "Do not stop. Do not fucking stop!" In the aftermath of the collision, it becomes clear that the obstacle, the threat, was a child. When the killing is finally revealed, it functions as the final clue in the mystery, one that would seem to explain the dramatic personality change that Mike experienced while in Iraq, the break in communication with his parents, and the violent conflict with his fellow soldiers. The child's body is the symbolic key to the soldiers' traumatic experience of the Iraq War, and the circumstances of the child's death reveal both the soldiers' perception of the incessant, ubiquitous threat of Iraq as well as the difficulty—or impossibility—of making good decisions in such an environment.

But it's *The Hurt Locker,* released in 2009, that takes the trope of the dead child to a new extreme. The story follows an Explosive Ordnance Disposal (EOD) unit, as they work to defuse the seemingly endless IEDs in Iraq.[1] Sgt. First Class William James (Jeremy Renner), the EOD team leader, is highly skilled at bomb disposal and has an excellent record of success. He also disdains protocol and is not at all averse to endangering himself and his teammates while trying to puzzle out the secret of a bomb's mechanism beyond the relative margin of safety. James is consumed by the puzzle, the challenge, the risk, and he pursues that risk at the expense of everything else.

In between jobs James befriends a young Iraqi boy who loves soccer and calls himself Beckham. James enjoys haggling back and forth over the pirated DVDs the boy sells, and the two have an easy repartee. When his EOD team searches a building said to be a laboratory for bomb makers, they come upon a truly grisly discovery. A child's body has been laid out on a table, a bomb implanted within the boy's torso. They call it a "body bomb." James is visibly shaken for the first time in the film as he realizes the boy is Beckham. He agrees with the other soldiers that they should exit the building and trigger the bomb rather than attempting to defuse it. But then he agonizes, struggling with the need to respect Beckham and the need to solve the puzzle, to uncover the mechanism. Finally the latter need wins, and he cuts into Beckham's body to defuse and remove the bomb. It's a messy task, and clearly an emotional one; afterward, he carries the body out of the building.

This, then, would seem to be the most extreme example of the trope of the dead child, innocence destroyed by the chaos of a war that will linger in the consciousness of the soldiers sent to fight it. This child has literally been violated by explosives—not killed by shrapnel or the stray shots of soldiers, but killed for the purpose of harboring a weapon, a deadly secret. And James, so hardened to threat and death and danger, is shaken. What would be the right decision? To leave Beckham's body for the explosion to incinerate, or to perform the autopsy and find the solution? The choice, as Fick puts it, is between bad and worse. James finds himself at a loss, and haphazardly pursues Beckham's killer by questioning locals vehemently but without success. Later, a child approaches him. It's Beckham, very much alive and ready to sell James DVDs or play soccer. James ignores him, and whatever his feelings are—frustration, shame, sadness—he hides them behind a blank stare.

Beckham's body, as it turns out, wasn't Beckham's. That child still lives, but it means that another has died, perhaps anonymously. The anonymous child's body indicates the brutal effects of war as well as the Americans' inability to properly "read" and understand Iraq. But it is, after all, a difficult text. *The Hurt Locker,* though set in 2004, is the most recent of the works covered in detail in this study and addresses the problems presented in the ongoing war by suicide bombers, sectarian violence, urban warfare, and explosives that can be triggered by seemingly innocuous people and technology. The film's opening sequence features a soldier who must decide in a matter of seconds whether an Iraqi man standing in a doorway with a cell phone is texting a friend or signaling a bomb to go off. The soldier hesitates, and it costs the life of his comrade, who dies in the ensuing explosion. *The Hurt Locker* emphasizes the way that the rules of engagement change dramatically when something as simple as a cell phone can be a deadly weapon.

Figure 8. In the opening sequence of *The Hurt Locker* (Summit Entertainment, 2009), a deadly explosion is detonated by a man holding a cell phone.

In Vietnam War films noted above, protagonists kill another soldier who has gone so far into the abyss of war that they request death by another's hand. The main characters are left dazedly contemplating that loss and their own responsibility for it, representatives of a nation also contemplating the unfamiliar double burden of loss and responsibility. The dead children in *The Hurt Locker* and other representations of the Iraq War are indications of even greater loss—of Iraqi and American innocence, but also of agency, the ability to make deliberate choices, and an understanding of who, exactly, is responsible for those losses in the first place. David Zimmerman's novel *The Sandbox,* published in 2010, follows *The Hurt Locker's* lead in adding additional levels of complexity to the trope of the dead child, which is the novel's opening image: "The body of the naked child lies in the center of the highway" (1). The young girl is initially assumed to be white, because her body has been covered in lye. Who she is and where she came from is a mystery to be solved, as is the identity of another Iraqi child who lives in an abandoned toy factory and occasionally reveals himself to the protagonist, Private Toby Durrant. Yet another boy dies after engaging in a firefight with the American soldiers, and meanwhile Durrant struggles with his girlfriend's ambivalence about her pregnancy. Iraq is figured as a nation of children, but Durrant is as helpless as a child himself when he is framed for treason and devastated by his girlfriend's decision to abort their baby.

The Hurt Locker, The Sandbox, and other Iraq War stories dramatize the frustrations American soldiers feel as they struggle to properly decode their environment, the same frustrations that reporter Dexter Filkins writes about in *The Forever War* (2008). Officers would often speak in acronyms, Filkins writes, like AQI for "Al-Qaeda in Iraq" or AIF for "Anti-Iraqi Forces," just as reporters would use terms like "insurgents" and "guerrillas" as if they meant something, "as if these were distinct groups, as if they were wearing uniforms and carrying flags" (122). But Iraqis could fight one day and not the next, change alliance, provide reliable or unreliable information depending on circumstance. "It drove the Americans crazy," Filkins writes. "They would drive through a village and spot an Iraqi man standing on the roadside, marking the convoy's time and speed as it passed. Working for the insurgency, no doubt, but how do you shoot a guy for looking at his watch?" Ask a local about an explosion or other attack, and he would invariably say that the wrongdoer lived in the next village rather than in the next house. "It wasn't just that the Iraqis lied," Filkins explains. "Of course they lied. It was that they had more to consider than the Americans were ever willing to give them credit for" (123). Homes, neighborhoods, children, families. These things necessitate a kind of double life, as Filkins puts it. But for the Americans—in their second lives as soldiers, combatants, sometimes-killers—it meant that things just got more complicated.

But the war had been complicated almost from the beginning. Concerns about WMDs at the war's outset bled into worries about IEDs and suicide bombers, especially after a bomber struck the U.N. headquarters in Iraq in August 2003. News of the Abu Ghraib scandal broke in 2004, and in February 2006 an attack on a Shiite shrine in Samarra by Sunni extremists sparked a wave of sectarian violence. Iraqis fought the Americans, but they also fought other Iraqis. David Finkel (who is, like Filkins, a Pulitzer Prize-winning war reporter) writes in *The Good Soldiers* (2009) about infantry soldiers fighting in Iraq during "the surge," an increased commitment of troops and effort announced in January 2007. Though many have argued that the surge was ultimately successful in improving security in Iraq, Finkel tells the story of Ralph Kauzlarich, an initially optimistic, enthusiastic Army lieutenant colonel who led a battalion into Baghdad as part of this initiative. "His soldiers weren't yet calling him the Lost Kauz behind his back," the book begins. Finkel continues this retrospective introduction:

> The soldiers of his who would be injured were still perfectly healthy, and the soldiers of his who would die were still perfectly alive. A soldier who was a favorite of his, and who was often described as a younger version of him, hadn't yet written of the war in a letter to a friend, "I've had enough of this bullshit." Another soldier, one of his best, hadn't yet written in a journal he kept hidden, "I've lost all hope. I feel the end is near for me, very near." Another hadn't yet gotten angry enough to shoot a thirsty dog that was lapping up a puddle of human blood. Another, who at the end of all this would become the battalion's most decorated soldier, hadn't yet started dreaming about the people he had killed and wondering if God was going to ask him about the two who had been climbing a ladder. (3)

Reporters like Filkins, Finkel, and Mark Boal confirm what many soldiers say in their first-person accounts—that all the grit and good intention in the world can't always make things right. Boal's *The Hurt Locker* questions those good intentions as well, at least in the figure of William James. James may be a genius with the wires and trigger mechanisms of bombs, and he can certainly think his way into a bomb maker's mental process, but he's not very good with people—of any nationality. When crouched in front of a bomb, James is in his element, and his work saves lives. But at other times, he takes unnecessary risks, endangering his comrades for the sake of the thrill of the hunt. When he at last returns home to his wife and baby boy, he inhabits their lives listlessly, realizing that what he really loves is risk, adrenaline—war. He leaves his family behind and signs on for another tour, trading his son's jack-in-the-box for more dangerous surprises. The final shot of the film shows him walking in the bomb suit toward yet another puzzle, his face alive and happy, loud heavy metal celebrating him on the soundtrack.

The Hurt Locker itself was celebrated widely during the 2010 awards season, which ended with the film receiving Academy Awards for Best Picture and Best Director for Kathryn Bigelow. Though its commercial success was dwarfed by that of the hugely popular *Avatar,* critics praised *The Hurt Locker*'s gritty realism and willingness to address the difficult subject of the Iraq War's effects on soldiers. In the run-up to the Oscars, however, some criticized the film for its *lack* of realism. Writing in *Newsweek,* Paul Rieckhoff, an Iraq War veteran and leader of the organization Iraq and Afghanistan Veterans of America, took issue with plot developments that involved the EOD team on patrol (rather than simply doing the highly specialized work of bomb disposal) and William James leaving his base alone and unauthorized on a foray into an Iraqi neighborhood. Rieckhoff argues that these aspects of the story reveal a "lack of research [and] ultimately respect for the American military." He does admit, however, that *The Hurt Locker* "does a good job of articulating the challenges returning troops face when they are coming home and trying to assimilate back to normal life." Similarly, Julian Barnes, Ned Parker, and John Horn reported in the *Los Angeles Times* that many active members of the military scoffed at the film's depiction of bomb disposal and the excitement of combat, though they expressed appreciation that audiences were reminded of their efforts overseas. Barnes, Parker, and Horn also note that the government was originally slated to offer production consultation and assistance to the film, but pulled out at the last minute due to objections over scenes they felt were unflattering to the troops. Conversely, they report Defense Secretary Robert Gates's enthusiasm for the movie, which he has called both authentic and compelling. Everyone, it seemed, had an opinion about *The Hurt Locker,* and some even speculated that the controversy over the film's realism was generated as a pre-Oscars smear tactic (Vanairsdale). In any case, the American soldier's experience in Iraq was news again—and worldwide entertainment news, no less.[2]

William James can't return home, and so he returns to war, to the work and the world he loves. Perhaps he does find a kind of transcendence— though it's different from that which the other soldiers discussed in this book desire but fail to achieve. Instead of wanting to live virtually, or challenge gender norms, or communicate across the boundaries of nation and culture, or use technology to move beyond the body's limitations, James craves excitement. Instead of worrying about how to properly meld the identities of a father, husband, and soldier, James simply commits himself fully to the latter. And so he begins another tour, rising above concerns about domesticity, comradeship, and friendship. But it's not a transcendence that's particularly appealing, nor does it offer a solution for other soldiers struggling to reconcile differing responsibilities, loyalties, and interests.

"By making a film about an unpopular war that still gives the audience someone to root for," notes the *Economist,* "[Bigelow] may have struck gold. Perhaps the return of John Wayne is what people have been waiting for" ("Waiting for John Wayne" 79). William James, however, is no John Wayne—at least, not in the sense that this writer intends. We don't quite root for him in the way we do for Wayne in so many Westerns (like *Stagecoach*) and World War II movies (like *The Flying Leathernecks*). But we may watch James with the same fascinated and troubled eye that we do when Wayne plays Ethan Edwards in *The Searchers. The Hurt Locker* interrogates and critiques James's addiction to risk in the same way that *The Searchers* critiques Edwards's addiction to his quest, and the dogged toughness that is both productive and corrosive. If at the end of the more recent film we move to the heavy beat of the soundtrack and cheer the handsome "wild man," we do so by overlooking the nuances of the portrait Boal and Bigelow give us. We miss the point, as does the *Economist,* and ultimately *The Hurt Locker* may have as much to say about audiences' addiction to representations of risk as it does about James's obsession with the real thing.

Rising above all other concerns is one response to the problems and complications of the war experience, but tuning everything out for the sake of entertainment doesn't do much good for anyone—neither individuals nor the communities they inhabit. "Attention must be paid," implored Linda Loman, but was it ever more true? War can indeed be a spectacular show, but as all these storytellers emphasize, there's a lot more to it than that. War alters the shape of our families, communities, and nation—it is, as ever, a breaking point for history, politics, art, and the very ways we talk to one another. It matters, and soldiers' stories tell us why and how. Then and now, we have to listen.

NOTES

Introduction

1. These observations might be guided by a writer like Jonathan Shay, whose book *Achilles in Vietnam* notes the parallels between Achilles's experience of the Trojan War as described by Homer and the oral histories of Vietnam War veterans. Both ancient and modern warriors feel the sting of a commander's betrayal, the surreal thrill of a berserker rage, and the devastation of losing a close comrade. Homer also has much to teach us, argues Shay, about the importance of honoring the enemy and the necessity of grieving for the dead.

2. I have written about Jones's description of combat numbness, and how that phenomenon is left out of both the 1964 and 1998 film adaptations of *The Thin Red Line,* in an article titled "The Other World of War: Malick's Adaptation of *The Thin Red Line."*

3. O'Brien's is one of the more sophisticated answers to what Frederic Jameson has called war's "nominalist dilemma: the abstraction from totality or the here and now of sensory immediacy and confusion" (1532). Jan Mieszkowski has written similarly about the relation between "a battle as something processed with the senses (the 'visibility') and a battle as something grasped through logical or narratological abstractions (its 'recountability')" (1649). O'Brien embraces that dilemma.

4. Tom Schatz treats this subject in some detail in "World War II and the Hollywood 'War Film.'"

5. Another blog, "Sgt. Stryker: Support Our Troops," with entries dating back to March 2007, seems to be unrelated.

6. In a footnote, he notes a sixth type of content, the "dissenting soldier testimony: Iraq war veterans bearing public witness to dark war experiences, such as killing unarmed civilians with the consent of their superiors." This final type of video, however, does not actually show images documenting the controversial aspects of war, and thus falls outside of the scope of his article.

7. Quotations from Salam Pax and Riverbend are drawn from the published versions of their blogs—*Salam Pax: The Clandestine Diary of an Ordinary Iraqi* and *Baghdad Burning: Girl Blog from Iraq*. The blogs are still accessible online at dear_raed.blogspot.com and riverbendblog.blogspot.com, but not all of the original entries have been maintained. The published books also include introductions and, in the case of Riverbend's, historical commentary to provide context for her entries.

8. The military has adapted games for its own use, and game companies have likewise earned huge profits creating scenarios based on war and the military. Chris Suellentrop has written that video games about the wars in Afghanistan and Iraq are "blockbusters," and that in 2010 games like *Call of Duty: Modern Warfare 2* are "the most popular fictional depictions of America's current wars" (62).

1. Lines of Sight

1. In some ways, Swofford and Buzzell are doing the opposite of what Tania Modleski has argued should be done with horror movies. Horror is often characterized as fairly vapid, a vehicle for insipid pleasure and the affirmation of mainstream values. But, Modleski argues, films like *Halloween* should be watched with an eye to the ways they can be critically energizing, "as apocalyptic and nihilistic, as hostile to meaning, form, pleasure, and the specious good as many types of high art" (771). Swofford and Buzzell reverse that directive—instead of watching seemingly pleasurable films for critical purposes, they take films intended as critical and political statements and watch them purely for pleasure.

2. Baudrillard misses the potent combination of satisfaction and anticipation that watching war can evoke, particularly when he claims that "the Persian Gulf War did not take place." According to him, it was a "virtual war," a war "stripped of its passions," watched but not felt—at least not by the American government or the audience of noncombatants (*Gulf War* 64). American civilians may indeed have found the Gulf War "empty," an "unreal war where nothing is extreme," and thus neither compelling nor satisfying, but the soldier's perspective is notably different (33). Representations of war can become empty for soldiers as well, though not as a result of the "multiplication of fakes and the hallucination of violence" that Baudrillard diagnoses (*Gulf War* 75), the loss of distinction between the real and the image that he also sees in films like *Apocalypse Now* (*Simulacra* 59–60). Instead, those representations empty out precisely because they differ so much from the experience of real war.

3. See Kakutani, Malcolm Jones, and Caldwell.

4. Mulvey argues that the tension between the scopophilic gazer, who takes pleasure in watching an objectified other, and the narcissistic self, which identifies with and recognizes the figures onscreen, can be explained along gender lines; the default cinematic gaze is male, and the camera watches women as objects of viewing pleasure and men as reflections of the watcher. But Swofford's gaze isn't strictly gendered. The other here is not only the female body, seducing and surrendering to the male gaze, but the male and female bodies of the enemy that are targeted by this military gaze.

5. As Joel Rudinow puts it, "[t]he voyeur seeks a spectacle, the revelation of his object of interest, that something or someone should be open to his inspection and contemplation; but no reciprocal revelation or openness is conceded, for the voyeur requires at the same time to remain hidden" (176).

6. A number of studies have addressed this issue. See, for example, Jeffords and Rabinovitz; Bennett and Paletz; and Taylor.

7. Quotations used in this chapter from the blog are drawn from *My War: Killing Time in Iraq,* the published book, because Buzzell's original blog entries have been taken off-line. The book includes those entries, as well as additional writing about his war experience, and encapsulates the story of the blog itself, its popularity, and its eventual termination.

8. For a discussion on the public debate about the Internet's pornographic content, see Chun. One of the first viral videos that directly affected the public perception of a political candidate, and thus the ensuing election, was George Allen's 2006 "macaca" outburst, which is widely believed to have cost him his seat in the Senate.

2. Making a Military Man

1. In *Gender Trouble,* Butler argues that gender "ought not to be construed as a stable identity or locus of agency from which various acts follow; rather, gender is an identity tenuously constituted in time, instituted in an exterior space through a *stylized repetition of acts*" (191). Gender, then, is performative rather than expressive.

2. Given this, one might take O'Brien's striking story "Sweetheart of the Song Tra Bong" as the exception that proves the rule.

3. His posts include such varied offerings as thoughts on war writing, bourbon, and brands of cigarettes named after Conrad, Kafka, and Tolstoy.

4. A few pages later he reveals a familiarity with Steven Pressfield's popular novelization of the battle of Thermopylae, *Gates of Fire* (48). Pressfield's is one of many such treatments, more recently including Frank Miller's graphic novel series of 1998 and the enormously successful film *300* in 2007. That film is an unapologetic celebration of hardness, of (relative) whiteness, and highly eroticized male-on-male violence. Aptly, A. O. Scott titled his review of *300* "Battle of the Manly Men."

5. See Stoff, Botchkareva, Stockdale.

6. See Alvarez, "G.I. Jane Breaks the Combat Barrier"; Myers, "Living and Fighting Alongside Men, and Fitting In"; Alvarez, "Wartime Soldier, Conflicted Mom"; Myers, "A Peril in War Zones: Sexual Abuse by Fellow G.I.s"; Cave, "A Combat Role, and Anguish Too."

3. Consuming the Other

1. This poem, as well as "Here, Bullet," were featured in the 2007 PBS documentary *Operation Homecoming: Writing the Wartime Experience.*

2. *Phantom Noise* thus continues the work of *Here, Bullet* in a somewhat different vein, and certainly invites further study beyond this brief mention.

4. One of U.S.

1. In Mockenhaupt's *Esquire* article "What I've Learned," Bryan Anderson voices similar concerns. Though he insists that his status as an amputee "doesn't define me" and isn't "who I am," he also thinks about the challenges he faces. If he should choose to have children someday, "I'm not going to be able to pick up my kids," he reflects. "I've thought about that a lot. It's going to be hard" (81). Comments like these from Halfaker and Anderson are reminders of how young many of these disabled veterans are, and how much of their lives are still in front of them.

2. Ali Jaafar has noted that Hank's mission and his determination echo those of Ethan Edwards, John Wayne's character in *The Searchers*—another competent, experienced man whose understanding of the world is turned upside down by what he eventually finds ("Casualties of War").

3. At this point in the film the investigatory procedure is fully underway, and requires both technology and expertise in manipulating that technology, which here consists of the extrication

of images. Think of the similar narrative significance of visual clues and the technology of photography in other murder mysteries like *Rear Window* (1954) or *Blow-Up* (1966). Obviously, the figure of the technology-savvy expert has taken on new life in the contemporary wave of investigatory television, such as the many versions of TV series *Law and Order* and *CSI,* where the forensic scientist, the lab technician, and even the criminal psychologist all play a vital role in uncovering the truth of the crime.

Conclusion

1. The script was written by Mark Boal and based on his article "The Man in the Bomb Suit," which he wrote after being embedded with a bomb squad; Boal also wrote the article that was the basis for the story of *In the Valley of Elah.*

2. Brian Turner chimed in as well, commenting on this film that shares a title with one of his poems. He agreed in one respect with Rieckhoff that the story's real value is in its portrait of a soldier who "cannot completely return to America," who is in Iraq no matter where he goes ("The Bomb Within Us").

BIBLIOGRAPHY

300. Dir. Zack Snyder. Perf. Gerard Butler, David Wenham. Warner Brothers, 2007. Film.

Ahlaam. Dir. Mohamed Al-Daradji. Perf. Aseel Adil, Basher Al-Majidi, Mohamed Hashim. Pathfinder Home Entertainment, 2005. Film.

Alive Day Memories: Home from Iraq. Dir. Jon Alpert and Ellen Goosenberg Kent. HBO Films, 2007. Film.

All Quiet on the Western Front. Dir. Lewis Milestone. Perf. Louis Wolheim, Lew Ayres. Universal Pictures, 1930. Film.

Alvarez, Lizette. "G.I. Jane Breaks the Combat Barrier." *New York Times,* 16 August 2009: A1. Print.

——. "Wartime Soldier, Conflicted Mom." *New York Times,* 27 September 2009: A1. Print.

Amichai, Yehuda. "The Diameter of the Bomb." In *The Selected Poetry of Yehuda Amichai,* 118. Trans. Chana Bloch and Stephen Mitchell. Berkeley: University of California Press, 1996. Print.

Andén-Papadopoulos, Kari. "US Soldiers Imaging the Iraq War on YouTube." *Popular Communication* 7, no. 1 (2009): 17–27. Print.

Antoon, Sinan. *The Baghdad Blues.* Brownsville, VT: Harbor Mountain Press, 2007. Print.

Apocalypse Now. Dir. Francis Ford Coppola. Perf. Martin Sheen, Marlon Brando. American Zoetrope, 1979. Film.

Au, Wagner James. *The Making of Second Life: Notes from the New World.* New York: HarperCollins, 2008. Print.

Avatar. Dir. James Cameron. Perf. Sam Worthington, Zoe Saldana. Twentieth Century Fox, 2009. Film.

Bakir, Vian. "Tele-Technologies, Control, and Sousveillance: Saddam Hussein— De-Deification and the Beast." *Popular Communication* 7, no. 1 (2009): 7–16. Print.

Barlett, Jonathan. "Broken Mirror." *Alive Day Memories: Home from Iraq.* HBO Films, n.d. http://www.hbo.com/documentaries/alive-day-memories-home-from-iraq/index. html#/documentaries/alive-day-memories-home-from-iraq/bios/jonathan-bartlett/ index.html. Web.

Barnes, Julian, Ned Parker, and John Horn. "War Movie Sets Off Conflict: Soldiers Disagree on Authenticity of *The Hurt Locker.*" *Los Angeles Times,* 25 February 2010: A1. Print.

The Battle of Manila Bay. Dir. J. Stuary Blackton. Vitagraph, 1898. Film.

Baudrillard, Jean. *The Gulf War Did Not Take Place.* Trans. Paul Patton. Bloomington: Indiana University Press, 1995. Print.

——. *Simulacra and Simulation.* 1981. Trans. Sheila Faria Glaser. Ann Arbor: University of Michigan Press, 1994. Print.

Baum, Dan. "The Price of Valor." *New Yorker,* 12 and 19 July 2004: 44–52. Print.

Bellafante, Ginia. "When the War Comes Home." *New York Times,* 8 September 2007: B14. Print.

Bennett, W. Lance, and David L. Paletz, eds. *Taken by Storm: The Media, Public Opinion, and U.S. Foreign Policy in the Gulf War.* Chicago: University of Chicago Press, 1994. Print.

The Best Years of Our Lives. Dir. William Wyler. Perf. Frederic March, Harold Russell. RKO Radio Pictures, 1946. Film.

Blow-Up. Dir. Michelangelo Antonioni. Perf. David Hemmings, Vanessa Redgrave. MGM, 1966. Film.

Boal, Mark. "Death and Dishonor." *Playboy* 51, no. 5 (2004): 108+. Print.

——. "The Man in the Bomb Suit." *Playboy* 52, no. 9 (2005): 70+. Print.

Boellstorff, Tom. *Coming of Age in Second Life: An Anthropologist Explores the Virtually Human.* Princeton: Princeton University Press, 2008. Print.

Born on the Fourth of July. Dir. Oliver Stone. Perf. Tom Cruise, Kyra Sedgwick. Universal Pictures, 1989. Film.

Botchkareva, Maria. *Yashka: My Life as Peasant, Exile, and Soldier. As told to Isaac Don Levine.* New York: Frederick A. Stokes, 1919. Print.

Bourke, Joanna. *An Intimate History of Killing: Face to Face Killing in 20th Century Warfare.* New York: Basic Books, 1999. Print.

Bragg, Rick. *I Am A Soldier, Too: The Jessica Lynch Story.* New York: Vintage Books, 2003. Print.

Bray, Chris. "From America's Post-9/11 Battlefields in Iraq and Afghanistan, Harrowing and Sometimes Ennobling Tales of Arms and the Man (and Woman)." *Washington Post,* 16 October 2005: T8. Print.

Bridge on the River Kwai. Dir. David Lean. Perf. Alec Guinness, William Holden. Columbia, 1957. Film.

Brockes, Emma. "What Happens in War Happens." *Guardian,* 3 January 2009: 14. Print.

Broyles, William. "Why Men Love War." *Esquire* (November 1984): 55–65. Print.

Burden, Matthew Currier, ed. *The Blog of War: Front-Line Dispatches from Soldiers in Iraq and Afghanistan.* New York: Simon and Schuster, 2006. Print.

Burroughs, William S. *Cities of the Red Night.* New York: Macmillan, [1981] 2001. Print.

Butler, Judith. *Gender Trouble: Feminism and the Subversion of Identity.* New York: Routledge Classics, [1990] 2006. Print.

Buzzell, Colby. *My War: Killing Time in Iraq.* New York: Berkeley Caliber, 2006. Print.

———. "Welcome Back." *Esquire* (September 2008): 172–212. Print.

Caldwell, Gail. "Memoirs Show War's Paradoxes: *Jarhead* Captures Complex Truths." *Boston Globe,* 19 March 2003: D1+. Print.

Cave, Damien. "A Combat Role, and Anguish Too." *New York Times,* 1 November 2009: A1. Print.

Chun, Wendy. "Screening Pornography." In *Control and Freedom: Power and Paranoia in the Age of Fiber Optics,* 77–127. Cambridge: MIT Press, 2006. Print.

von Clausewitz, Carl. *On War.* Ed. Anatol Rapoport. New York: Penguin, [1832] 1982. Print.

Cole, Sarah. "Enchantment, Disenchantment, War, Literature." *PMLA* 124, no. 5 (2009): 1632–47. Print.

Collins, Billy, ed. *Flowers of Flame: Unheard Voices of Iraq.* East Lansing: Michigan State University Press, 2008. Print.

Coming Home. Dir. Hal Ashby. Perf. Jon Voight, Jane Fonda. United Artists, 1978. Film.

Conroy, Thomas, and Jarice Hanson. "Freedom of Expression and Voices of War: Blogging as an Alternative to Mainstream Media." In *Constructing America's War Culture: Iraq, Media, and Images at Home,* ed. Thomas Conroy and Jarice Hanson, 15–32. Lanham, MD: Lexington Books, 2008. Print.

Cooper, Christopher. "Army Blogger's Tales Attract Censor's Eyes." *Wall Street Journal,* 9 September 2004: B1. Print.

Courage under Fire. Dir. Edward Zwick. Perf. Meg Ryan, Denzel Washington. Fox Pictures, 1996. Film.

Crane, Stephen. *The Red Badge of Courage and Other Stories.* New York: Penguin, [1895] 1991. Print.

Crawford, John. *The Last True Story I'll Ever Tell: An Accidental Soldier's Account of the War in Iraq.* New York: Riverhead Books, 2005. Print.

Davis, Lennard. *Bending Over Backwards: Disability, Dismodernism, and Other Difficult Positions.* New York: New York University Press, 2002. Print.

The Deer Hunter. Dir. Michael Cimino. Perf. Robert DeNiro, Christopher Walken. Universal Pictures, 1978. Film.

The Dreams of Sparrows. Dir. Hayden Mousa Daffar. IraqEye Group, 2006. Film.

Edwards, Martha. "Philoctetes in Historical Context." In *Disabled Veterans in History,* ed. David Gerber, 55–69. Ann Arbor: University of Michigan Press, 2000. Print.

Fahrenheit 9/11. Dir. Michael Moore. Lions Gate Entertainment, 2004. Film.

Feaster, Felicia. "*All Quiet on the Western Front.*" Turner Classic Movies, n.d. http://www.tcm.com:80/tcmdb/title.jsp?stid=67079&category=Articles. Web.

Fick, Nathaniel. *One Bullet Away: The Making of a Marine Officer.* Boston: Mariner Books, 2006. Print.

Fiedler, Leslie. *Freaks: Myths and Images of the Secret Self.* New York: Anchor, [1978] 1993. Print.

Filkins, Dexter. *The Forever War.* New York: Vintage Books, 2008. Print.

Finkel, David. *The Good Soldiers.* New York: Sarah Crichton Books, 2009. Print.

The Fugitive. Dir. Andrew Davis. Perf. Harrison Ford, Tommy Lee Jones. Warner Brothers, 1993. Film.

Full Metal Jacket. Dir. Stanley Kubrick. Perf. Matthew Modine, Vincent D'Onofrio. Warner Brothers, 1987. Film.

Fussell, Paul. *The Great War and Modern Memory.* London: Oxford University Press, 1975. Print.

Garber, Marjorie. *Vested Interests: Cross-Dressing and Cultural Anxiety.* New York: HarperCollins, 1993. Print.

Gellman, Barton. "U.S. Bombs Missed Seventy Percent of Time." *Washington Post,* 16 March 1991: A1. Print.

Generation Kill. Dir. Susanna White, Simon Cellan Jones, and Patrick Norris. Perf. Alexander Skarsgård and James Ransone. HBO. 13 July–24 August 2008. Television.

Gerber, David. "Disabled Veterans: Why Are They Different? What Difference Does It Make?" *The Disability History Association Newsletter* 3, no. 1 (2007): 14–26. Print.

———. "Introduction." In *Disabled Veterans in History,* ed. David Gerber, 1–51. Ann Arbor: University of Michigan Press, 2000. Print.

Gilbert, Michael. "Stryker Brigade Slammed by Insurgents." *Tacoma News Tribune,* 10 August 2004: A1+. Print.

Gourevitch, Philip, and Errol Morris. *Standard Operating Procedure.* New York: Penguin Press, 2008. Print.

The Green Berets. Dir. John Wayne, Ray Kellogg, John Gaddis. Perf. John Wayne, David Janssen. Warner Brothers, 1968. Film.

Grossman, Dave. *On Killing: The Psychological Cost of Learning to Kill in War and Society.* Boston: Little, Brown, 1995. Print.

Grossman, Lev. "Meet Joe Blog." *Time,* 21 June 2004: 65–68. Print.

Guadalcanal Diary. Dir. Lewis Seiler. Perf. Preston Foster, Lloyd Nolan. Twentieth Century Fox, 1943. Film.

Guest, Tim. *Second Lives: A Journey through Virtual Worlds.* New York: Random House, 2007. Print.

Gunner Palace. Dir. Michael Tucker, Petra Epperlein. Palm Pictures, 2005. Film.

Halberstam, Judith. *Female Masculinity.* Durham: Duke University Press, 1998. Print.

Halter, Ed. *From Sun Tzu to Xbox: War and Video Games.* New York: Thunder's Mouth Press, 2006. Print.

Hammond, Mary, and Patrick Bagley. "An Interview with Brian Turner." Alice James Books, 13 May 2007. http://www.poemoftheweek.org/id29.html. Web.

Haraway, Donna. "A Cyborg Manifesto: Science, Technology, and Socialist-Feminism in the Late Twentieth Century." In *Simians, Cyborgs, and Women: The Reinvention of Nature,* 149–81. New York: Routledge, 1991. Print.

Hartley, Jason Christopher. *Just Another Soldier: A Year on the Ground in Iraq.* New York: Harper, 2005. Print.

Hasford, Gustav. *The Short-Timers.* New York: Bantam, 1980. Print.

Hatem, Adam. "That Is My Life." In *Flowers of Flame: Unheard Voices of Iraq,* ed. Sadek Mohammed et al., 37–39. Trans. Haider Al-Kabi. East Lansing: Michigan State University Press, 2008. Print.

Hearts of the World. Dir. D. W. Griffith. Perf. Lillian Gish. D. W. Griffith Productions, 1918. Film.

Hedges, Chris. *War Is a Force That Gives Us Meaning.* New York: Anchor, 2003. Print.

Heinemann, Larry. *Paco's Story.* New York: Penguin, 1989. Print.

Heller, Joseph. *Catch-22.* New York: Scribner, [1961] 1996. Print.

Herman, Judith. *Trauma and Recovery.* New York: Basic Books, [1992] 1997. Print.

Herr, Michael. *Dispatches.* New York: Vintage Books, [1997] 1991. Print.

Hersh, Seymour. "Torture at Abu Ghraib." *New Yorker,* 10 May 2004: 42–47. Print.

Herz, J. C., and Michael Macedonia. "Computer Games and the Military: Two Views." *Defense Horizons* 11 (2002): 1–8. Print.

Hevey, David. "The Enfreakment of Photography." In *The Disability Studies Reader,* ed. Lennard Davis, 367–78. 2nd ed. New York: Routledge, 2006. Print.

Hockenberry, John. "The Blogs of War." *Wired* 13, no. 8 (2005). http://www.wired.com/wired/archive/13.08/milblogs.html. Web.

Holmes, Richard. *Acts of War: The Behavior of Men in Battle.* New York: Free Press, 1985. Print.

Holsinger, M. Paul. "Tearing Down the Spanish Flag (Film)." In *War and American Popular Culture: A Historical Encyclopedia,* ed. Paul Holsinger, 190–91. Westport, CT: Greenwood Press, 1999. Print.

Homer. *The Iliad.* Trans. Stanley Lombardo. Indianapolis: Hackett, 1997. Print.

hooks, bell. "Eating the Other: Desire and Resistance." In *Black Looks: Race and Representation,* 21–39. Boston: South End Press, 1992. Print.

The Hurt Locker. Dir. Kathryn Bigelow. Perf. Jeremy Renner, Anthony Mackie. Summit Entertainment, 2009. Film.

Hynes, Samuel. *The Soldiers' Tale: Bearing Witness to Modern War.* New York: Allen Lane, 1997. Print.

In the Valley of Elah. Dir. Paul Haggis. Perf. Tommy Lee Jones and Charlize Theron. Warner Independent Pictures, 2007. Film.

Iraq in Fragments. Dir. James Longley. Typecast Releasing, 2006. Film.

Jaafar, Ali. "Casualties of War." *Sight and Sound* 18, no. 2 (2008): 16–20, 22. Print.

———. "Home Truths." *Sight and Sound* 18, no. 2 (2008): 18–19. Print.

James, David. "Rock and Roll in Representations of the Invasion of Vietnam." *Representations* 29 (1990): 78–98. Print.

Jameson, Frederic. "War and Representation." *PMLA* 124, no. 5 (2009): 1532–47. Print.

Jarhead. Dir. Sam Mendes. Perf. Jake Gyllenhaal and Peter Sarsgaard. Universal, 2005. Film.

Jeffords, Susan. *The Remasculinization of America: Gender and the Vietnam War.* Bloomington: Indiana University Press, 1989. Print.

———, and Lauren Rabinovitz, eds. *Seeing through the Media: The Persian Gulf War.* New Brunswick: Rutgers University Press, 1994. Print.

Jones, James. *The Thin Red Line*. New York: Delta Books, [1962] 1998. Print.

Jones, Malcolm. "That Other Gulf War." *Newsweek*, 3 March 2003: 59. Print.

Kakutani, Michiko. "A Warrior Haunted by Ghosts of Battle." Rev. of *Jarhead*, by Anthony Swofford. *New York Times*, 19 February 2003: E1+. Print.

Khedairi, Betool. *Absent: A Novel*. Trans. Muhayman Jamil. New York: Random House, 2007. Print.

Kovic, Ron. *Born on the Fourth of July*. New York: Pocket Books, 1976. Print.

Levin, Jerry. "Will the Real Ali Baba Please Stand Up?" In *West Bank Diary: Middle East Violence as Reported by a Former American Hostage*, 94–97. Pasadena, CA: Hope Publishing, 2005. Print.

Lonesome Dove. Dir. Simon Wincer. Perf. Robert Duvall, Tommy Lee Jones. Motown Productions. 5 February–8 February 1989. Television.

The Longest Day. Dir. Ken Annakin, Andrew Marton, Gerd Oswald, Bernhard Wicki, Darryl Zanuck. Perf. John Wayne, Henry Fonda, Robert Mitchum. 20th Century Fox, 1962. Film.

Mahler, Kim. "Interview with Brian Turner." *Cimarron Review* 155 (2006): 96–102. Print.

Mailer, Norman. *The Naked and the Dead*. New York: Henry Holt, [1948] 1998. Print.

Mann, Herman. *The Female Review: Life of Deborah Sampson, the Female Soldier in the War of the Revolution*. Boston: J. K. Wiggin and W. P. Lunt, [1797] 1866. Print.

Marshall, S. L. A. *Men Against Fire: The Problem of Battle Command*. Norman: University of Oklahoma Press, [1947] 2000. Print.

*M*A*S*H*. Dir. Robert Altman. Perf. Donald Sutherland, Elliot Gould. Aspen Productions, 1970. Film.

Maslin, Janet. "A Sharing of Chaos: 2 Soldiers, Same Iraq." *New York Times*, 18 August 2005: E1. Print.

Men in Black. Dir. Barry Sonnenfeld. Perf. Tommy Lee Jones, Will Smith. Amblin Entertainment, 1997. Film.

Mieszkowski, Jan. "Watching War." *PMLA* 124, no. 5 (2009): 1648–61. Print.

Mikhail, Dunya. *The War Works Hard*. Trans. Elizabeth Winslow. New York: New Directions, 2005. Print.

Mockenhaupt, Brian. "Rebuilding Bryan Anderson." *Esquire* (March 2008): 184–94. Print.

——. "What I've Learned." *Esquire* (January 2007): 76–81, 133. Print.

Modleski, Tania. "The Terror of Pleasure: The Contemporary Horror Film and Postmodern Theory." In *Film Theory and Criticism*, ed. Leo Braudy and Marshall Cohen, 764–73. 6th ed. New York: Oxford University Press, 2004. Print.

Mulvey, Laura. "Visual Pleasure and Narrative Cinema." *Screen* 16, no. 3 (1975): 6–18. Print.

Musser, Charles. "Film Truth in the Age of George W. Bush." *Framework* 48, no. 2 (2007): 9–35. Print.

Myers, Steven Lee. "Living and Fighting Alongside Men, and Fitting In." *New York Times*, 17 August 2009: A1. Print.

——. "A Peril in War Zones: Sexual Abuse by Fellow G.I.s." *New York Times*, 27 December 2009: A1. Print.

No Country for Old Men. Dir. Joel and Ethan Coen. Perf. Tommy Lee Jones, Javier Bardem. Mike Zoss Productions, 2007. Film.

No End in Sight. Dir. Charles Ferguson. Magnolia Pictures, 2007. Film.

O'Brien, Tim. *Going After Cacciato*. New York: Doubleday, 1978. Print.

——. *In the Lake of the Woods*. New York: Houghton Mifflin, 1994. Print.

——. *The Things They Carried*. New York: Broadway, 1990. Print.

"One in Five Iraq and Afghanistan Veterans Suffer from PTSD or Major Depression." News Releases, RAND Corporation, 17 April 2008. http://www.rand.org/news/press/2008/04/17/. Web.

"Operation Homecoming: Writing the Wartime Experience." *America at a Crossroads*. Dir. Richard Robbins. Perf. Robert Duvall and Beau Bridges. Public Broadcasting Service. 9 February 2007. Television.

Owen, Susan A., Sarah R. Stein, and Leah R. Vande Berg. *Bad Girls: Cultural Politics and Media Representations of Transgressive Women*. New York: Peter Lang, 2007. Print.

Owen, Wilfred. "Dulce Et Decorum Est." In *The Collected Poems of Wilfred Owen, 55*. New York: New Directions, 1963. Print.

Parenti, Christian. "Stretched Thin, Lied to and Mistreated." *Nation*, 18 September 2003. http://www.thenation.com/article/stretched-thin-lied-mistreated. Web.

Pax, Salam. *The Clandestine Diary of an Ordinary Iraqi*. New York: Grove Press, 2003. Print.

Peebles, Stacey. "The Other World of War: Malick's Adaptation of *The Thin Red Line*." In *The Cinema of Terrence Malick: Poetic Visions of America*, ed. Hannah Patterson, 153–63. London: The Wallflower Press, 2004. 2nd ed. 2007. Print.

Piedmont-Marton, Elisabeth. "Writing Against the Vietnam War in Two Gulf War Memoirs: Anthony Swofford's Jarhead and Joel Turnipseed's Baghdad Express." In *Arms and the Self: War, the Military, and Autobiographical Writing*, ed. Alex Vernon, 257–72. Kent, OH: Kent State University Press, 2005. Print.

Pilkington, Ed. "Iraq Veteran Wins Blog Prize as US Military Cuts Web Access." *Guardian*, 15 May 2007: 3+. Print.

Platoon. Dir. Oliver Stone. Perf. Charlie Sheen, Willem Dafoe. Herndale Film, 1986. Film.

Ponders, Kim. *The Art of Uncontrolled Flight*. New York: HarperPerennial, 2005. Print.

Pressfield, Steven. *Gates of Fire*. New York: Doubleday, 1998. Print.

Priest, Dana, and Ann Hull. "Soldiers Face Neglect, Frustration at Army's Top Medical Facility." *Washington Post*, 18 February 2007: A1. Print.

Pynchon, Thomas. *Gravity's Rainbow*. New York: Viking, 1973. Print.

Rear Window. Dir. Alfred Hitchcock. Perf. James Stewart, Grace Kelly. Paramount, 1954. Film.

Redacted. Dir. Brian De Palma. Perf. Kel O'Neill and Daniel Steward Sherman. Magnolia Pictures, 2007. Film.

Redmond, Sophie. *Free Speech in Iraq: Recent Developments*. Article 19: Global Campaign for Free Expression. August 2007. http://www.article19.org/pdfs/publications/iraq-free-speech.pdf. Web.

"Remarks by the Present in Address to the Nation on the End of Combat Operations in Iraq." The White House. 31 August 2010. http://www.whitehouse.gov/

the-press-office/2010/08/31/remarks-president-address-nation-end-combat-operations-iraq. Web.

Rieckhoff, Paul. "When Cinéma Vérité Isn't." *Newsweek* Online, 24 February 2010. http://www.newsweek.com/2010/02/23/when-cin-ma-v-rit-isn-t.html. Web.

Riverbend. *Baghdad Burning: Girl Blog from Iraq.* New York: Feminist Press, 2005. Print.

Robbins, Major Elizabeth L. "Muddy Boots IO: The Rise of Soldier Blogs." *Military Review* 87, no. 5 (2007): 109–18. Print.

Al-Rubaiee, Abdul Razaq. "Tomorrow the War Will Have a Picnic." In *Flowers of Flame: Unheard Voices of Iraq,* ed. Sadek Mohammed et al., 16–19. Trans. Sadek Mohammed. East Lansing: Michigan State University Press, 2008. Print.

Rudinow, Joel. "Representation, Voyeurism, and the Vacant Point of View." *Philosophy and Literature* 3, no. 2 (1979): 173–86. Print.

The Sands of Iwo Jima. Dir. Allan Dwan. Perf. John Wayne, John Agar. Republic Pictures, 1949. Film.

Saving Private Ryan. Dir. Steven Spielberg. Perf. Tom Hanks, Tom Sizemore. Amblin Entertainment, 1998. Film.

Scarry, Elaine. *The Body in Pain.* New York: Oxford University Press, 1985. Print.

Schatz, Tom. "World War II and the Hollywood 'War Film.'" In *Refiguring American Film Genres: History and Theory,* ed. Nick Browne, 89–128. Berkeley: University of California Press, 1998. Print.

Scott, A. O. "Battle of the Manly Men: Blood Bath with a Message." *New York Times,* 9 March 2007: E8. Print.

———. "Seeking Clues to a Son's Death and a War's Meaning." *New York Times,* 14 September 2007: E1. Print.

The Searchers. Dir. John Ford. Perf. John Wayne, Natalie Wood. Warner Brothers, 1956. Film.

"Secretary Rumsfeld Remarks on ABC 'This Week with George Stephanopoulos.'" United States Department of Defense, Office of the Assistant Secretary of Defense (Public Affairs), 30 March 2003. http://www.defense.gov/transcripts/transcript. aspx?transcriptid=2185. Web.

Serlin, David. *Replaceable You: Engineering the Body in Postwar America.* Chicago: University of Chicago Press, 2004. Print.

Shay, Jonathn. *Achilles in Vietnam: Combat Trauma and the Undoing of Character.* New York: Simon and Schuster, 1995. Print.

Shulman, Holly Cowan. "The International Media and the Persian Gulf War: The Importance of the Flow of News." In *Seeing through the Media: The Persian Gulf War,* ed. Susan Jeffords and Lauren Rabinovitz, 107–20. New Brunswick: Rutgers University Press, 1994. Print.

Silverman, Jason. "Films Capture Iraq's Brutal Truth." *Wired* 13, no. 06 (2005). http://www.wired.com/entertainment/music/news/2005/06/67741. Web.

Sipress, Alan, and Sam Diaz. "A Casualty of War: MySpace." *Washington Post,* 15 May 2007: A1. Print.

"Soldiers' Iraq Blogs Face Military Scrutiny." National Public Radio, 24 August 2004. http://www.npr.org/templates/story/story.php?storyId=3867981. Web.

South Pacific. Dir. Joshua Logan. Perf. Rossano Brazzi, Mitzi Gaynor. 20th Century Fox, 1958. Film.

Spector, Mike. "Soldiers' Online Journals Come under Increased Scrutiny." Columbia News Service, Stryker Brigade News, 11 May 2006. http://www.naplesnews.com/news/2006/may/11/soldiers_online_journals_under_deeper_scrutiny/?neapolitan. Web.

Stalag 17. Dir. Billy Wilder. Perf. William Holden, Don Taylor. Paramount, 1953. Film.

Standard Operating Procedure. Dir. Errol Morris. Sony Pictures Classics, 2008. Film.

Staub, Michael. Personal interview. 28 November 2009.

Stockdale, Melissa K. "'My Death for the Motherland Is Happiness': Women, Patriotism, and Soldiering in Russia's Great War, 1914–1917." *American Historical Review* 109, no. 1 (2004): 78–116. Print.

Stoff, Laurie. *They Fought for the Motherland: Russia's Women Soldiers in World War I and the Revolution.* Lawrence: University Press of Kansas, 2006. Print.

Stryker, John. "About Me." Sgt. Stryker's Daily Briefing. n.d. http://aboutstryker.blogspot.com/. Web.

Suellentrop, Chris. "War Games." *New York Times Magazine,* 12 September 2010: 62+. Print.

Sun Tzu. *The Art of War.* Trans. Samuel B. Griffith. London: Oxford University Press, 1963. Print.

Swofford, Anthony. *Jarhead.* New York: Scribner's, 2003. Print.

Taylor, Philip. *War and the Media: Propaganda and Persuasion in the Gulf War.* Manchester: Manchester University Press, 1998. Print.

Tearing Down the Spanish Flag. Dir. J. Stuart Blackton. Vitagraph, 1898. Film.

The Thin Red Line. Dir. Terrence Malick. Perf. Jim Caviezel, Sean Penn. 20th Century Fox, 1998. Film.

Thirty Seconds Over Tokyo. Dir. Mervyn LeRoy. Perf. Van Johnson, Robert Walker. MGM, 1944. Film.

This Is the Army. Dir. Michael Curtiz. Perf. George Murphy, Joan Leslie. Warner Brothers, 1943. Film.

The Three Burials of Melquiades Estrada. Dir. Tommy Lee Jones. Perf. Tommy Lee Jones, Barry Pepper. EuropaCorp, 2005. Film.

Three Kings. Dir. David O. Russell. Perf. George Clooney, Mark Wahlberg. Village Roadshow, 1999. Film.

Thucydides. *Thucydides.* Trans. Benjamin Jowett. London: Oxford University Press, 1881. Print.

Tritle, Lawrence. *From Melos to My Lai: War and Survival.* London: Routledge, 2000. Print.

Trumbo, Dalton. *Johnny Got His Gun.* New York: Bantam Books, [1939] 1989. Print.

Turner, Brian. "The Bomb within Us." *New York Times,* 4 March 2010: Home Fires. http://opinionator.blogs.nytimes.com/2010/03/04/home-fires-the-bomb-within-us/. Web.

——. *Here, Bullet.* Farmington, Maine: Alice James Books, 2005. Print.

——. "Mountains of the Moon." *New York Times,* 23 September 2007: Home Fires. http://opinionator.blogs.nytimes.com/2007/09/23/mountains-of-the-moon/. Web.

——. "The Night Visitors." *New York Times,* 20 December 2009: Home Fires. http://opinionator.blogs.nytimes.com/2009/12/20/the-night-visitors/. Web.

——. *Phantom Noise*. Farmington, Maine: Alice James Books, 2010. Print.

——. "Requiem for the Last American Soldier to Die in Iraq." *New York Times*, 31 October 2007: Home Fires. http://opinionator.blogs.nytimes.com/2007/10/31/requiem-for-the-last-american-soldier-to-die-in-iraq/. Web.

——. "Verses in Wartime (Part 2: From the Home Front)." *New York Times*, 24 October 2007: Home Fires. http://opinionator.blogs.nytimes.com/2007/10/24/verses-in-wartime-part-2-from-the-home-front/. Web.

——. "The War in Present Tense." *New York Times*, 5 June 2007: Home Fires. http://opinionator.blogs.nytimes.com/2007/06/05/the-war-in-present-tense/. Web.

Turnipseed, Joel. "About Joel Turnipseed." Hotel Zero, 2007. http://hotelzero.typepad.com/hotel_zero/author.html. Web.

——. *Baghdad Express: A Gulf War Memoir*. St. Paul, MN: Borealis Books, 2003. Print.

Twain, Mark. *More Maxims from Mark*. Ed. Merle Johnson. Privately printed, 1927. Print.

Tyson, Ann Scott. "For Female Gis, Combat Is a Fact: Many Duties in Iraq Put Women at Risk Despite Restrictive Policy." *Washington Post*, 13 May 2005: A1. Print.

United States Army. Operations and Signal Security. Army Regulation 530–31. Washington: Department of the Army, 2007. Print.

Vanairsdale, S. T. "Are *Hurt Locker* Foes Using Troops to Take Down the Oscar Front-Runner?" Movieline, 26 February 2010. http://www.movieline.com/2010/02/are-hurt-locker-foes-using-troops-to-take-down-the-oscar-front-runner.php. Web.

"Waiting for John Wayne." *Economist*, 30 August 2008: 78–79. Print.

Wake Island. Dir. John Farrow. Perf. Brian Donlevy, Robert Preston. Paramount, 1942. Film.

Weschler, Lawrence. "Valkyries Over Iraq." *Harper's Magazine*, November 2005: 65–77. Print.

Wheelwright, Julie. *Amazons and Military Maids: Women Who Dressed as Men in the Pursuit of Life, Liberty and Happiness*. London: Pandora Press, 1989. Print.

Why We Fight Series. Dir. Frank Capra. U.S. Army Special Service Division, 1943–1945. Film.

Williams, Kayla. *Love My Rifle More Than You: Young and Female in the U.S. Army*. New York: W. W. Norton, 2005. Print.

Wright, Evan. *Generation Kill: Devil Dogs, Iceman, Captain America, and the New Face of American War*. New York: Berkeley Caliber, 2004. Print.

Zimmerman, David. *The Sandbox*. Soho Press, 2010. Print.

Index